Richard Meier Architect

*Essays by Kenneth Frampton
and Joseph Rykwert*

1992/1999

Richard Meier Architect

RIZZOLI
NEW YORK

First published in the United States
of America in 1999 by
Rizzoli International Publications, Inc.
300 Park Avenue South
New York, NY 10010

Library of Congress
Cataloging-in-Publication Data
Meier, Richard, 1934–
Richard Meier, architect. Volume 3 / essays
by Kenneth Frampton and Joseph Rykwert.
p.   cm.
Includes bibliographical references.
ISBN 0-8478-1996-5 (hc.)
ISBN 0-8478-2048-3 (pbk.)
1. Meier, Richard, 1934–
—Themes, motives.
2. Architecture, Modern—
20th century—United States—
Themes, motives.
I. Frampton, Kenneth, 1930–
II. Rykwert, Joseph, 1926–   III. Title.
NA737.M44A4   1999
720'.92—dc21   95-30707   CIP

Editor: Lisa J. Green
Design: Massimo Vignelli
Design Coordinator: Abigail Sturges

Printed and bound in Italy

For my present and former collaborators

Acknowledgments

I recently traveled extensively in Europe and America lecturing about architecture, and this gave me the opportunity to reflect on some of the ideas and aspirations that brought us to where we are today in my own practice, which began in December of 1963 in the small two-room apartment where I lived and worked.

Looking back now, thirty-five years later, I realize that the projects far outnumber the realized buildings. But I also see that the importance of the projects lies in the ideas they contain, that the process of making architecture is a continual one that must include one's entire body of work.

In the making of space, there is always a concern for the way in which the public nature of a place is defined in human terms, and this means that there must always be an emphasis on the character of the whole. In responding to society's needs, one must be concerned with constructing a physical fabric that is equally durable, rational, and architecturally vibrant.

Fourteen years have passed since volume one of my monograph was published, where the first discussion I had with my children, Joseph and Ana, regarding "what is white?" was included. This has been an ongoing dialogue with them that has taken on a life of its own. But now that they are in or about to be in college, it is time that they continue this discourse individually, in whatever way is best for them.

The work of the last eight years, since volume two was published, shows an evolution of ideas, and of a vocabulary in architecture, with the fourteen-year involvement in the design and construction of the Getty Center being the most absorbing project from both a professional and a personal point of view. This book is a reflection of those ideas, which have evolved in both the built and unbuilt work. It is a reflection of the work of many talented and dedicated people who have worked with me for years in the most responsible and conscientious manner, their efforts being of consummate quality.

My appreciation goes to Lisa Green, who was the master organizer of this book; to Massimo Vignelli, the visionary director and chef du graphic design; to Abigail Sturges, the outstanding person responsible for the final layouts; and to Rizzoli's editors, who carefully corrected and oversaw this third volume. And finally, I wish to thank Kenneth Frampton, the most articulate architectural critic of our generation, and Joseph Rykwert, the peerless historian, architect, and teacher; and the ingenious architect Arata Isozaki, who understands as well as anyone I know the relationship between practice and theory. All of you, most importantly, are my very dear friends who share with me this eventful and fulfilling time in architectural discourse at the close of the millennium.

Richard Meier

New York
December 1998

Contents

Preface

Architecture is a social art. It is concerned with the quality of life, and this concern must find form through the nature of our work. At best the architect possesses an innate ability to transcend function and accommodation, going beyond the superficial attributes of style to express our human concerns poetically through space and material form.

Subject to history and to the never-ending interplay between interpretation and innovation, architecture also remains an opportunity and a responsibility. If we are to create new and meaningful places within our cities, we need to have not only a sense of our common social and spiritual aspirations but also a feeling for the traditions from which our society stems. Our cities are in a constant state of evolution. All of us are part of changing urban patterns that affect our work, play, commerce, communication, and travel. That is why it is so essential for us to relate architecture and urban design to the urgent issues of our time: to the problems of economic and social deprivation, to inadequate housing, and to the concomitant loss of freedom in the broadest possible sense. The art of city building has never been so crucial to our future, yet an awareness of that need has all but disappeared from today's political arena. There is a discernible weakening of public mission in this regard, not only in the United States but elsewhere.

It is our responsibility as architects to attempt to deal with the neglected and squalid sections of our cities. We must find a way to reach out to these sectors, to enliven and enhance them, and to bestow new energy upon the form of the urban fabric. I think that there are many ways in which we may achieve this. Every situation offers its own potential, whether we are building in Paris, Los Angeles, or New York. Louis Kahn said the city should be "a place where a little child walking through the streets can imagine what he or she would like to be some day." I think that this is the kind of city we should aspire to create. Imagine a city where schools, libraries and hospitals, workplaces, and recreational and cultural facilities are all capable of giving full expression to the human need for self-realization at the highest level. But for that to happen, we must create what Kahn called the *availabilities*. Such institutions must be seen as readily accessible. We know that cities are meeting places, which we value because of everything they offer us. To the degree that institutions remove themselves from the public, to the degree that they keep people at arm's length and make themselves inaccessible, the very concept of the *res publica* dies.

Our meeting places must embody the sense of inspiration that lies at the very heart of the urban idea. An institutional space must not only accommodate human activity but also contribute actively to the shaping of human action, thereby helping to transform it into something that we are able to recognize as meaningful and rewarding. These are the twin essentials of city life: *accessibility*, combined with the drive to give form to our ideals; that is, to create the *availabilities*. It is our task as architects to promote the growth of such values. One fundamental way to do this is through an *architecture of connection*, an architecture that weaves together the urban plazas, streets, and parks that still make up much of the urban fabric.

It is our responsibility to develop civic ideas in which there is a physical sense of sharing that permeates the urban space and the contingent architectural form. I look forward to seeing our profession reaffirm its traditional concern for the urban fabric as a matrix for gathering and energizing the essence of the public realm. We need to remind ourselves continually of our mission to recognize and improve upon those patterns of civic behavior that already exist but that need a certain formal definition. Our task may not always be to invent a new sense of place from the ground up; sometimes it may be more important for us to modify, to alter, and to reconstruct within an existing fabric. In either case, the civic space in question must grow logically out of each particular situation, and out of its physical, historical, and social contextuality.

One way to achieve this goal is to adopt a collagist approach toward urban design. With such a strategy it is possible to differentiate clearly between public and private places, between interior and exterior volumes, and to mediate in a subtle way between these opposing elements. Such a mediation will have to deal with movement and passage, with components that cross the city and interconnect its various parts, sometimes bringing the old into direct confrontation with the new. Such an architecture of connective tissue cannot afford to be unduly concerned with fashion or style. It is an architecture that searches for clarity rather than surface effect, an architecture that is committed to civic culture rather than divorced from it, a *parti pris* that has the capacity to recompose our cities and to liberate our lives. All too often today, this potential is totally neglected. New buildings are perceived as little more than free-standing commodities, with little connection to either the community or the topography.

In recent years a new kind of public space has emerged spontaneously in our society. We may encounter this only too directly in the new shopping centers, sports arenas, office complexes, and government facilities that populate the megalopolis. Within such institutions we may find spaces that, while privately managed, still persist in combining private and public uses. They are of great social relevance to our everyday experience of urban life. One of the challenges that architecture now faces is to design these new public spaces in such a way as to convey a sense of collectivity, enabling them to become an integral part of the urban experience. As always, the best way to achieve this may not necessarily be the cheapest.

In my experience, the quest for economy does not always spring from a drive toward elegance and simplicity. It arises just as often from the desire to create works that are capable of enduring across time. In this regard it may often be necessary to find additional money—and indeed to spend such funds on the finest possible material—in order to achieve a durable result. As advocates for the city, we should be prepared to argue in favor of achieving quality and durability over expediency. Today, we have access to extremely sophisticated technology as well as a desire to deal with problems that have not been tackled before. What we always need and often lack are sufficient funds to arrive at an appropriate and long-lasting solution to these problems. Our aim should be to demand the best and not just the cheapest, so that, through our art, we can render the civic realm as a democratic space of human appearance in every sense of the word.

Richard Meier

August 1998

Three Tropes in the Later Work of Richard Meier

Kenneth Frampton

Palace of the Assembly, Chandigarh, India. Le Corbusier, 1955. Sketch

Sydney Opera House, Sydney, Australia. Jørn Utzon, 1957. Section

They (some friends) tell me that I do not have a theoretical framework or a method. That I give no clues about the direction to be taken. And that this is not being pedagogical. A kind of ship at the mercy of the waves, that inexplicably does not always sink (which is something else they tell me). I do not give our ships' planks a good try out on the open sea. Excesses break them up into pieces. I study the currents, eddies. I look for the heavens before taking risks. I can be seen walking alone up and down on the deck. But the entire crew and all the equipment is there, the captain is a ghost. Whenever the pole-star is only just visible, I do not dare take the helm. I cannot point to any clear way. The ways are not clear.

— Alvaro Siza, *Professione poetica*[1]

Atectonic

Although Richard Meier has long since acknowledged the neo-Corbusian character of his architecture, other tropes from the trajectory of the new have also emerged in his work. One may discern not only undulating forms drawn from the works of Alvar Aalto and Oscar Niemeyer but also the occasional plastic syncopation reminiscent of neoplasticism, not to mention a trace here and there of constructivism. One thinks of Jean Prouvé, whose characteristic window with rounded corners surfaced in the Bronx Development Center (1977), or of such obscure figures as Oscar Nitschke, whose Maison de la Publicité of 1936 seems latent in the dematerialized curtain walls of Meier's later work: for example, the horizontal fenestration of the Museum of Contemporary Art in Barcelona (1995) or the Canal+ television headquarters (1992) in Paris. In an interview with Charles Jencks, Meier openly conceded the influence of constructivism, prompting one to take particular note of such features as freestanding spiral stairs rising up into saw-toothed skylights or dog-leg stairs and flying ramps lined with wire-mesh balustrades. Elsewhere Meier's articulation of columns, beams, and panels appears to be in a state of oscillation, while his white-enameled paneling often seems on the verge of dematerializing under light. Meanwhile, his habitual atectonic articulations of the surface of a building in terms of a square grid recall the work of Josef Hoffmann.

As with the architecture of Fumihiko Maki, to which Meier's work may be readily compared (one thinks in particular of Maki's Tepia Pavilion, Tokyo [1990], and his Museum of Modern Art, Kyoto [1986]), this approach to revetment seems simultaneously both to express the latent structure of the building and to deny it. Meier occasionally offsets this modulated ambivalence with a continuous plastic form made from homogenous material. In the Museum of Contemporary Art in Barcelona a freestanding gallery, amoeba-shaped in plan, floats in front of the striated, lightweight, brise soleil facade. Like the conical cooling tower within (a trope borrowed from Le Corbusier's assembly building in Chandigarh), this form asserts itself as a foil to the rampway behind the curtain-wall front.

As Werner Blaser implied in his 1990 essay "Architectural Principles for a New Aesthetic in the Work of Richard Meier," a tectonic dimension has slowly come into being in Meier's recent work. This is particularly evident in three exceptional pieces: the Federal Building and United States Courthouse, Phoenix, Arizona, designed in 1995, the Neugebauer House, Naples, Florida, recently completed, and his winning entry in the competition for a Church of the Year 2000, dating from 1996 and scheduled to be completed for the millennium in a working-class district of Rome. In each instance, structural form comes to the fore as the main expressive element, a tectonic focus that in the courthouse is associated with one of the most rigorous pieces of modular planning of Meier's recent career. Here against an L-shaped armature of law courts and offices, Meier has set a lightweight, ferro-vitreous atrium of such elegance as to

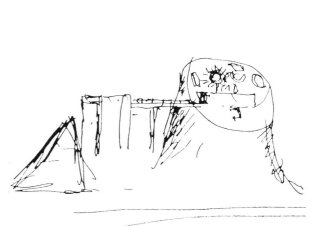

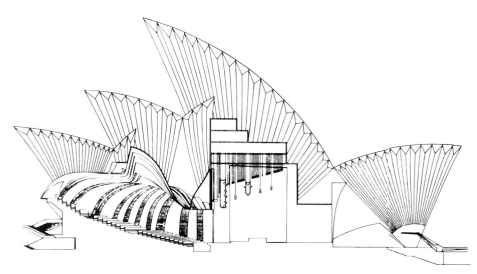

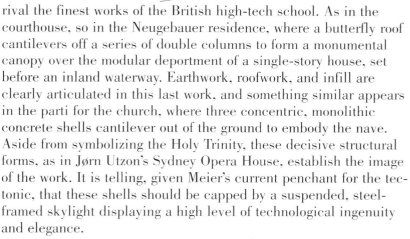

rival the finest works of the British high-tech school. As in the courthouse, so in the Neugebauer residence, where a butterfly roof cantilevers off a series of double columns to form a monumental canopy over the modular deportment of a single-story house, set before an inland waterway. Earthwork, roofwork, and infill are clearly articulated in this last work, and something similar appears in the parti for the church, where three concentric, monolithic concrete shells cantilever out of the ground to embody the nave. Aside from symbolizing the Holy Trinity, these decisive structural forms, as in Jørn Utzon's Sydney Opera House, establish the image of the work. It is telling, given Meier's current penchant for the tectonic, that these shells should be capped by a suspended, steel-framed skylight displaying a high level of technological ingenuity and elegance.

Res Publica
One of the largest enclosed public spaces in Europe, Meier's City Hall and Central Library in The Hague is a seminal work indebted not only to Frank Lloyd Wright's Larkin Building but also to Giuseppe Mengoni's famous Galleria Vittorio Emanuele in Milan, built in 1877. While exceeding the Galleria in overall scale, Meier's building resembles it in that it is a microcosmic public realm built at the scale of the surrounding urban fabric. Moreover, both works possess parallel political connotations, with the former proclaiming the triumph of the Risorgimento and the latter consolidating the self-conscious awakening of the Dutch capital from its genteel era, as it tries to rival, in high-tech construction, the booming skyline of Rotterdam.

Meier's urban mandate, although never stated as such, was to unify and consolidate the city's new megalopitan character. Thus the city hall is a megaform of sufficient height, length, and horizontal continuity to hold its own against the random, mediocre high-rise office slabs that have been loosely superimposed on the preexisting urban grain. Yet, as with most of Meier's interventions in historic urban cores, contextuality is a moot point, for while on the one hand it would be difficult to imagine a building more alien to the Dutch tradition than this large structure, clad in a tessellated enameled skin, on the other, this new municipality seems to be uncannily sympathetic to Dutch culture—which may be explained in part by the Dutch assistants who worked on the project throughout. Thus, the Dutch new objectivity was somehow implicit in this building from the beginning. Who could deny its reference to the Van Nelle factory of 1929, even if its structural rhythm and its tapering, 10.5-degree format derive from the urban fabric? The fenestration provides, in accordance with Dutch law, a specific number of operable windows both within the atrium and without. However, these opening lights do not simply meet the legal requirement: their detailing recalls in terms of scale and profile the proportions of the work of neoplastic cabinetmaker Gerrit Rietveld. Aside from this subtle reference, Meier's design conforms to Dutch domestic tradition as a whole, with its constant attempt to optimize natural light. His use of tubular-steel and wire-mesh balustrades seems thus equally native, evoking the early work of Herman Hertzberger. Last but not least, the aerial *passerelles* that traverse the atrium to provide convenient access from one side of the office complex to the other are reminiscent of the glazed conveyor belts of the Van Nelle factory. This reference is reinforced by the freestanding glazed elevator shafts that recall the constructivist space-time ethos of the late 1920s.

Historical contextuality is evident in the galleria itself, which, given the perennially grey Dutch climate, makes one think of Hermann Boerhaeve, who formed the greenhouse principle at the beginning of the seventeenth century. However, one of the ultimate local references arises from the sense of collective consensus that pervades

Spatial Development: dome sections (Johann Friedrich Geist, Arcades, Cambridge, Mass., The MIT Press, 1983), with overlay of The Hague City Hall

1. *Paris, Galerie Vivienne, 1825.*
2. *Paris, Galerie Colbert, 1826.*
3. *Berlin, Kaisergalerie, 1873.*
4. *Milan, Galleria Vittorio Emanuele, 1877.*
5. *The Hague, Passage, 1885.*
6. *Naples, Galleria Umberto I, 1891.*
7. *Berlin, Friedrichstrassenpassage, 1908.*
8. *The Hague, City Hall, 1995.*

the atrium, for here the designers rendered public amenities immediately accessible from the galleria, and even where such access is restricted for security reasons, mutually interpenetrating lines of sight prevail. This popular panoptic dimension is also part of Dutch tradition. It goes along with that particular admixture of conformism with anarchy that pervades The Netherlands. Culture and commerce join to frame the main entry: a giant portico composed of the central library and the Hulshoff's furniture emporium. Equally panoptic inside and out, this largely transparent, elevated rotunda and trapezoid are also penetrated by sightlines. Thus, one catches glimpses of the library from the elevated corridors and bridges of the galleria and vice-versa. This open-stack library, flooded with light on all levels, is equipped with continuous escalator access between floors. This makes for an unceasing flow of pedestrian movement at every level, bestowing a level of accessibility rarely found in contemporary libraries, where book-lined volumes, artificially lit, often convey a sense of exclusion and constraint.

On entering through the monumental southwestern portico of the structure one passes into the cubic, all-glass lobby of the city hall, which is deftly inserted into the twelve-story, glazed screen that closes this end of the atrium. This vertical welded space-frame, made out of square-sectioned tubular steel, is a structural tour de force that immediately imparts a feeling of heroic grandeur. It is also the first in a series of permeable planes extending the full height of the atrium. These virtual planes, composed of perforated balustrades and passerelles, are simultaneously present and absent. They are, in a sense, "tectonic mirages," hovering like haze in the middle of the space. As such, they counter the false perspective created by the 10.5-degree difference between the flanking walls of the atrium. While delaying the foreshortening of the space, they also paradoxi-

1 5 3 2   7   6 4 8

cally prolong it. They virtually disappear like a mirage as one approaches each set of aerial bridges in succession, only to reappear behind one, hovering in the air with the persistence of sea mist.

This work recalls Moholy-Nagy's light-space modulator of 1930, since each atomized component creates a constantly changing proliferation of light and shade. The full-height, steel-framed curtain wall on the southwestern end casts its strident shadow on the drum of the council chamber, just as the deep beams carrying the skylights over the atrium modulate the vast volume through constantly changing patterns of shadow. The wire-mesh balustrades of the aerial bridges refract sunlight in every conceivable direction, creating a veiled luminosity through which the eye tries to capture the momentous totality of the volume. All of this is further activated by the white-enameled panels of the flanking walls, which iterate a series of highlights and reflections that further diffuse the ephemerality of the aerial walkways.

This modulation of space by light changes with height, and to this end the architects have installed cantilevered balconies that open off the elevator lobby on each floor, providing vantage points from which to contemplate the spectacle of the space. Diminutive elements like these bestow upon the vast scale a reassuring and surprising intimacy. They also encourage our active perception of the space, which at one instant appears to be vast and at another, relatively small. Such perceptual instability often indicates a building of quality.

These multiple vistas collapse when one views the space laterally or diagonally across the axis. From here one can read the building programatically, as a city in miniature. On one side, one proceeds from the entry past the café terrace and the long public service counter to

two shops topped by the drum of the wedding hall, reached via a monumental stair. On the other flank one first encounters the information center and then the curved stair leading to the council chamber above. This overture is followed by a public reception facility and an entrance to the subterranean exhibition space. On the first floor a wide access gallery runs along the northwestern side of the atrium, serving a series of private offices and interview rooms. These private suites are subtly illuminated during the day by full-height glass-block walls. These syncopated, paired cubicles are rhythmically counterpointed by a large serial abstract sculpture by the Dutch artist Fortuyn O'Brien comprised of marble cylinders and benches. The opposite side of the atrium features a hairdresser's salon and other retail facilities. The commercial potential of this space seems to have been deliberately underplayed as opposed to the greater availability of such space on the exterior.

One of the pleasures of this building resides in being able to overlook various activities of the city hall from an elevated position. Thus one may observe the top of the council chamber, where the general public meets with councilors on a one-to-one basis. This elevated, semipublic arena is offset by a recessed four-story café terrace let into the interior face of the atrium, much like the "eye" set into the elevation of Le Corbusier's Cartesian skyscraper of 1938. Since this loggia is reserved solely for municipal employees, the general public may only view this space obliquely, at a distance. Meier insisted on including a council chamber in the final brief for the building, arguing that a municipality without this representational space could not be fully consummated as a city hall. Meier acted similarly when he designed the Hartford Seminary, where at his insistence a chapel was finally included in the brief. Is it not symptomatic of our age that in both instances the clients were initially indifferent to the absence of such essential symbolic elements?

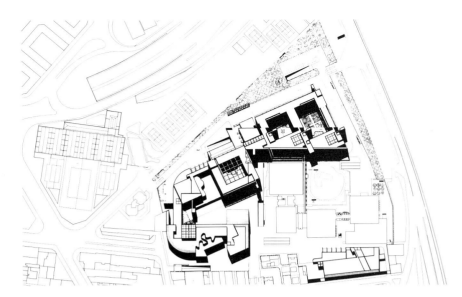

Renault Administrative Headquarters, Boulogne-Billancourt, France. Richard Meier, 1981. Site Plan

The Getty Center, Los Angeles, California. Richard Meier, 1984-1997. East Elevation

This structure displays a tessellated surface inside and out; the logic of its grid determines the entire fabric. Even where the standard square-panel module is reduced in size, as in the glazing of the elevator cabins, the grid still prevails. In this instance the quadratic module allows the cabin to serve as a cursor that registers its precise movement against the grid of the atrium as it rises and falls, opposing its own dynamic volume to the stasis of the atrium. This pervasive modularity seems less successful externally. While the panel module increases in size on the windowless parts of the structure, this doubling-up seems incapable of modulating such a large structure. It simply cannot bracket into larger perceptual wholes a building of such oceanic proportions, particularly when viewed from the narrow streets surrounding it. Nevertheless, existing street alignments have been meticulously respected throughout, just as points of ingress and egress relate precisely to the grain of the city. Thus, Herman Hertzberger's cultural center, offset by an entire block, is subtly drawn into the orbit of the city hall, as is the plaza that it encloses in conjunction with Carel Weeber's hotel and Rem Koolhaas's dance theater. This plaza is all but literally sucked into the gap separating the city hall from the central library. Meanwhile, the library rotunda points to the one other modern building of caliber in the vicinity, P. L. Kramer's brick-faced, copper-clad department store built for the de Bijenkorf chain in 1926.

I have dealt with the City Hall and Central Library at length because I am convinced it is the most significant public building of Meier's career to date, not withstanding his major museum buildings and his equally consequential law courts as these now near completion. In these last we seem to be witnessing the emergence of a new characteristic type, an L-block plan formation enclosing a freestanding cylinder. This type seems to have found its ideal content in the program of the modern courthouse. In The Hague, on the other hand, Meier adapted the galleria type to the predominantly bureaucratic character of the late-twentieth-century municipality. At the same time, this atrium was able to condense into a single building the role previously performed by a traditional urban core. Thus today it is "The Heart of the City," to quote the title of CIAM VIII (1951). The creation of such micro-urban realms is surely preferable to more comprehensive urban renewal schemes that invariably destroy the existing fabric through the inevitable cacophony of mediocre buildings. Instances of this are too numerous even in The Netherlands; I have in mind the recent redevelopment of the Weena district in Rotterdam. The renewal of the center of The Hague, with its ill-assorted office buildings, is a consequence of the same kind of indifferent speculation. By and large it has few redeeming features aside from Meier's city hall, with its capacity to serve as a "social condenser" for the city as a whole.

Idyll

When one looks back over Meier's production, one is immediately struck by the detailed nature of his site plans. Over time, these have become increasingly topographic. This sensibility first appeared in Meier's proposal for an Olivetti training center in Tarrytown (1971), and again appeared in the dormitories that he designed for Cornell University three years later. Topography is primary in The Atheneum of 1979 in New Harmony, Indiana, where the freely undulating form of the western elevation echoes the undulating course of the nearby Wabash River. This preoccupation with the countervailing role of landscape seems to be confirmed by Meier's sharp response to Charles Jencks's contention that New Harmony totally lacked the color and decorative rhetoric of the baroque that inspired it. As Meier remarked, "Superimposition of color would have created a whole new spatial instrument which I felt would be destructive to the building in relation to the landscape."

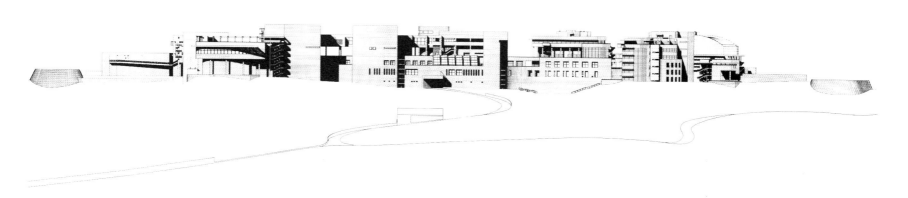

The full incarnation of the topographic in Meier's architecture came with his Museum for the Decorative Arts in Frankfurt (1985), where the building extends into the adjacent parkscape through a series of paved walkways. Here, in a manner evocative of the Roman cardo and decumanus, two intersecting axes rotate 3.5 degrees about their point of intersection to correspond to the shift in the alignment of the river frontage as the River Main swings to the north. In the former back gardens of a series of nineteenth-century villas running the length of the Schaumainkai, Meier created an elegiac arboretum out of an existing tree-studded space between the two street frontages. This quasi-leftover space was to have been unified by a long pedestrian accessway, paralleling neither the river nor the Villa Metzler. Meier's site plan for his unrealized ethnographic museum, projected in 1989 as part of the new cultural complex for the city of Frankfurt, further defines this concept. Here, with the aid of an enclosed bridge, the pedestrian network would have extended beyond the confines of the block, as in a knight's move in chess. However, neighboring homeowners perceived the two museums linked by walkways as a Trojan horse, capable of transforming the entire residential district into a public domain.

The interstitial megastructure as a subversive strategy came into its own with Meier's 1981 proposal for the new Renault Administrative Headquarters in Boulogne-Billancourt, France. In this extremely subtle scheme it is difficult to identify where the internal space-form of the building ends and the topography of the site begins. Structured about two countervailing orthogonal grids—one coming off the Seine and the other off the street grid—Meier's proposal is a montage in section as well as in plan. Innumerable serpentine walls modulate this heterotopic intersection, while an undulating figure rises to become the dominant image of the assembly at its western end, where the two grids converge. Here Meier exploited the serpen-tine motif to signify the larger public volumes of the complex, the technological and artistic exhibition spaces that would have opened off the main foyer. As his site plan indicates, greenery would have infiltrated this spatial overlay in different ways to create a repertoire of lawns, parterres, roof terraces, and mazes, bounded by an avenue of trees in the French classical manner.

Boulogne-Billancourt set the key for much of the 1980s, from Meier's entry for the Lingotto factory in Turin to an infill office complex for Siemens in Munich adjacent to the old Siemens headquarters. The first instance was a witty work playing with the theme of motopia, the second a typological exercise structured about a standard perimeter block. The latter, designed in 1983, led to a second, somewhat more dynamic project for Siemens in the same city, on Hoffmannstrasse. Now partially realized, this project once again posited a city in miniature together with a landscape palette that assured overall unity. Throughout the 1980s, Meier's topographic sensibility varied according to the context: at times rationalist, as in his Bicocca proposal for Milan of 1986, at times organic, as in the remarkable interstitial scheme that he proposed for the Spanish Quarter of Naples in the same year.

All these civic exercises find their fulfillment in the Getty Center, finally completed in the Brentwood area of Los Angeles at the end of 1997. Laid out on a 110-acre "acropolis" running parallel to the San Diego Freeway, the Getty Center is once again a city in miniature, although siting, scale, and format could hardly be more removed from the comparatively modest intervention that Meier achieved in The Hague. Most of the buildings that make up this low-rise, hilltop complex are structured about two ridges that meet at a 22.5-degree angle. This angle happens to correspond to that of the San Diego Freeway as it bends north out of Los Angeles toward the

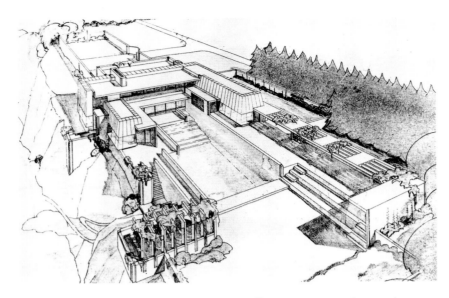

Sepulveda Pass, an inflection that recalls Meier's reaction to the changing angle of the River Main in Frankfurt.

In many respects the Getty Center is structured about a sequence of courtyards, ramps, steps, pools, and parterres, not to mention the systematic forestation of the surrounding slopes, all of which are as much part of the poetics of the place as the buildings themselves. The design was constrained by severe height restrictions imposed by the Brentwood Homeowners Association, and perhaps no twentieth-century landscape is so sectionally orchestrated, with one recessed courtyard stepping down into another as the buildings hug the contours of the site. All of this becomes immediately apparent as soon as one boards the tramway rising to the acropolis from the visitors' parking below. This rail access is a linear garden in itself, starting with the station environs and the retaining wall that parallels the track. The scheme recalls both the plan for Boulogne-Billancourt and the undulating dormitories projected for Cornell. The upper terminus is the propylaeum of the campus, giving immediate access to the museum and the 450-seat auditorium, together with the administration building and Getty Conservation Institute. From this entry plaza the main substance of the center unfolds, with the restaurant and the Getty Research Institute for the History of Art and the Humanities spread out to the right along a single ridge. Straight ahead, up a monumental flight of steps, one encounters the museum complex built along its own appointed ridge. In this way one passes from the restaurant, with its view of the ocean and the mountains, to the largely top-lit museum sequence, interrupted here and there by terraces with views over the mountains and the city. Moving away from the museum and the restaurant, one is deflected toward the third term of the complex: the Research Institute for the History of Art and the Humanities. Its circumferential library curls around a cylindrical patio before the land falls away into a ravine, culminat-

ing in the lower central gardens which cascade to the lowest level of the site. Each of these structures is a microcosm in itself in which the difference between one building and the next, and even between one floor and the next, is as much about the treatment of the interior as about the configuration of the exterior.

As cities in miniature, it is hard to imagine two works less alike than The Hague City Hall and the Getty Center, even if both are centers of institutional power: one is local, democratic, and integrated into the fabric of an existing city, the other is global, oligarchic, and detached from the megalopolis. Despite the Getty's aloof stance, which is reinforced by the tramway approach and by the discreet but elite presence of a helicopter landing pad behind the administration building, the Getty Center has become an instant popular success. The administration is currently hard-pressed to handle the twenty thousand people who visit the site daily—almost three times the number of visitors initially anticipated.

Aside from the distant allusion to an Italian hill town, there is nothing typological about this work, even if the individual components appear typified in themselves. The unifying ethos of the piece is its carefully orchestrated landscape, structured about an informal promenade that permeates every aspect of the site. The visitor passes from the cylindrical entrance foyer of the museum complex into the courtyard and then into the first nine-square gallery sequence clustered around a top-lit court. From this cluster the route continues out onto a terrace and then via a connecting canopy into the next nine-square pavilion. Set across from an angled, free-standing cube devoted to temporary exhibitions, this second gallery cluster encloses an open-air pool. From here one approaches the third and fourth nine-square clusters that make up the exhibition itinerary as it bounds the museum court. The visitor is allowed every

opportunity to escape onto the perimeter terraces, which afford spectacular views over the surrounding landscape.

This constant alternation between foyer and loggia runs throughout the site. Thus in the Conservation Institute one passes from loggia to foyer and then into an open-air access corridor before entering the air-conditioned volumes of its library and offices. These in turn face private terraces looking out over the San Diego Freeway. Comparable counterchanges between loggia, foyer, and terrace also occur in the restaurant/café and the Research Institute for the History of Art and the Humanities, and this more than the baroque syntax of the architecture evokes the Southern Californian tradition, so lyrically formulated by Frank Lloyd Wright and his émigré pupils, Rudolph Schindler and Richard Neutra.

A similar alternation occurs between the gridded surface of the lightweight paneling and the stack-bonded, almost fused character of the cleft stone that faces the outer shell of the complex. Thus the contradictory legacy of the tectonic comes down to us: on the one hand, the essence of immateriality in the non-load-bearing, enameled skin suspended in front of a skeletal steel frame; on the other, a similarly suspended materiality of Italian travertine rudely torn from the surface of the earth. Both cases manifest the representational act of cladding, *Bekleidung*, as Gottfried Semper understood the term: an atectonic rain screen in the travertine, totally removed from Wright's textile block houses built in Southern California in the mid-1920s.

Compromised by the client's refusal to allow the Italianate form of Meier's central gardens to function as the unifying matrix of the entire complex, the Getty Center nonetheless belongs to that long and remarkable American tradition of cultural enclaves where the economic instrumentality that otherwise dominates the entire continent finds itself momentarily suspended. Like Stanford, Harvard, Wellesley, and Cranbrook, to cite only a handful of the more idyllic campuses of this nation, the Getty Center is a heterotopia that still proclaims the patrician values of a bourgeois America before the rise of global modernization. As Meier is only too aware, it is unlikely that such an extravagant act of patronage will ever be repeated, certainly not in this century and even in the next, for the new commodified surplus of our digital age is hardly oriented toward this kind of culture. Possibly, then, this is the last idyll, certainly as I have depicted it here and even further as the architect has imagined it over his long and illustrious career.

Notes
1. Alvaro Siza, *Professione poetica, Quaderni di Lotus* (Milan: Electa, 1986).

The Third Installment

Joseph Rykwert

Federal Building and United States Courthouse, Phoenix, Arizona. Richard Meier, 1994-2000. Section through courtrooms

Federal Building and United States Courthouse, Islip, New York. Richard Meier, 1993-1999. Section through atrium

Looking back over three decades of Richard Meier's work, I find it increasingly clear that he is—and I think always has been—doing architecture his own way, not following any style. Which style historians will foist on him in the future is therefore none of his business.

Of course Meier has been quite explicit and specific about his debt to the European architecture of the 1930s, especially Le Corbusier —and this hardly needs saying; he has always been very clear (as some of those architects who liked the label "functionalist" were not) about his own specific concern with formal problems, formal devices, his analytical approach to program, and his use of proportion. Hence his primary interest in the composition of certain typeforms. In recent projects, he has enhanced this with a shifting emphasis on the procession through the building, the unfolding of the building to its user and visitor. Yet the more obvious planar concerns still preoccupy him and give his drawings—even sketches for study purposes—an easy elegance that the finished presentation projects of many of his contemporaries cannot possibly rival.

Meier has become—as will be obvious from this volume—an established European architect: Paris, The Hague, Hilversum, Luxembourg, Frankfurt, Ulm, Barcelona, and Basel now have Meier public buildings, and these cities will soon be joined by Rome, with a church and a museum. This third volume of his work commemorates these—but also his return home. The major buildings are now in the United States, and one of them is his biggest project to date: the Getty Center at the intersection of the San Diego Freeway and Sunset Boulevard in Los Angeles. His recent clients have not just been the private-house builders and corporations who commissioned him in the past but also the Federal government. For the first time Meier will be creating public buildings and "political" spaces in his own country.

Over the last decade a new factor has marked his work. While taking account of the constraints imposed by site and construction has always been an aspect of his formal approach, Meier has recently become increasingly concerned with nonmechanical climate control; increasingly, too, he has mastered something that has always been recognized as a particular skill: the filtering of natural daylight. In dealing with light and climate, he does not regard his solutions as more or less ingenious engineering devices but gives them a highly visible role in the conception and elaboration of a project. In particular, it has inspired him to vary the configurations of the roof and to develop the brise soleil.

The American work seems to me to open a new period (I am even tempted to call it a style) in Meier's work. Take the Federal Building and United States Courthouse in Islip, Long Island. At first sight it may perhaps look more like his older work: it is generally configured as a slab building facing north and south. The north face, with its cunning pattern of small syncopated openings, screens the smaller offices and faces a parking lot, but the south face with its deep brise soleil is gently curved. Within that curved screen run the main public passages that look out to the ocean beyond and connect the various courtrooms. The building's salient feature is a slim, truncated cone rising its full height, its glistening white-enameled metal sheathing foiled by the softer limestone of the other walls and of the sun screens. It is a grand entry hall for the building, formally announcing (even to the passing motorist) that this is no ordinary office block. Although it does not rise above the roofline, the cone works as a landmark, almost as if it were a bell tower or watchtower. It marks a caesura in the block, emphasized by a limestone east-west wall dividing the district courts from the smaller area of the fiscal ones, and the placement of the special proceedings courtroom. The paved public forecourt between the building and the roadway is

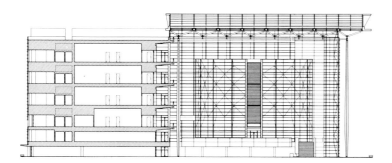

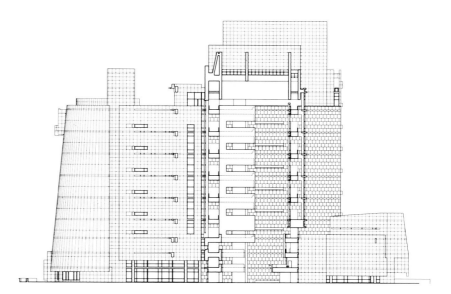

outlined by a range of trees that turns it into a narthex to emphasize the civic and very public nature of the federal courthouse.

The sense of entering a space that belongs to the people at large is something that the old *salles des pas-perdus* (and to some extent the halls of railway stations) often made rather oppressive. In The Hague City Hall and Central Library Meier has attempted to communicate that very sensation and seems to have done so clearly and without overpowering the visitor. He seems to have achieved it in more difficult circumstances in the Federal Building in Phoenix, Arizona.

Phoenix has a more perplexing climate than Long Island, with extremes of heat and cold and very dry air. It also has none of the site advantages offered by Islip, so the federal courthouse there seems sited almost randomly on a block within the urban grid. Meier has chosen to enclose that whole block and to create one of the first atria in which the problems and the value of this new type have been fully realized. An enclosed L-shaped element contains the office accommodation and the subsidiary court chambers on the south and west sides. The atrium completes the rectangle of the block and has a glazed front to the north and east. Its southern face is the leg of the L and is treated internally as an open street elevation, though the atrium has an independent columnar structure carrying a faceted glass roof that serves as the main ventilating device. Climatically, the problem was not just to control the temperature but also to moisturize the air. The solution relies on humidifying hot, dry air drawn in from the exterior at a high-level port in the atrium. As the moisture evaporates, the air cools and drops to the occupied floor below. This process, aided by overflow air vents near the base of the atrium, induces a natural air flow that continuously replenishes itself, creating a climate of relative comfort between the exterior extremes and the fully air-conditioned courtrooms.

The atrium is laid out as a garden court and articulated by an internal entry pavilion and the bank of elevators; its main element—which takes up about a third of its area—is a platform at the level of the second floor, approached by a wide stairway. This supports the glazed cylinder of the special proceedings courtroom that rises almost the full height of the building. This commanding formal element also plays a part in controlling the microclimate, since the warmer air from the air-conditioning helps draw the moisturized cold air down. This interplay of the formal and representational with climatic considerations results in one of Meier's most innovative recent buildings.

On a smaller, domestic scale, the Neugebauer House (1998) in Naples, Florida, where community rules imposed a sloping roof, inverts the usual double-pitch into a butterfly shape. The long and low house faces south to the sea, and its brise soleil is framed as an independent screened and louvered structure: the roof seems to float over it, giving the whole house a sense of being aerated by the sea breeze—which indeed it is.

Such are the new factors clearly legible in Meier's recent designs. However, another and more important change has been shaping his plans for some years. Although to many of his critics and admirers he is primarily a designer of object-buildings (and they have tended to read even such projects as the Getty Center as an assembly of objects), Meier has been moving into the more exacting role of urbanist-architect. And that is how the Getty plan must be read: as a public and an urban complex.

The ex-urbanizing of the Getty Center by siting it on a hilltop almost inevitably imposed the grouping of the various component institutions around an internal space, which therefore becomes the com-

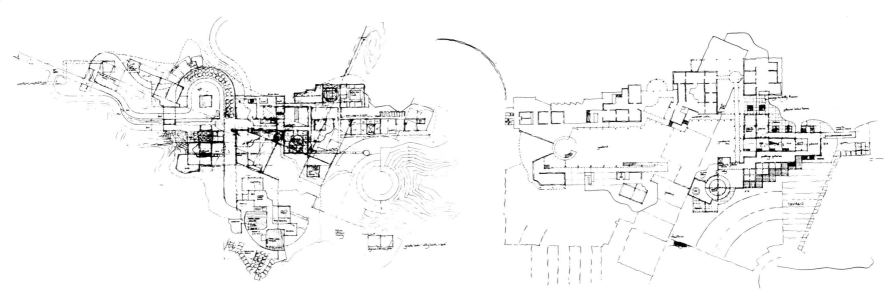

plex's main public "room." The layout takes up two main directing lines: the north-south line follows the grid lines of much of Los Angeles. The other, inclined to it by 22.5 degrees, takes up the lines of the San Diego Freeway by which most visitors will arrive at the site, as well as of West Los Angeles, which lies immediately below.

Marrying the superimposed grids with the site contours determined the arrangement of the different buildings and therefore the main outlines of the public space. This cannot be read as a series of architectural promenades—a mere negative of the built form. It is the animating core of the Getty Center, its essential nexus and binder. It is also the instrument that Meier uses cunningly to counterbalance and refract the prodigious bulk that the scale of the enterprise inevitably imposes on him—along with variations in texture.

Visitors arriving at the Getty Center by the tram that enters the site parallel to the freeway see the travertine retaining wall of the terraces and above it the more private parts of the complex: the Getty Conservation Institute, the Getty Education Institute for the Arts, and the J. Paul Getty Trust offices, which, like the Research Institute for the History of Art and the Humanities, are aligned on the north-south grid. The restaurant/café and the outer envelope of the J. Paul Getty Museum follow the San Diego Freeway, like the monorail, and that line continues into the gentle stairways that take visitors up to the museum. There the entrance canopy leads into a cylindrical and translucent hall through which visitors can appreciate the whole museum complex, planned around an internal garden courtyard. The museum pavilions are arranged partly chronologically and partly according to medium or style. The upper level, which is directly skylit, houses paintings and sculptures, while more light-sensitive drawings, engravings, and decorative objects of the same period are housed in the lower level. The sequence is

interrupted between the pavilions by balconies and terraces that allow visitors to reestablish contact with the outside world. The articulation of the several pavilions plays on differences of scale. The plan of the museum epitomizes the whole center, since Meier used the contrast between the two grids to enliven it. The main group of pavilions and the outside walls of the museum obey the freeway axis while others, facing the gardens, fraction the museum's internal facade by following the north-south direction and so connect to the circular building of the Research Institute. The gardens continue up between the museum and the Research Institute. Below the brow of the hill was to have been an open-air theater, but that concept was replaced by a water-sculpture garden from which visitors will have a spectacular view of Los Angeles. The Research Institute, on their right, features a cylindrical inner court that can be read as a negative, or counterpoint, to the museum's cylindrical entry hall. The main rooms of the institute radiate from this circular hollow.

The surface most in evidence at the Getty Center is honey-colored travertine, a stone of which much of Rome was built. It is used for paving and for the facing of many of the walls as well as for the pergolas and the colonnades, sometimes smooth-cut, but in the retaining wall and patios, split and left rough. Against this naturally rough surface, the smooth but matte-white or buff-colored metal panels offer a sharp but agreeable contrast of texture: lighter buildings seem to grow out of or over the stone core.

In the Getty plan the cylinder form—positive and negative—plays a pivotal but secondary role. Meier's cunning use of the cylinder is a relatively recent innovation. In the Ulm Exhibition and Assembly Building (1993), it organizes the whole building; in other projects—particularly when the site is irregular—the cylinder

(usually translucent) may act as a link or hinge. This is very clear in the small Museum of Television & Radio (1996) on the corner of Little Santa Monica Boulevard and North Beverly Drive in Beverly Hills. The building is in fact a conversion, and this imposed certain constraints, though the main architectural problem lay in relating a quasi-public building to the rather unwelcoming street pattern. Projecting the cylindrical entry hall from the facade created a minimal but usable public space, while a pool and a low bench act as tokens of civility. All this is important, as the main activity of the museum goes on at screen booths and in small private theaters; it is therefore the movement about the building that shows its vitality. Two of Meier's "type" elements—the cylinder and the ramp—here create a building in which movement is constantly visible. A staircase coils up on the inner face of the cylinder, above the entry point, to connect the second and third floors, while a more impressive internal movement is displayed by the long ramp that moves up the facade behind its brise soleil from the ground to the second floor.

I have considered this rather small but recent building in some detail here because it is a useful miniature realization of Meier's development. Analogous things might have been said about the Museum of Contemporary Art in Barcelona (1995) or the Euregio Office Building in Basel (1998). On a smaller scale again, this approach governs the Espace Pitôt in Montpellier, France (1995), a mixed-use development. One might equally find such virtues of urbanity in the recent private houses, particularly in the Rachofsky House in Dallas (1996); among contemporary architects, Meier is perhaps the one to whose work the old saw applies: he knows "the house to be a small city and the city a large house."

The design of the Church of the Year 2000 in Rome has led Meier to interpret his analytic and compositional approach in symbolic terms

by considering the implications of his type-forms. This development, and his consideration of the ludic element in building, show another aspect of his talent that has always prompted him to devote some time every day to making collages and, more recently, sculptures. Only a great assurance and maturity could have led him to consider such a development.

Whatever the surprises this new departure will bring, it can only add to his achievement. Meier's mastery of his formal language is now so complete that every new invention is satisfying. As his commissions grow in both size and number, the real surprise is that he still finds ever more perfect solutions within his approach and is open enough to look at each problem in a new way.

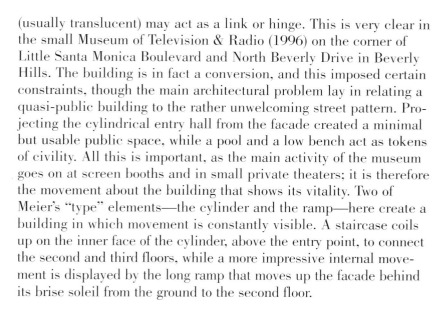

Private Buildings and Projects

Rachofsky House

Dallas, Texas
1991–1996

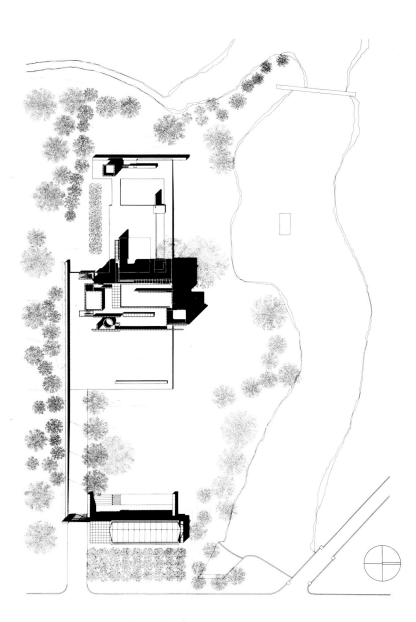

Set in a suburban landscape, this house/private museum is anchored to the ground by a podium faced in black granite that extends both in front of and behind the main body of the building. The white form of the house hovers on pilotis above the podium like an opaque plane, pierced by a number of discrete openings. A succession of spatial layers recedes from this taut surface to accommodate the house's principal volumes. The metal-faced front elevation that shields the living volume gives way on the north and west elevations to taut curtain walls that, together with the opaque front, inflect the interior layered space toward a small body of water to the southwest. Two sheets of water—a reflecting pool and a swimming pool—penetrate the podium at the rear of the house. The swimming pool, plus a cubic pool house and a low wall, effectively terminate the sitework at the western end.

Two separate stairs provide access to the three floors of the house: an enclosed spiral stair to the south and an open switchback stair to the north. This contrast between private and public circulation is echoed consistently in the organization of the volumes within. Thus the public stair opening off the gallery foyer leads directly to the double-height living room on the first floor, while the cylindrical private stair ascends to the library on the second floor and the master suite on the floor above. Two separate volumes on the third floor, a suspended study and an exercise room, afford views of the living volume and the garden. All glass walls that are exposed to low-angle western light are protected by electrically operated shades.

Stairs giving access from the swimming pool and to the roof terrace, along with a two-car garage under the guest suite on the south side of the house, complete the symmetrical repertoire. The exterior of the house is clad in white-enameled aluminum panels with aluminum fenestration and insulated glazing.

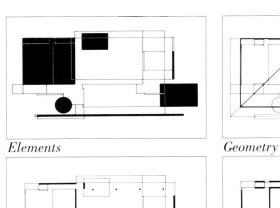

Elements

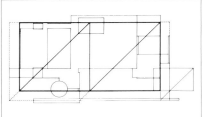

Geometry

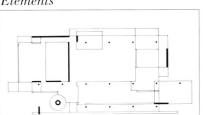

Structure

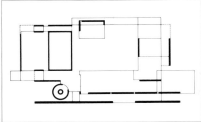

Enclosure

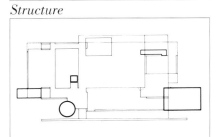

Circulation

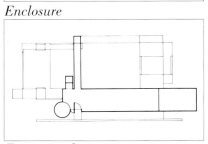

Entry circulation

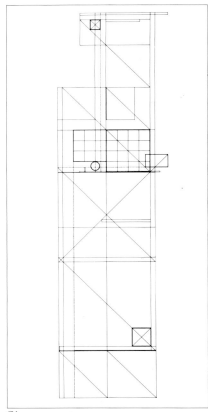

Site geometry

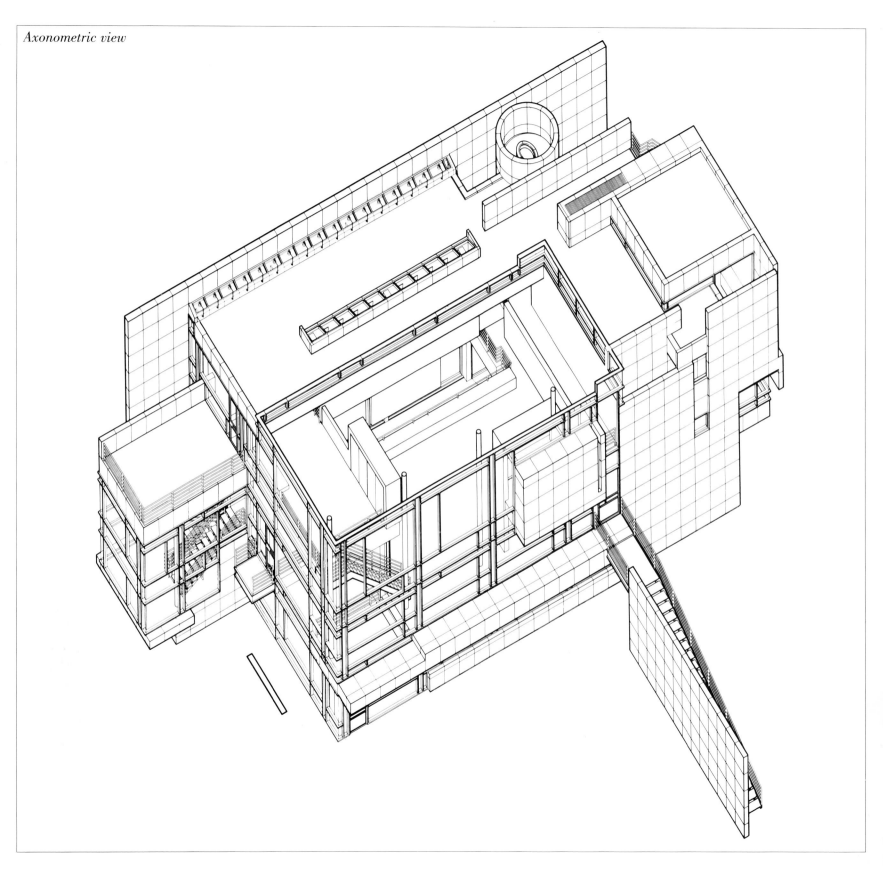

Axonometric view

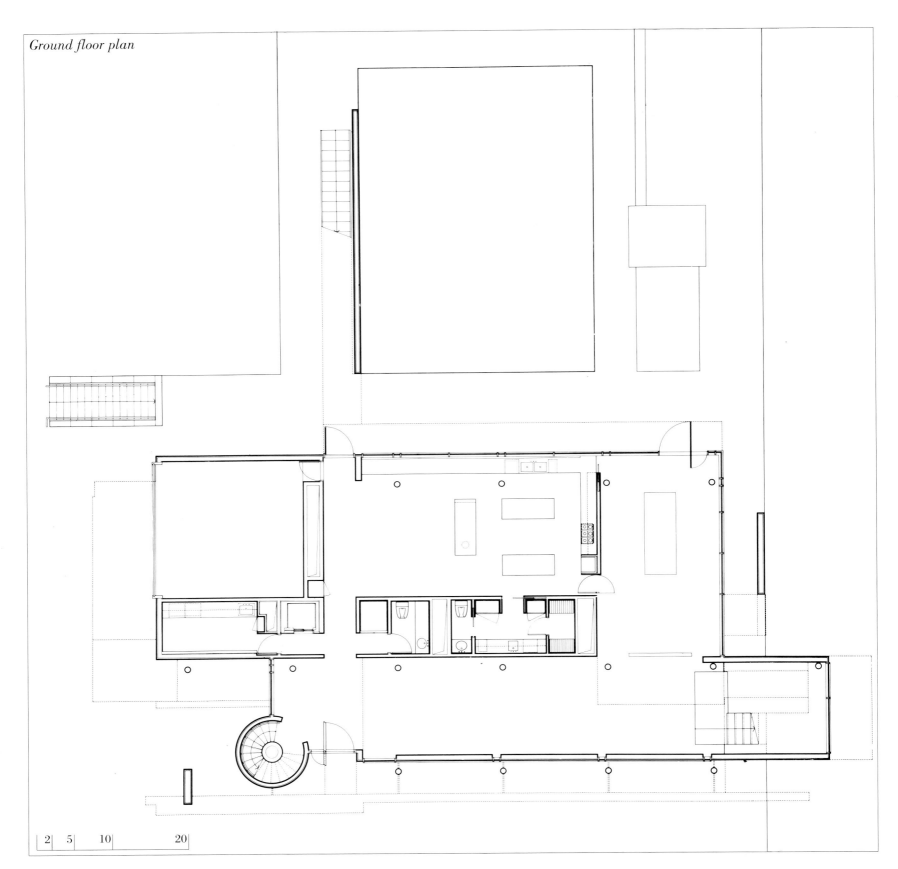

Ground floor plan

| 2 | 5 | 10 | 20 |

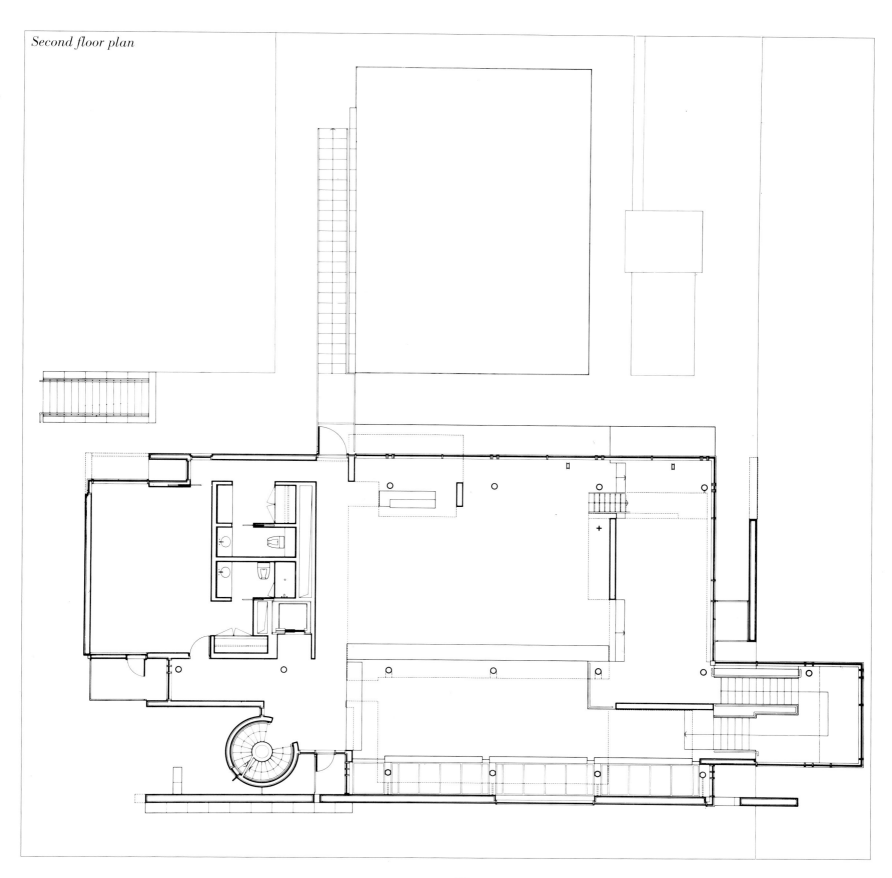

Second floor plan

33

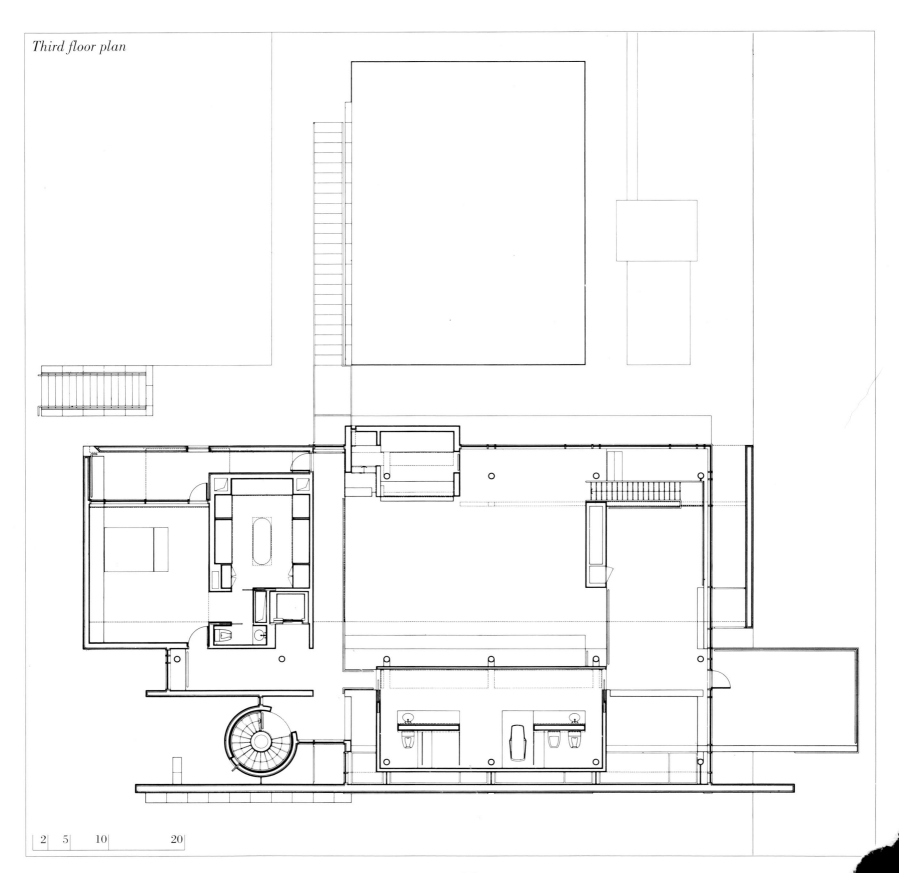

Third floor plan

2 5 10 20

East elevation

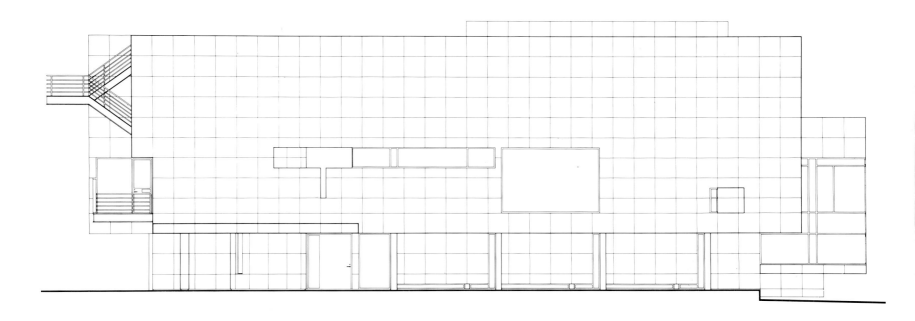

South elevation

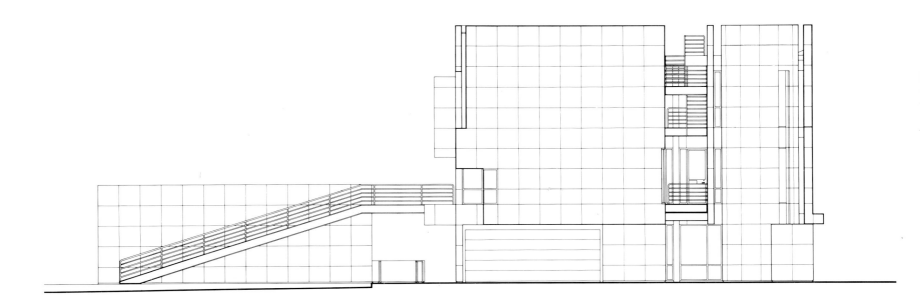

West elevation

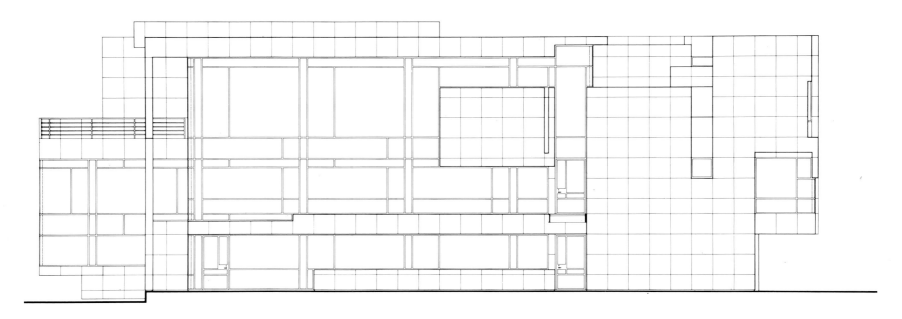

Longitudinal section

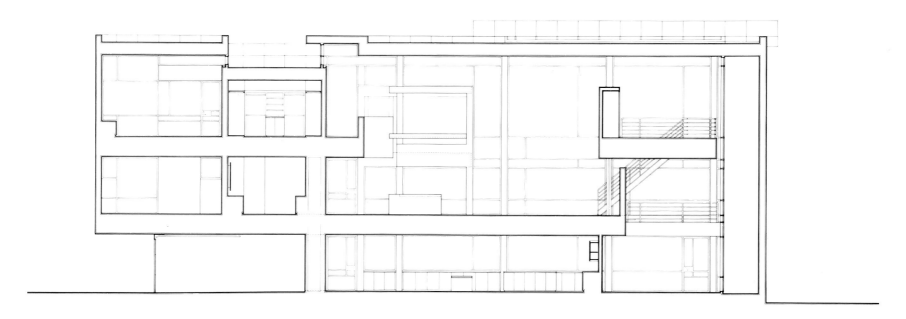

2 5   10   20

North elevation

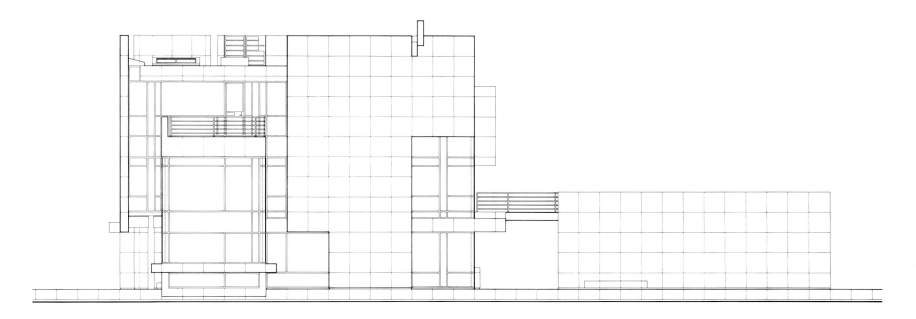

Cross section

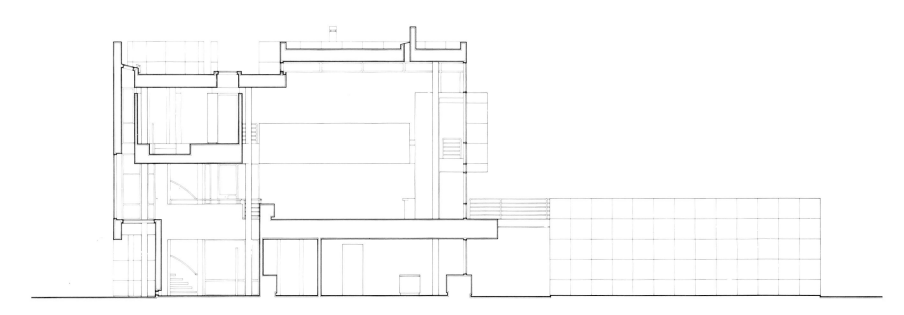

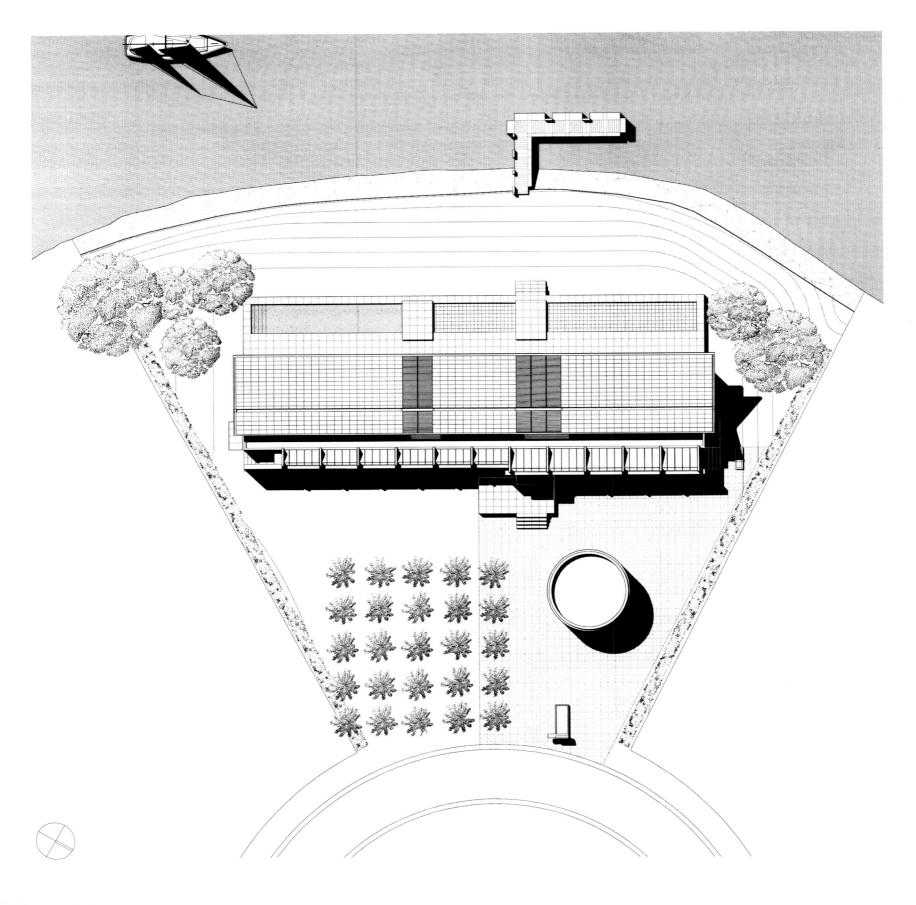

Neugebauer House

Naples, Florida
1995–1998

Located in a prestigious residential community on a one-and-a-half-acre waterfront site, this house spans the width of its wedge-shaped plot to face southwest across Doubloon Bay. One approaches the house from a winding access road lined with royal palm trees. The entrance is across the front lawn. This expanse of grass is uninterrupted except for an orthogonal cluster of royal palms and a low opaque cylinder faced with bent panels. This drum discreetly encloses a two-car garage. Since the turf is reinforced throughout, cars and pedestrians are free to circulate across the greensward at will. Beyond, effectively concealing a view of the water, lies the horizontal facade of the house itself, clad in two-foot by three-foot limestone slabs backed by concrete-frame and masonry construction. Pierced at regular intervals by vertical slot windows, this stone-faced facade conceals a wide, top-lit access corridor running the length of the house.

The inhabited volume of the house lies under a large steel-frame butterfly roof cantilevered off steel-box stanchions at 15-foot centers. The inverted roof pitch provided an unexpected way to meet the local design code's requirement of a pitched roof and at the same time reinforces the house's orientation toward the water. The double-layered roof is finished with two-foot by three-foot square panels in pulverized composite stone; its soffit is finished in plaster. The stone paneling on the roof serves solely as a rain screen, with water drained away beneath. The roof is also integrated into an elaborate sun-screening system made up of one-inch-diameter aluminum tubes placed at two-inch centers that screen the upper part of the oceanfront and span openings in the roof. The aluminum-subframe curtain walls are made of hurricane-resistant, $1^{5}/_{16}$-inch-thick laminated glass. The skylight glass is treated with a ceramic frit to provide additional sunscreening.

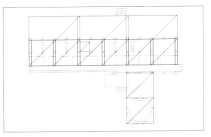

Geometry

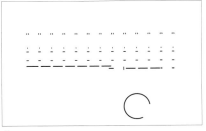

Structure

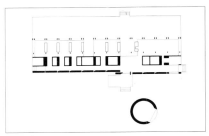

Enclosure

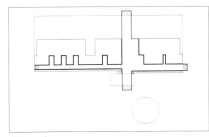

Circulation

Floor plan

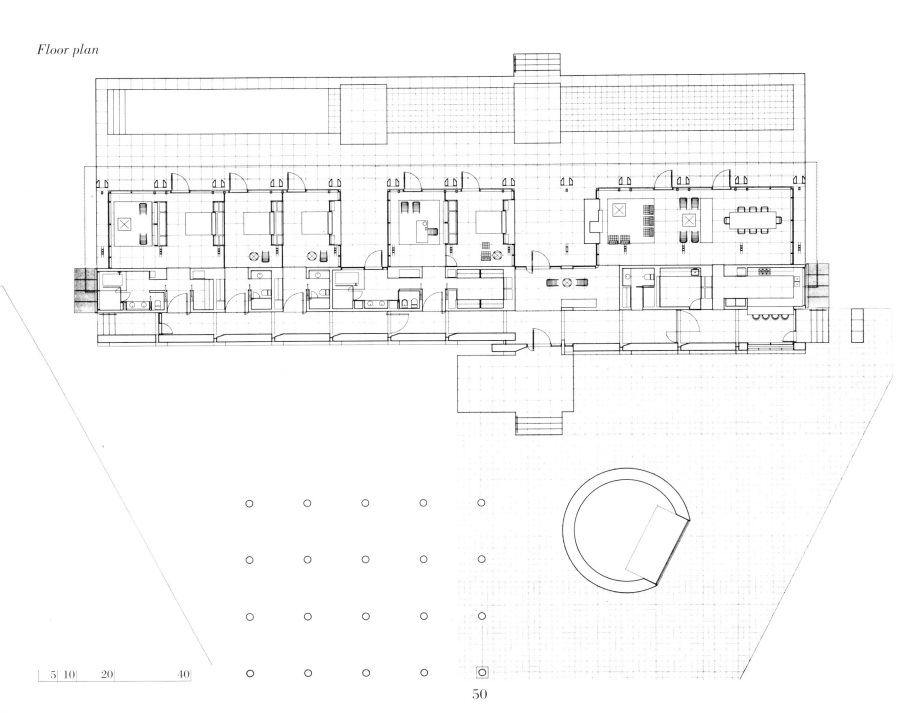

5 10   20   40

50

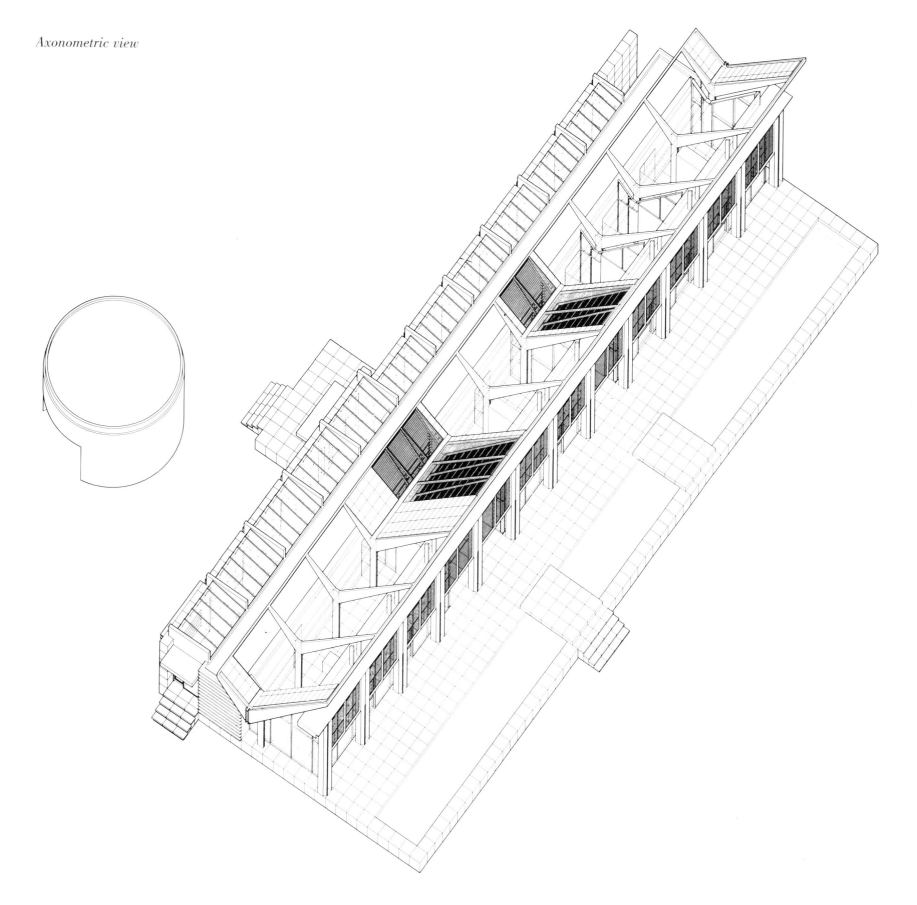

Axonometric view

North elevation

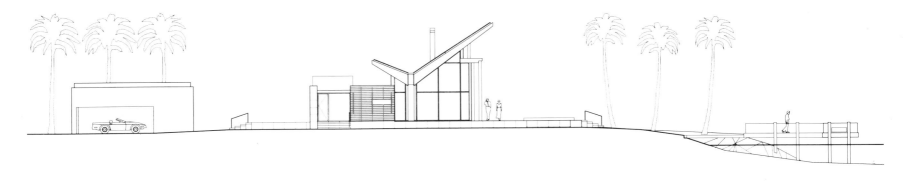

Cross section looking south

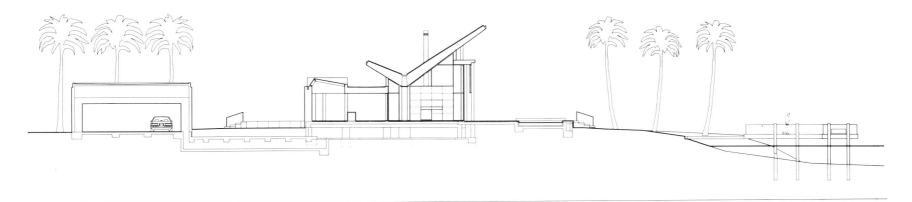

Cross section looking north

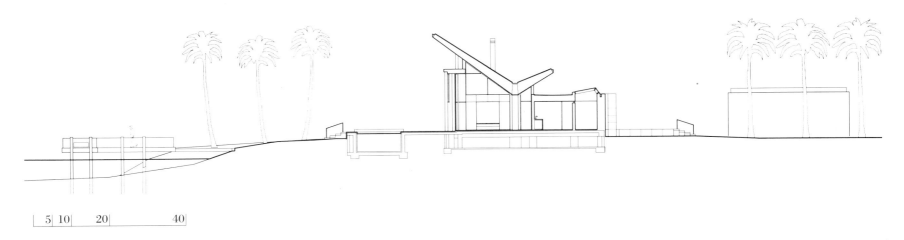

5	10	20		40	

West elevation

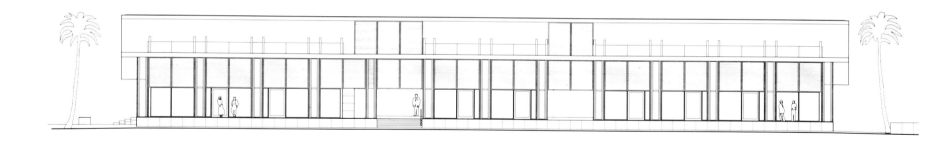

East elevation

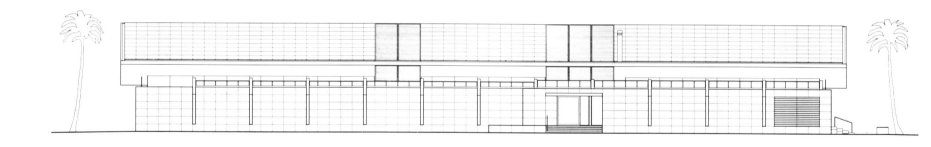

Longitudinal section through corridor looking west

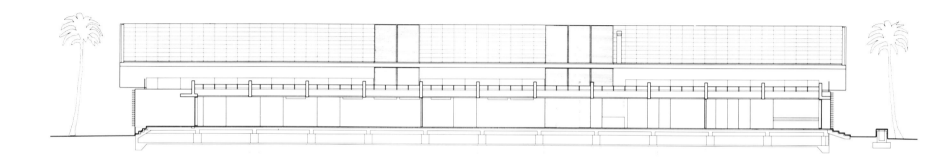

Public Buildings and Projects

Exhibition and Assembly Building

Ulm, Germany
1986–1993

Conceived as a programmatic and cultural complement to Ulm's Münsterplatz and the historic mass of its cathedral, this *Stadthaus* establishes a modest, secular, civic presence within the newly configured main square of the city. The building houses a visitors' information center, a ticket office, and a café terrace on the ground floor, and a top-lit, multilevel gallery space-cum-lecture hall on the floors above. With its striking cylindrical form capped by three prominent roof skylights, the building imparts a decisively civic character to the otherwise continuous commercial frontage of the square. The main body of the building derives its form from the geometry of the cathedral and the square. It is based on a nine-square structural bay system augmented on three sides by concentric peripheral walls modified and curtailed by intersecting axes and regulating lines. The main drum form functions as a counterpoint to the cathedral as one enters the square from the west and southwest. An asymmetrical stair and a freestanding elevator afford immediate access from the ground floor to the lecture hall and exhibition spaces above, while a loggia/bridge at the upper level links the restaurant to the entry foyer on the ground floor and the exhibition spaces above.

The building was designed to provide carefully framed views of the cathedral and the square. The construction is reinforced concrete frame and blockwork throughout, with the inner nine-square cube faced in natural stone and the outer concentric screen walls and the restaurant clad in stucco. The northwest perimeter of the square is planted with sycamore trees to create a more intimate pedestrian scale along the commercial frontage, while the *parvis* was re-created and repaved in accordance with a grid derived from the geometry of the cathedral.

Site plan

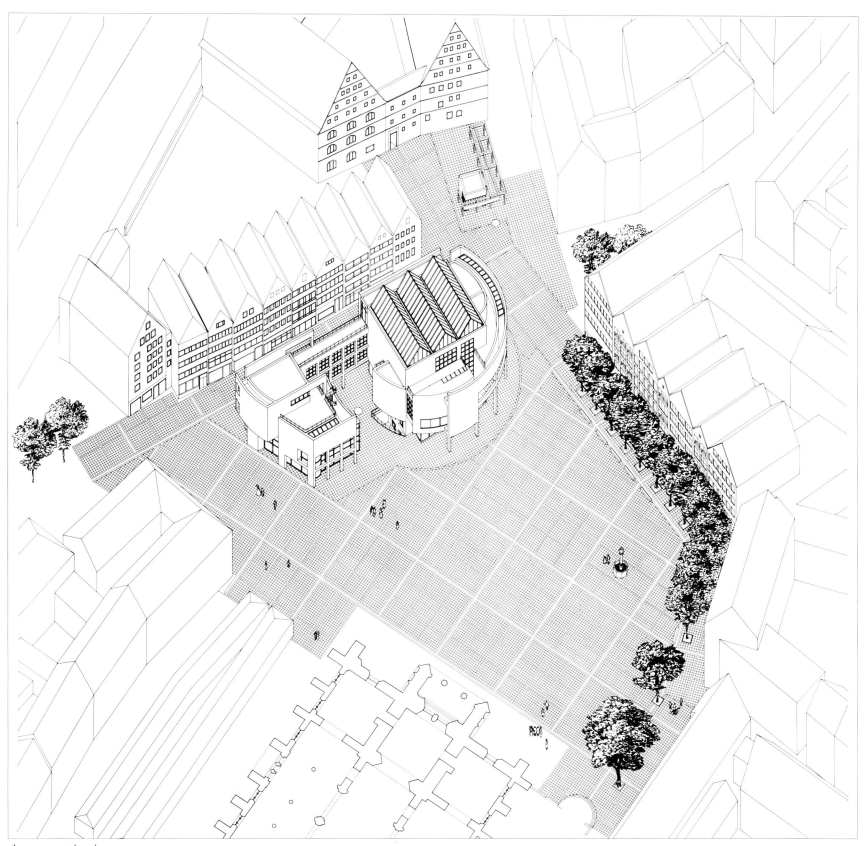

Axonometric view

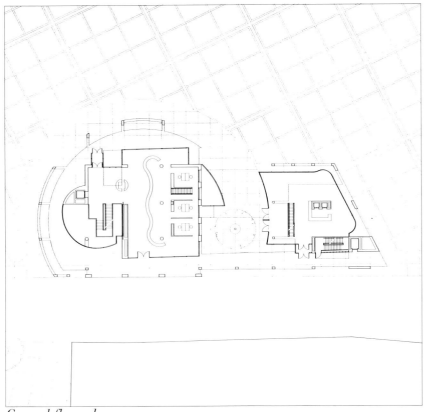

Ground floor plan

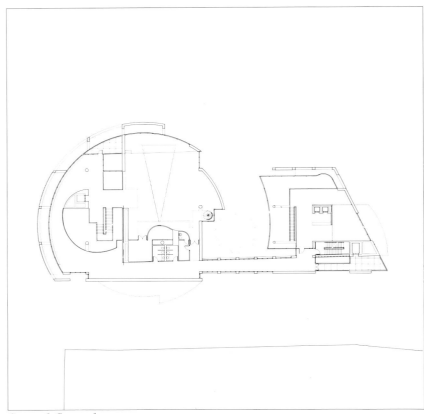

Second floor plan

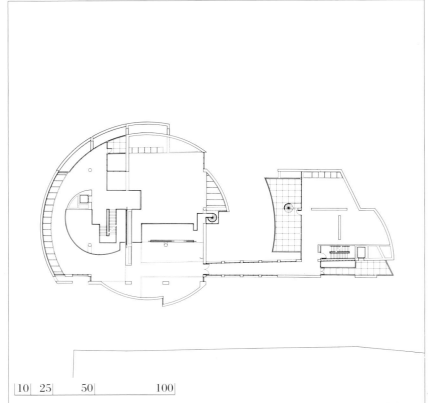

|10| 25| 50| 100|

Third floor plan

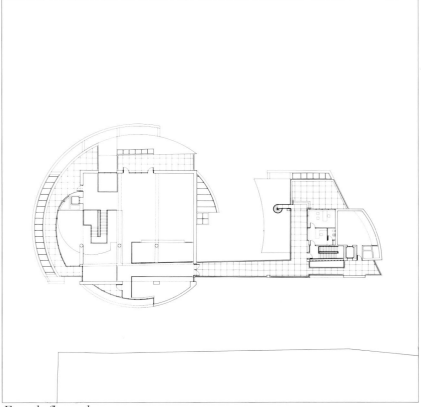

Fourth floor plan
62

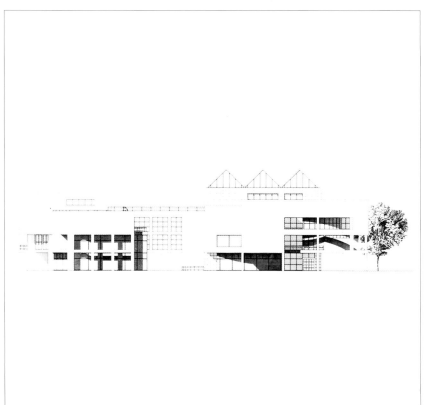

Northeast elevation

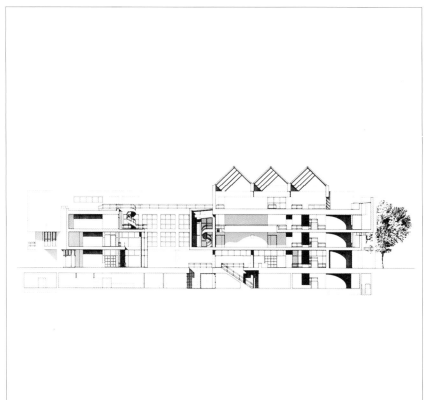

Cross section facing southwest

Southwest elevation

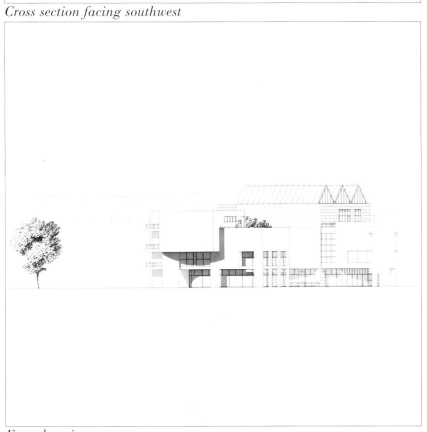

East elevation

63

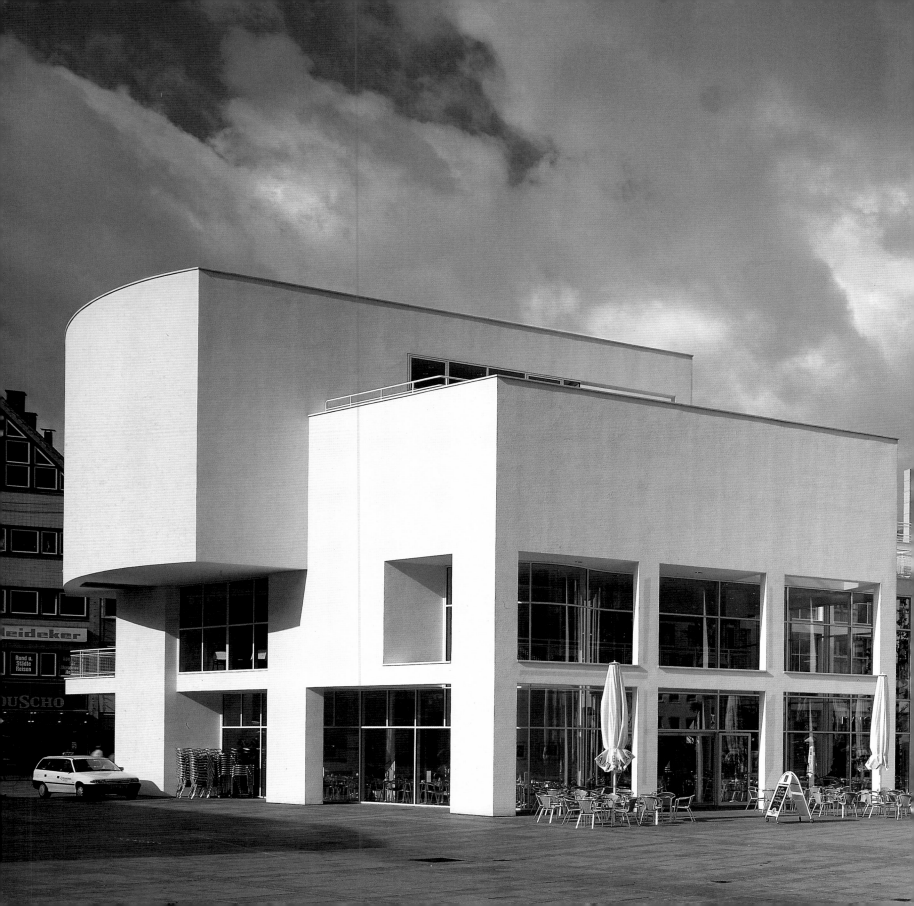

66

A vital aspect of the Stadthaus is its restaurant/café that opens onto the Münsterplatz, thereby catering directly to the most public events that occur in this space—to the visiting tourists as much as to the regular market-goers. This aspect provides for a constantly changing pageant on the square.

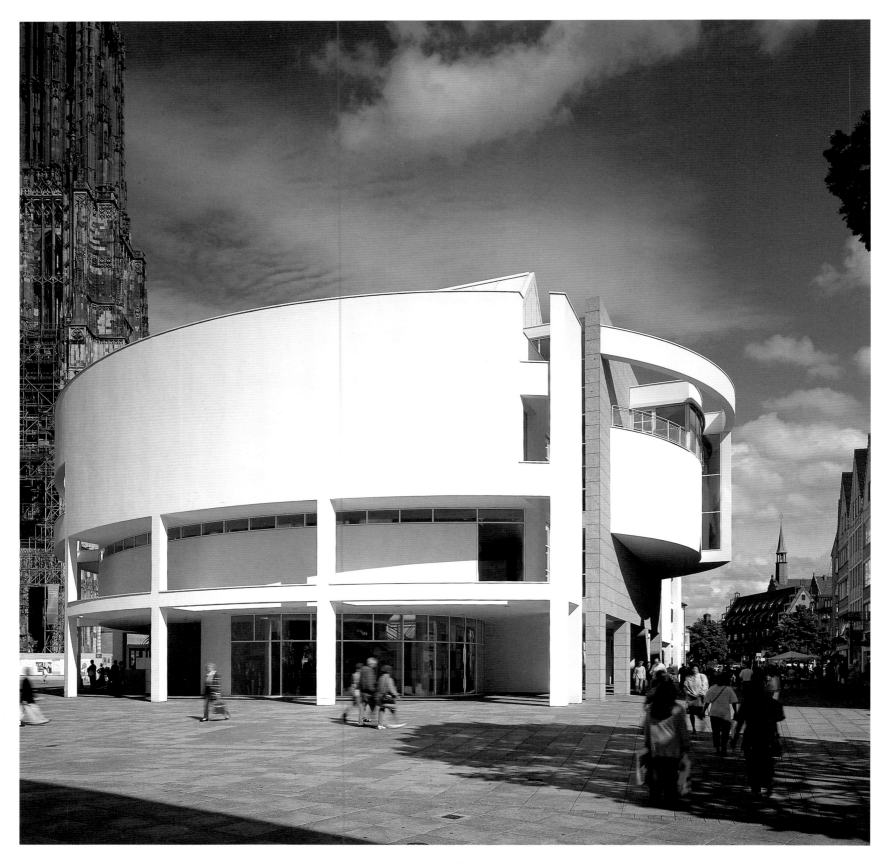

It may well be that the seemingly European character of my architecture arises from my particular feeling for cities and for the way in which the cultural history of a particular place may be read and experienced, almost in its entirety, by virtue of the architecture alone. The Münsterplatz in Ulm is just such a place where, as Max Bächer, chairman of the 1986 assembly building competition jury, put it, the spire of the cathedral soars upwards "not ad maiorem Dei but ad maiorem civitas gloriam." Thus, while constantly related to the cathedral, our cultural building is intended to reinforce the civic, secular nature of the main city square.

The heavy aerial bombardment inflicted on Ulm at the end of the Second World War effectively destroyed 80 percent of the city's original medieval fabric. The cathedral was one of the ten monuments fortunately spared. The pastiche postwar reconstruction of the surrounding buildings had the unfortunate effect of greatly enlarging the square, even to the extent of opening one end to a faceless parking lot. Our primary task was to design a building that, by virtue of its form, scale, and presence, would restore the somewhat compromised urban character of the Münsterplatz.

In Europe, history is visible in every city; it is there to be read. The history of architecture as well as the whole cultural history of a place is present and can be experienced. That is an obligation. Building in the context of history requires sensitivity, an acceptance of the place in each sense. The attention I pay to such questions perhaps makes me seem more European than many of my colleagues in the United States.

City Hall and Central Library

The Hague, The Netherlands
1986–1995

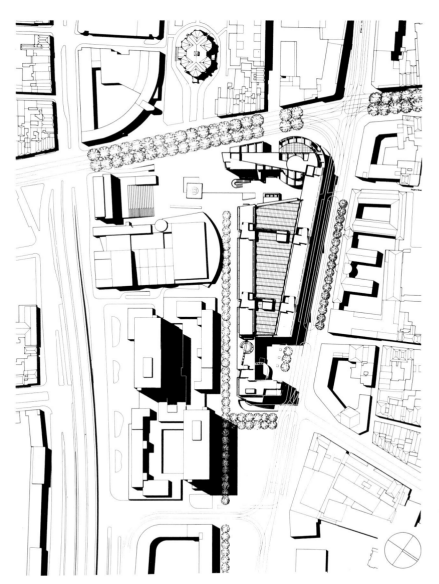

This continuous megastructural galleria, 800 by 250 feet, effectively establishes The Hague's new city center, together with a concert hall, hotel, and dance theater to the southeast and a multiuse cultural center to the south. Within its overall volume is the main public library, a council chamber, cafés, exhibition spaces, and a wedding room. The city hall provides office space on either side of the top-lit public galleria. This enclosed public realm extends into a semi-independent rental office building at its northeast end, while extensive, small-scale retail space runs throughout its ground floor.

The 10- and 12-story horizontal office slabs diverge at an angle of 10.5 degrees to match the grain of the city. The slabs flank a large internal atrium that forms the new *res publica* of the municipality known as the Citizens Hall.

The main library, with its concentric semicircular plan, is located at the northwest end of the complex, where its dynamic form gives definition to the intersecting streets. Opposite the library and adjacent to the main entrance to the city hall is a well-known local furniture store that occupies part of the space beneath the library. In the ground-floor foyer are a reception counter, a café, and free-standing escalators that serve the library floors above.

The monitor-lit glass roof of the atrium is carried on deep beams. Aerial bridges spanning the atrium at two points further interrupt the longitudinal axis. These are served by elevator shafts with fully glazed elevator cabins. These light, elegant structures in painted white steel are intended to appear as dematerialized screens subdividing the large perspectival volume into three different zones. The council chamber itself is situated prominently to one side of the main entrance. Its upper surface, visible from the flying bridges, provides an informal space for the councilors to meet the general public.

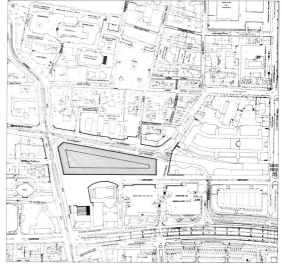

These six diagrams show the evolution of the design from the influence of the surrounding urban grain on the building module to the counterpoint between the internal galleria and the external civic spaces and monuments.

Building site

The new building is at the intersection of the city's two grids.

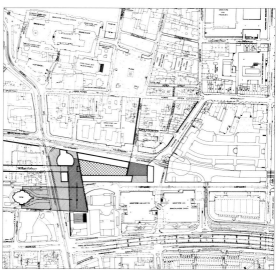

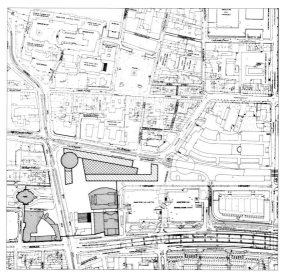

Open spaces on the site and in the building were created in response to the formal organization of the built environment.

The City Hall and Central Library completes the "culture square" precinct of The Hague.

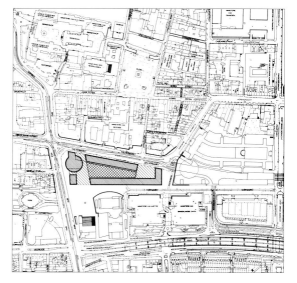

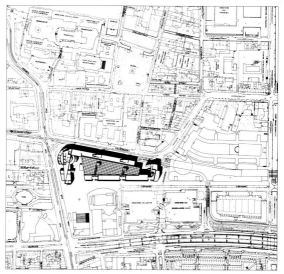

The location of open spaces on the site also relates to the building's main entrances.

Site plan within the city's urban fabric.

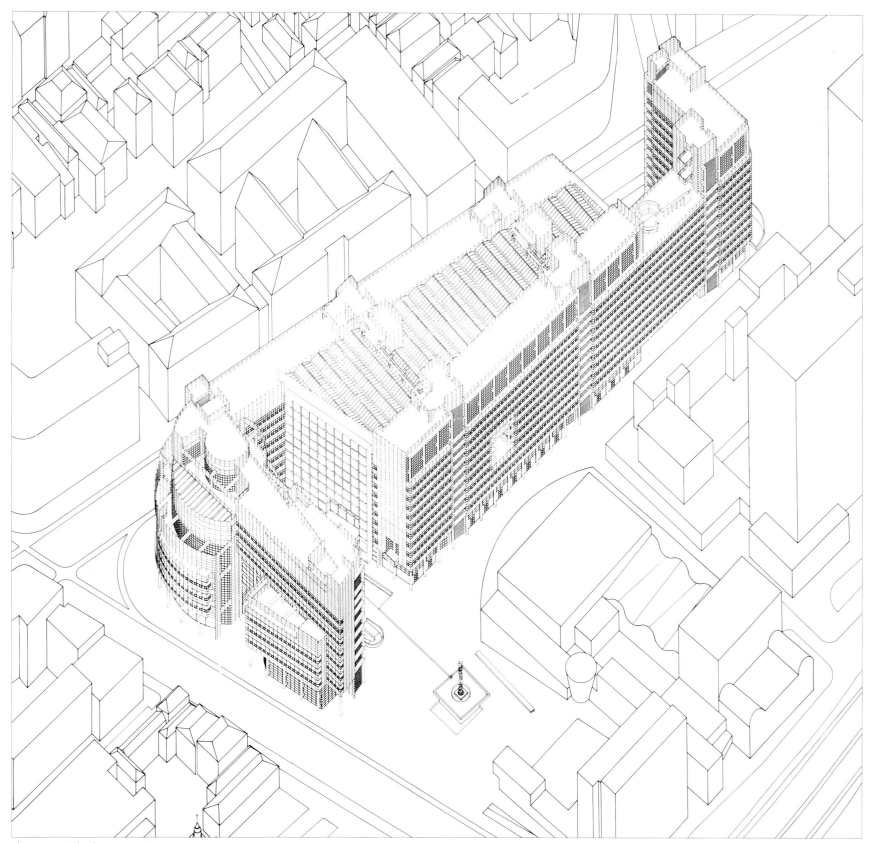

Axonometric in context

Ground floor plan

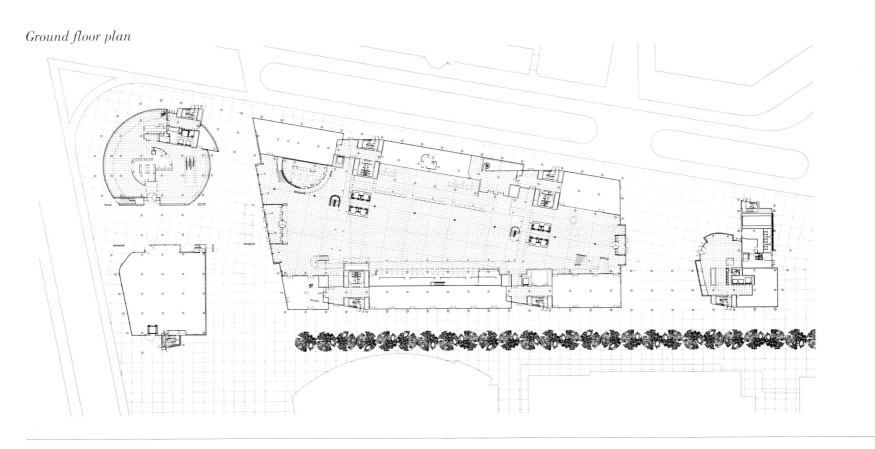

Second floor plan

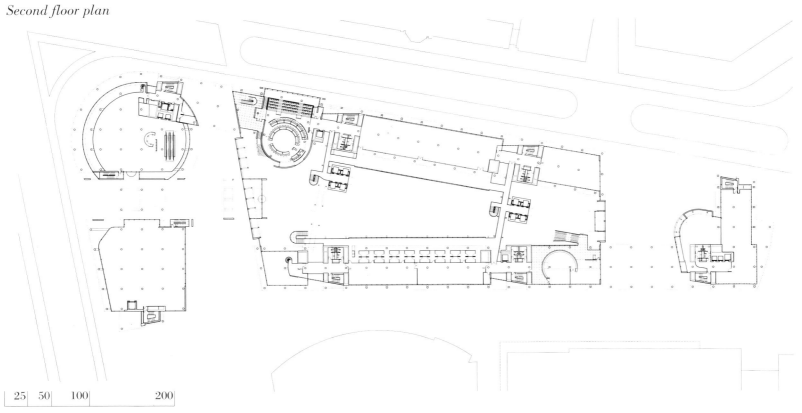

25 50 100   200

82

Seventh floor plan

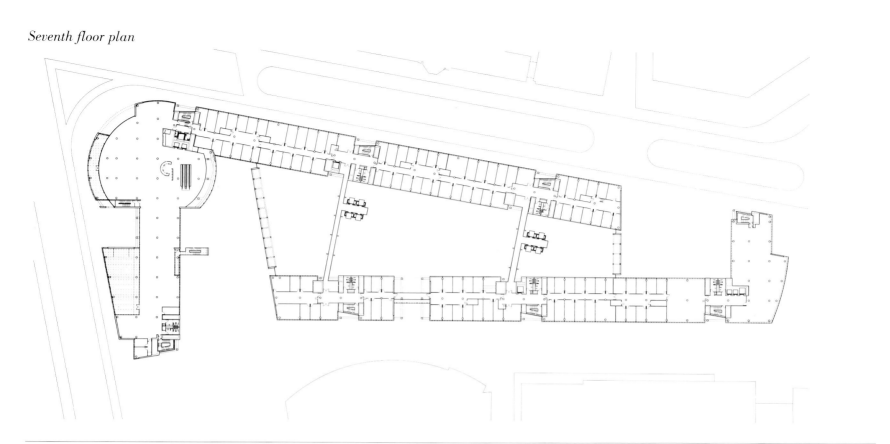

Eleventh floor plan

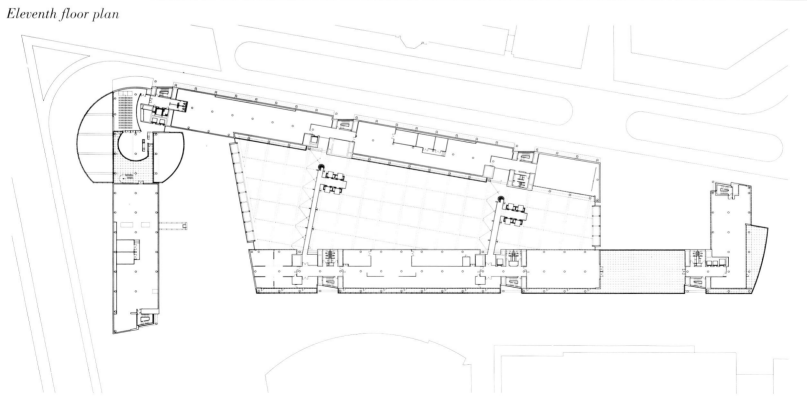

As the seat of Dutch government, the Hague has been restructured continually over the last two decades. Most of this urban renewal has taken place between the old core city and the railway station. Our city hall and library not only form the public heart of this Nieu Centrum, but also have become the catalyst for a great deal of new building by both Dutch and foreign architects. Hopefully this new construction will further reinforce pedestrian movement through the heart of the city.

By virtue of its extensive transparency the city hall reveals not
only the structure of its organization but also the essentially open
character of the city's form of
governance. The building
expresses civic dedication
through contrasting spatial
and tectonic elements that shift
constantly between public and
private, formal and informal,
light and dark, solid and void.

Architects working abroad, while bringing their professional experience and expertise to a site, must remain conscious of the need to create a place that responds to the indigenous environment. In the end, one must acknowledge that once construction is completed, the building sheds forever the influence of the architect and becomes part of the cultural patrimony of the neighborhood, city, and country where it is rooted.

When you look at Dutch landscape paintings, you sense at once that the sky is a large part of the image, an aspect that surely derives in large measure from the flatness of the land. This accounts for the overall gray and diffused character of Dutch light, which is quite different from that of Southern Europe or America. At the same time the light has a peculiar radiance, even on the grayest of days, and the clouds in The Hague are incredible. All of this is picked up by the refractive, translucent top-lit atrium that glows with a particular warmth when the sun breaks through.

Almost three years after the official opening of the Central Library, I was invited to lecture one evening in the atrium, thereby fulfilling a fantasy I had entertained ever since we first broke ground. For me it felt like a homecoming to speak to more than one thousand architecture aficionados in a glazed internal courtyard nearly the size of St. Mark's Square in Venice.

Weishaupt Forum

Schwendi, Germany
1987–1992

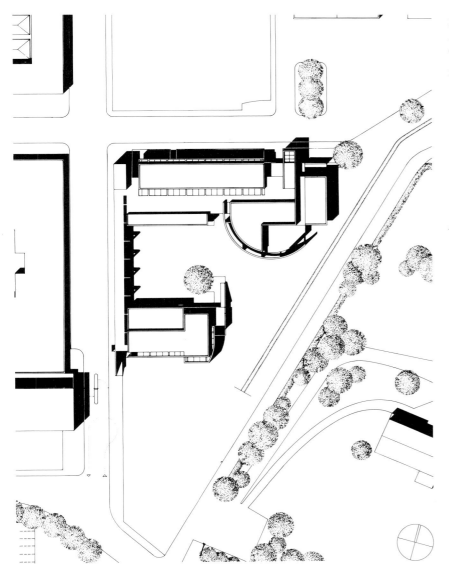

Set in Schwabian countryside on the edge of a small town, this complex is the representational building for a small industrial plant. The assembly was conceived as a communal and public reception facility, which, running parallel to the existing administration building, creates a new controlled street leading from the main entry to the interior of the plant. The new complex is made up of two principal structures: a cafeteria and a training center housed in a single-bar building, and a portico building opposite the existing offices. The portico building accommodates a product display area and a 50-seat orientation space at grade, with a gallery for the industrialist's collection of late-twentieth-century art above. This structure is linked to the cafeteria/training wing by a loggia/*passerelle* that comprises the third side of an inner grass-covered court. The covered causeway provides protection from the elements as employees come and go to the factory. It also affords access to the two guest dining rooms and the double-height, 260-seat staff cafeteria. The latter houses the main stair leading to two classrooms and a teaching laboratory on the floor above. The complex may be entered at both levels via dog-leg stairs at the external corners.

The inner court is framed by two first-floor terraces, one flanking the semicircular screen wall of the cafeteria and the other opening off the art gallery. These terraces impart an intimate feeling to the court, which is bounded on one side by the loggia and on the other by a stream that separates the forum from the owner's private residence to the southwest, at the extreme corner of the site.

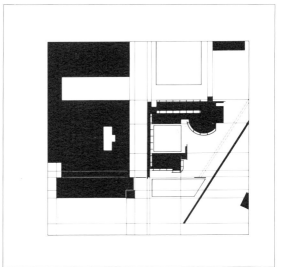

Site relationships

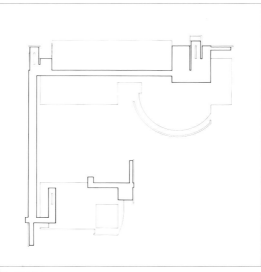

Program

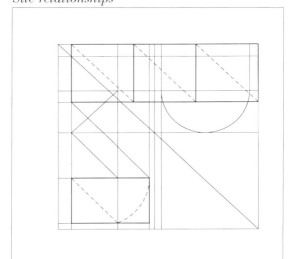

Geometry

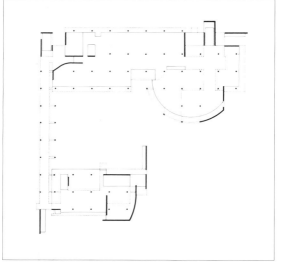

Structure

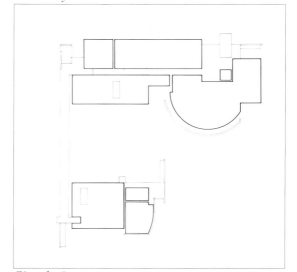

Circulation

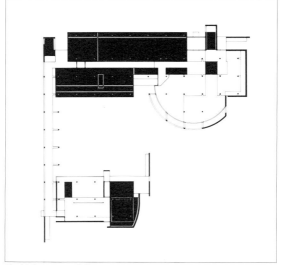

Solids vs. voids

Axonometric view

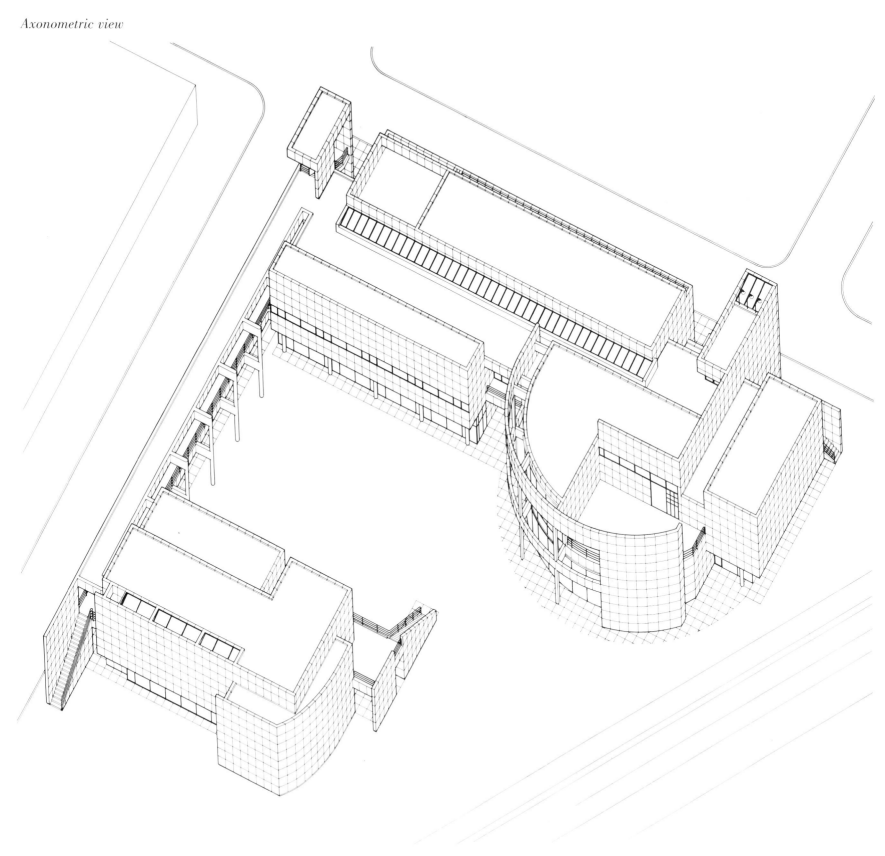

99

After World War II, many
American architects found
themselves asked to design
headquarters buildings for major
corporations. For the next three
decades, such buildings were
often regarded as representative
of corporate identity. This
practice has largely disappeared
in the United States, and only
one-off, small-scale European
works such as this one recover
something of the period when a
headquarters building was seen
as embodying the image of the
company.

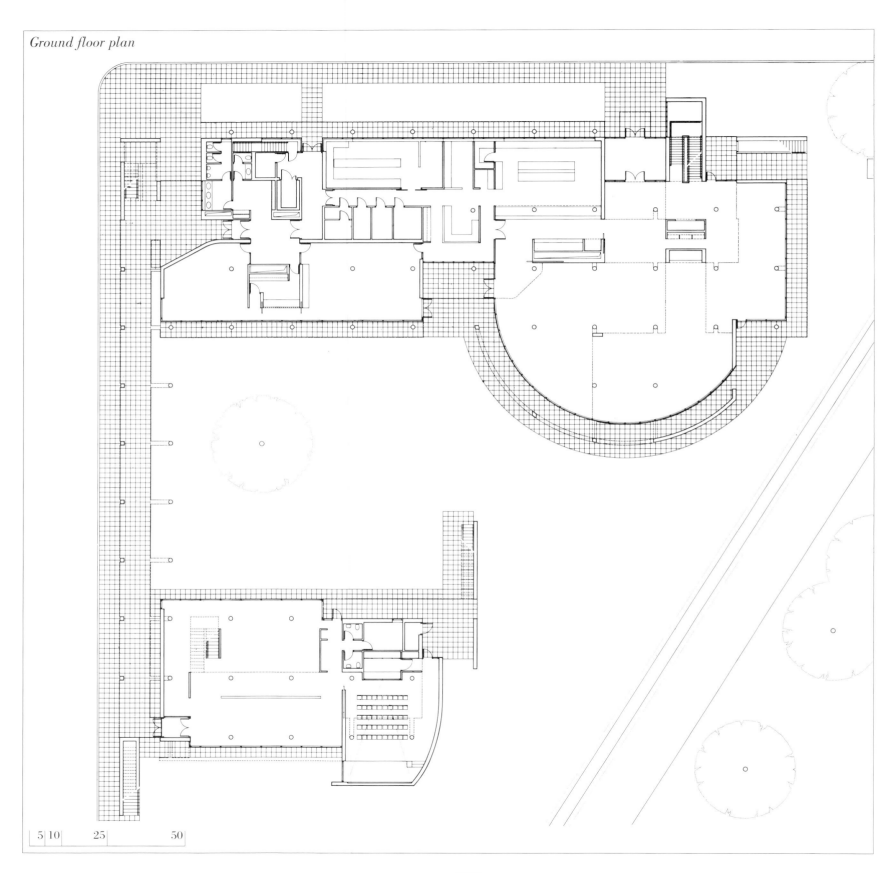

5 | 10   25   50

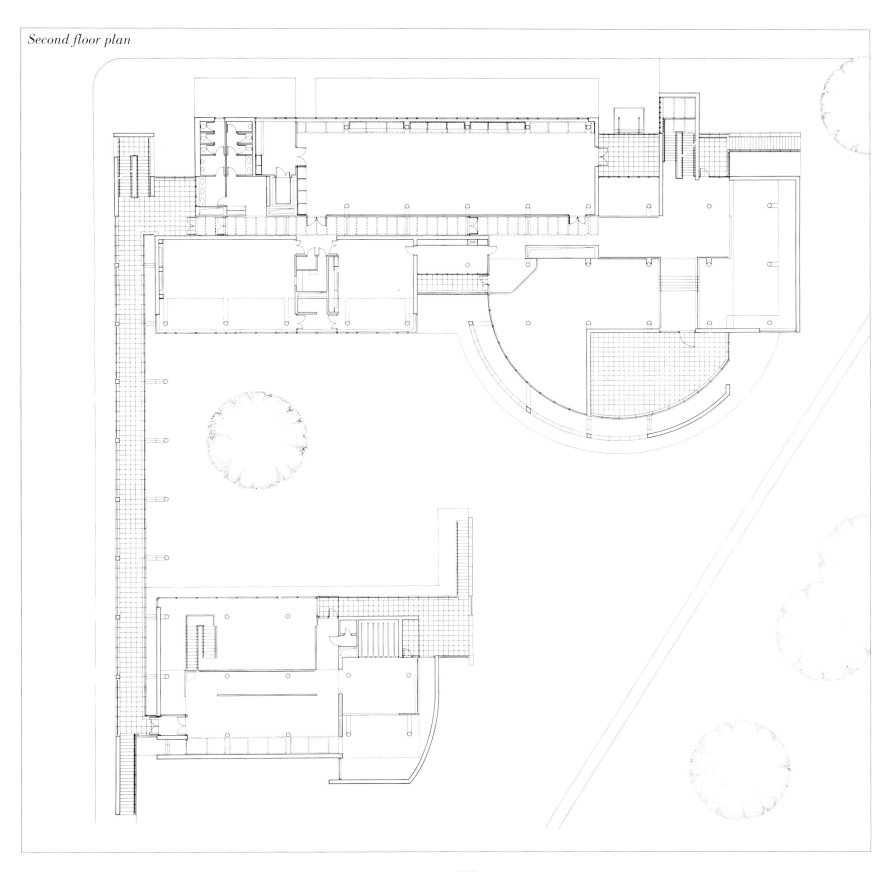

Second floor plan

The semipublic identity of the company is represented through two buildings that face each other across a green area: a two-story gallery that houses the owner's art collection, and a semicircular staff cafeteria.

Southeast elevation

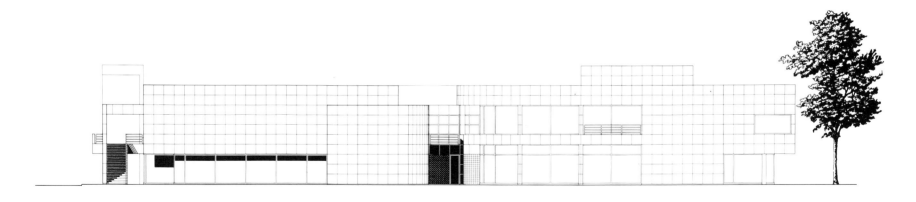

Southeast elevation of interior court

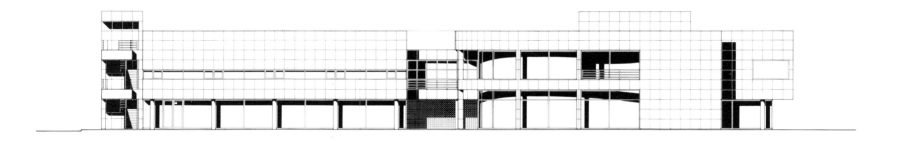

Northwest elevation

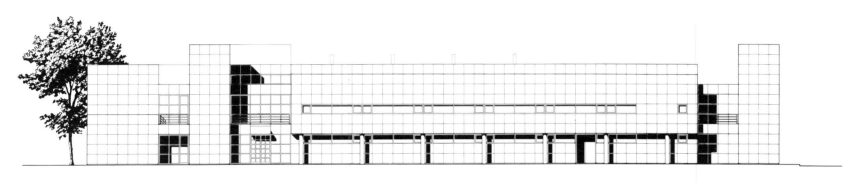

5|10| 25| 50|

Northwest elevation of interior court

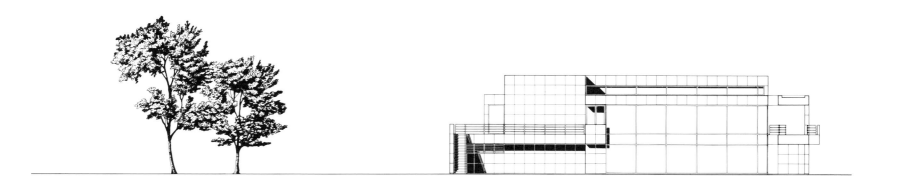

Northeast elevation

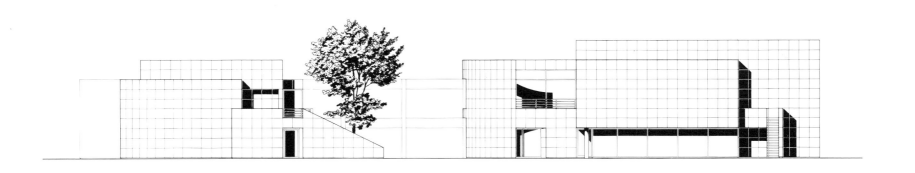

Southwest elevation

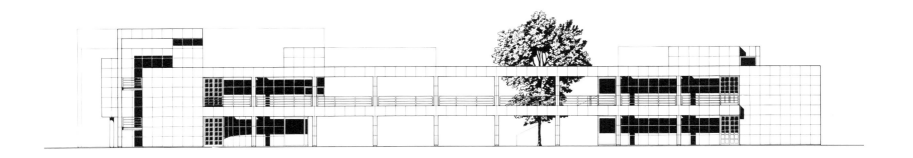

111

Every work of architecture represents the coming together of a variety of components. However, what is important to me is the way in which architecture expresses a unified whole. In addition to the site, the program, and the mores of the place, there must always be an aspirational vision. It is not possible to create a work of architecture without an enlightened client. In Schwendi, Siegfried Weishaupt had the will to achieve a great building of enduring value.

Royal Dutch Paper Mills Headquarters

Hilversum, The Netherlands
1987–1992

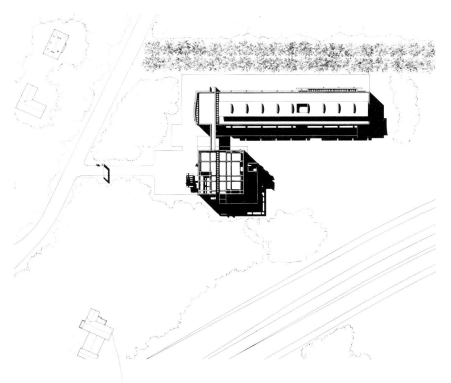

This headquarters for a prominent international paper company is set in a clearing in a densely wooded area. The building consists of two interconnected structures: a four-story cubic reception building and a two-story office slab elevated on pilotis. The former provides dining facilities on the lower two floors, with general staff convening in a double-height restaurant at grade and executives and visitors in mezzanine dining rooms above. These private dining spaces overlook the main space and open to terraces facing southwest and southeast. Guest offices and meeting rooms are on the second floor, with a 60-seat lecture hall and conference room above.

The building is organized volumetrically around two intersecting corridors: one runs northwest-southeast and is serviced directly by the elevator/mechanical core; the other, running northeast-southwest, affords access to offices on either side.

The two-story elevated office slab has two main entrances: one at the northeast end with an honorific stair, echoing a similar feature in the reception building, and another at midpoint equipped with an independent elevator core serving the executive offices in the southwest half of the slab. Both the executive and the staff offices are served from top-lit, double-height, double-loaded corridors with continuous access on one side and *passerelles* to office clusters on the other. The voids between *passerelles* illuminate lower corridors and unify the internal space.

Sophisticated in its exterior treatment, the office slab sets up a counterpoint between the main structure of freestanding cylindrical columns and the projecting concrete blades that maintain structural continuity in the spandrel wall. Horizontal strip windows plus horizontal sun screens add further syncopation to the facade.

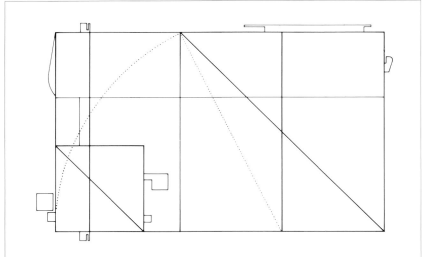

Geometry

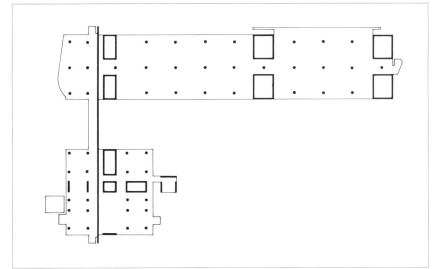

Structure

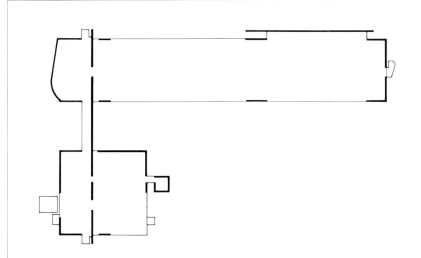

Enclosure

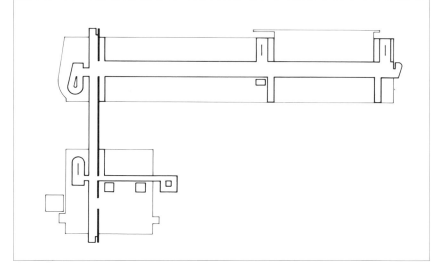

Circulation

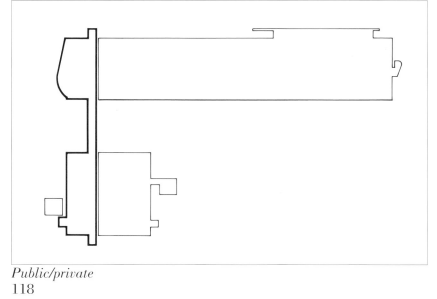

Public/private

118

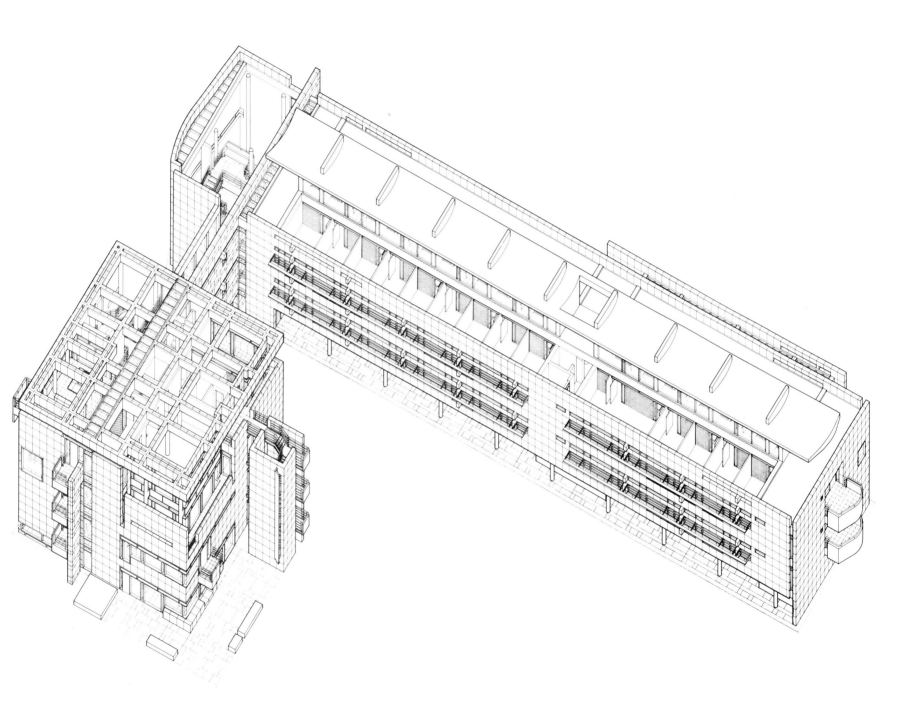

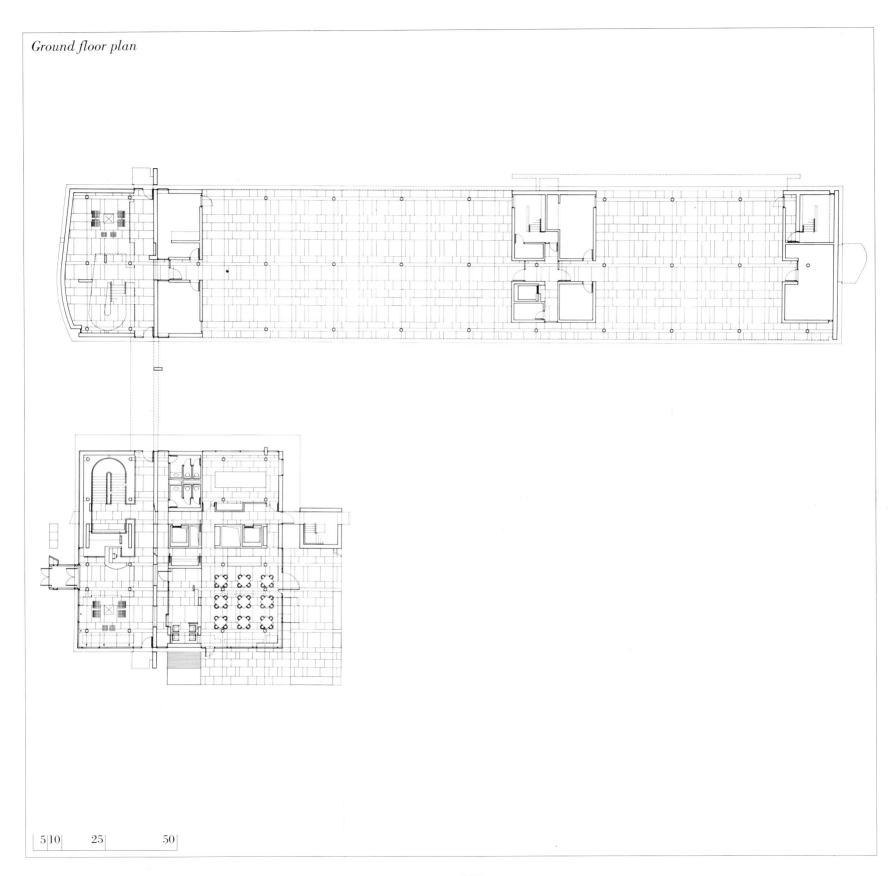

5|10   25| 50|

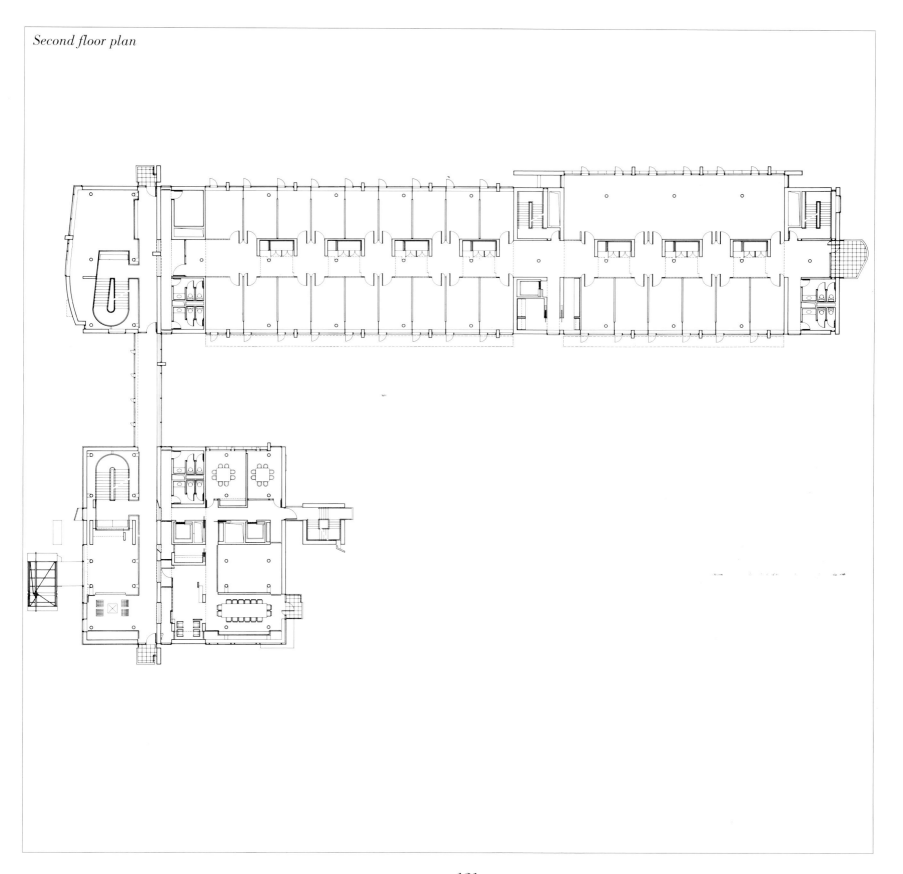

This complex, comprised of a two-story office building raised on pilotis and a four-story staff reception block, may be approached either straight on from the street or laterally from a parking lot to the rear of the offices. The reception block is paralleled by an avenue of trees linking the complex to the landscape, while the office building is a four-square cubic mass, similar in scale to the mass-form of the neighboring villas.

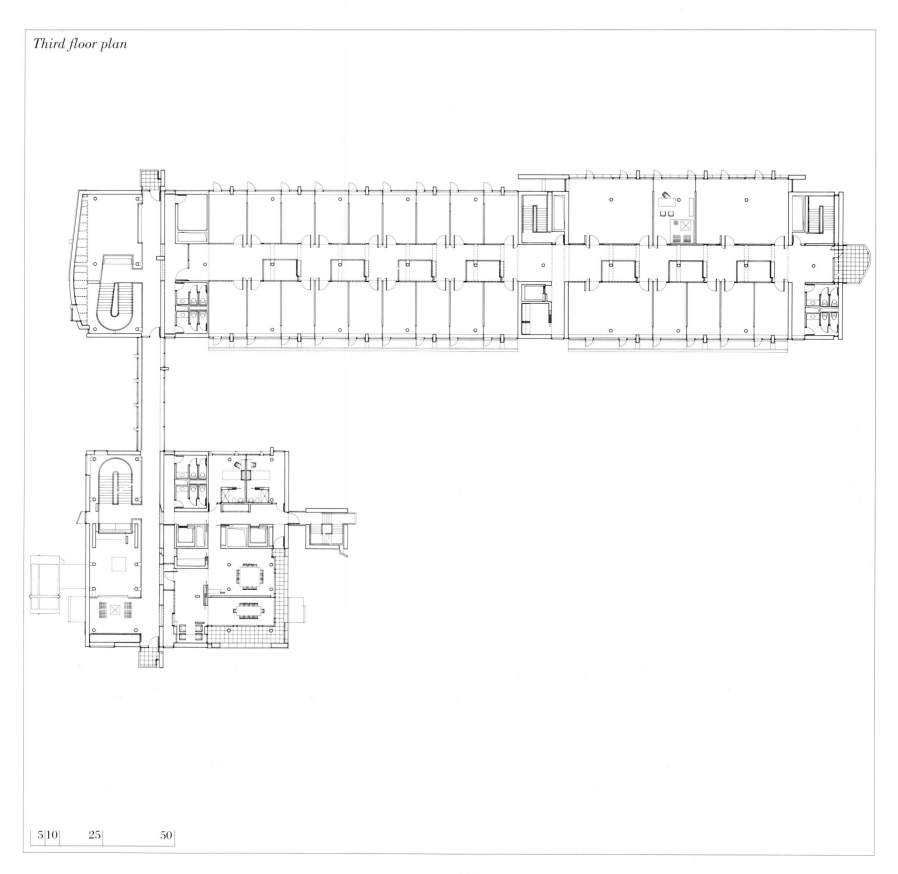

5|10| 25| 50|

Northeast elevation

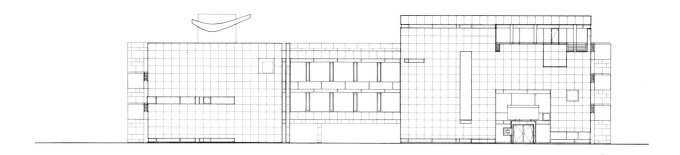

Southwest elevation

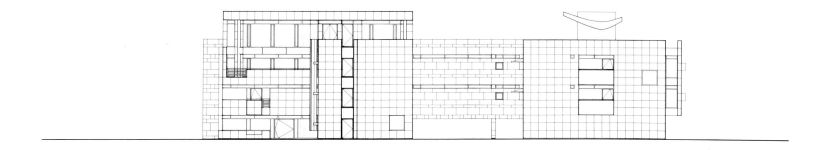

Northwest elevation

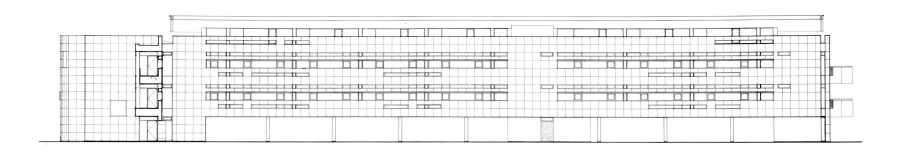

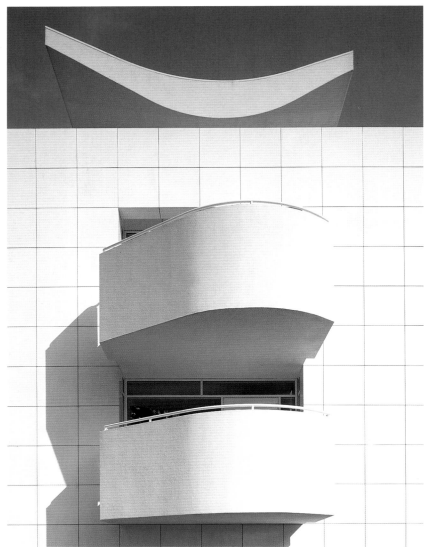

A few years after this headquarters building was completed, the corporate structure of the company changed and the new board decided to consolidate its office space in Amsterdam. The building was sold to a major media company, and I am pleased to say that it has respected the original design intentions and not made any significant changes. Perhaps the clear planning and organization of the space made this reuse possible.

I consistently find working abroad—whether in Europe or elsewhere—to be an adventure in cultural climates that are profoundly different from my own in New York. If architects are not sensitive to people's social codes, to the rhythm of their daily lives, to geographic distinctions, and to the unique quality of sunlight, they cannot responsibly design for a site abroad.

Museum of Contemporary Art

Barcelona, Spain
1987–1995

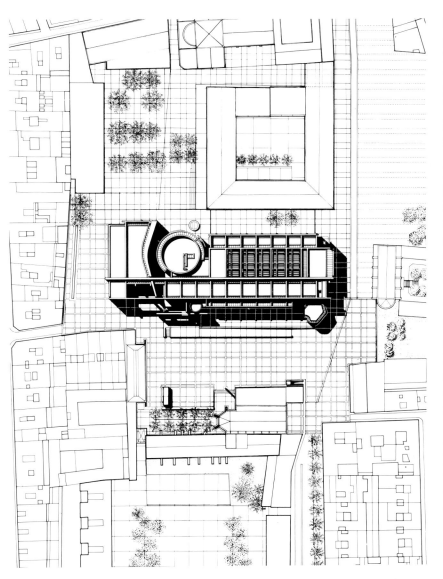

Contextually responsive in its scale and orientation, this museum plays a key role in restructuring the Gothic district of Barcelona. Together with the Casa de la Caritat cultural center and a new university building to the north of its sculpture court, the museum helps to consolidate this new arts quarter within the broader urban fabric. To this end, ground-floor circulation generates a new pedestrian pattern linking the new plaza in front of the building with an interblock pedestrian system serving the cultural center and the university.

Entry to the gallery space is through a cylindrical, top-lit gallery/foyer leading to a glazed, triple-height ramp-hall that faces the new Plaça dels Angels to the south. This hall, together with an intermediate corridor paved in glass block, enables the visitor to access six continuous loftlike spaces on successive levels. A semidetached wing at the eastern end of the block accommodates additional gallery space and the suite of curatorial offices.

The main galleries are partially lit from above, particularly at the top of the building where the loft space is covered with louvered skylights. Some of the light from this source filters down via glass-block floors and open slots to illuminate the lower levels. Where natural light enters from the south, it is screened in part by the external louvers, by a number of freestanding screen walls, and by the ramp itself.

Clad in white enameled-steel panels, the plaza elevation is animated by the horizontal louvers of the ramp-hall and by two plaster sculptural elements, a cut-out plane above the entrance and a free-form, top-lit special exhibitions gallery set in advance of the building at the eastern end of the main facade.

Context

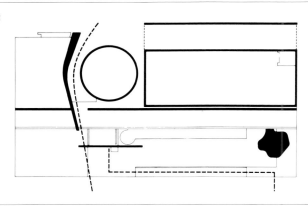

Program

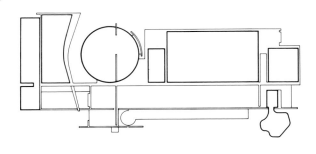

Geometry

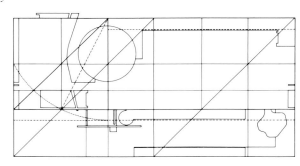

Structure

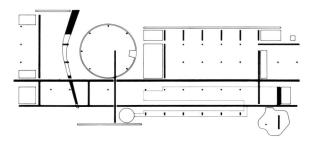

Enclosure

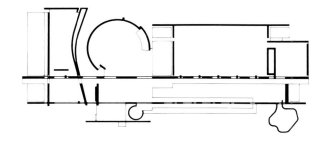

Circulation

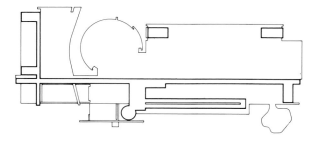

Entry circulation

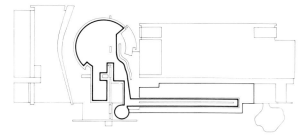

Objects

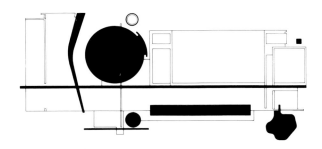

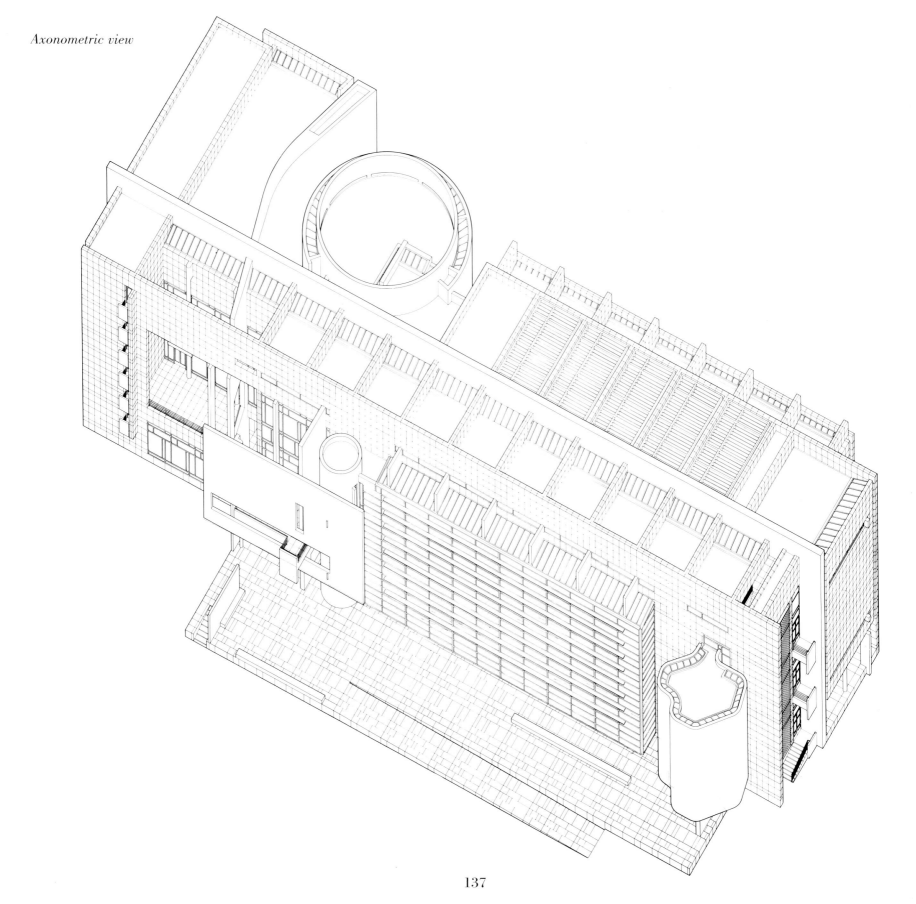

Axonometric view

Ever since the turn of the century and the heyday of Antonio Gaudí, Barcelona, like Chicago, has been a city in which architecture is valued by the citizenry to an exceptional degree. This cultural consensus supported the political will that made it possible to build a whole new sector to accommodate the Olympic city. Fortunately, it was the same impulse that enabled us to realize the Barcelona museum.

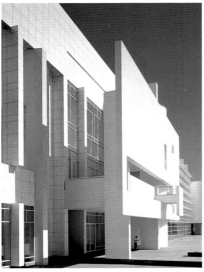

Ground floor plan

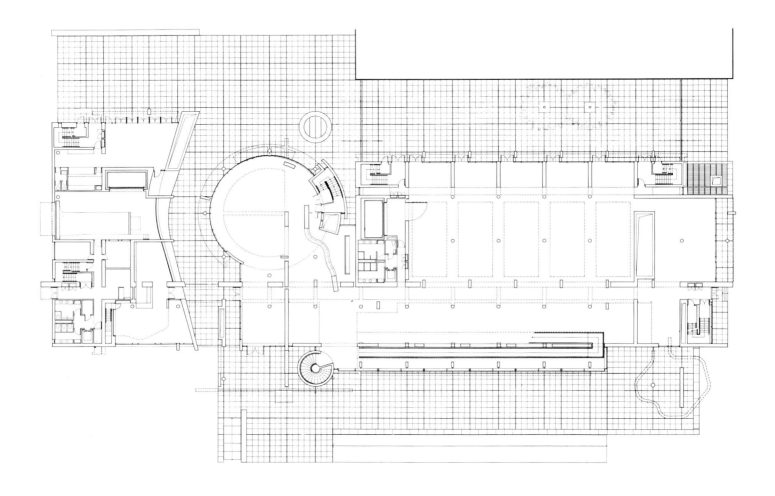

140

Second floor plan

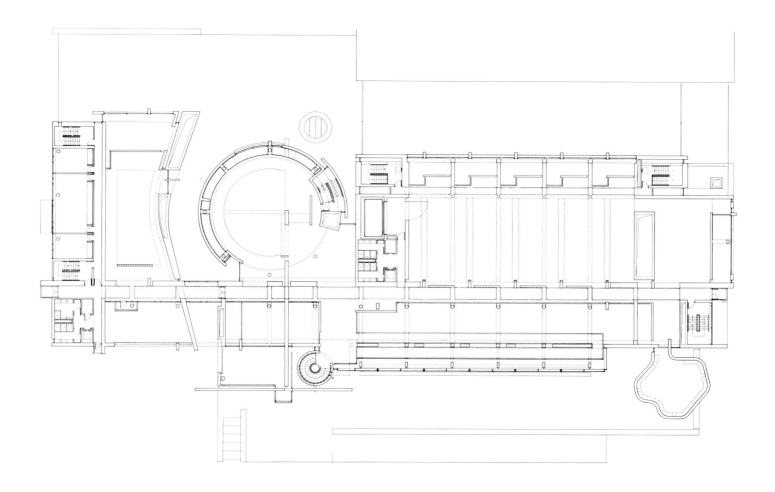

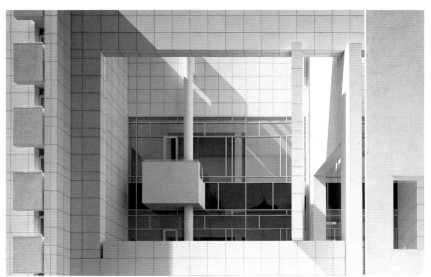

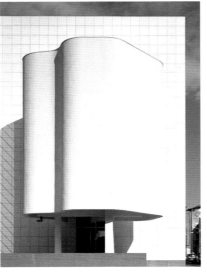

This building organizes circulation in relation to its urban location. The museum was the outcome of a well-considered and debated political decision orchestrated by then-mayor Pasqual Maragall. The Raval district historically has been a subject of discussion and controversy, as it is an area of enormous density with a high land occupancy rate. This design was seen as a way to inject new life into the rundown district, for by being opposite less elegant surroundings the museum openly connects with nearby structures. The contrast, it seems to me, is positive and provocative.

Third floor plan

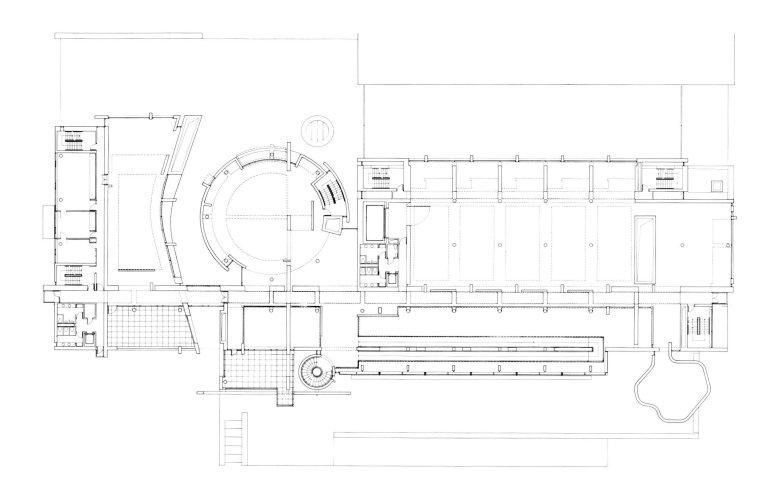

10 20   40   80

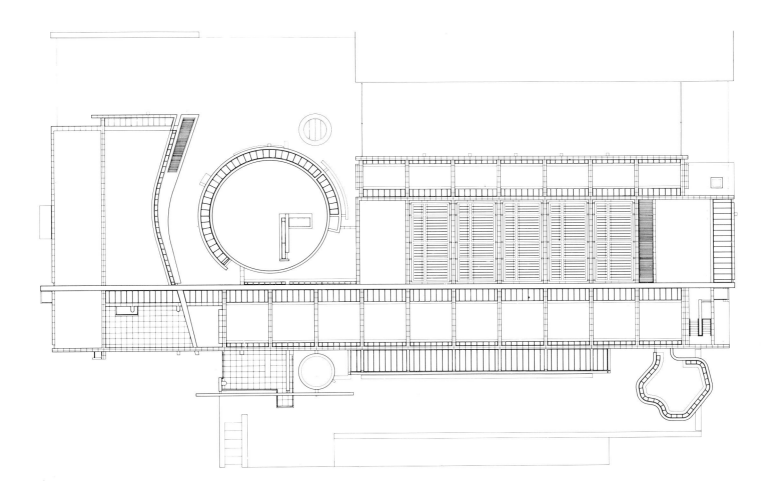

In this automotive, high-speed age, it is rare to encounter a city in which walking is still a way of life. In Barcelona, the paseo is an everyday social activity. Areas of the city where there is inadequate inducement or provision for walking are simply ignored. From this simple standpoint, one of the goals in building the museum may have been to help stimulate pedestrian movement throughout the area.

South elevation

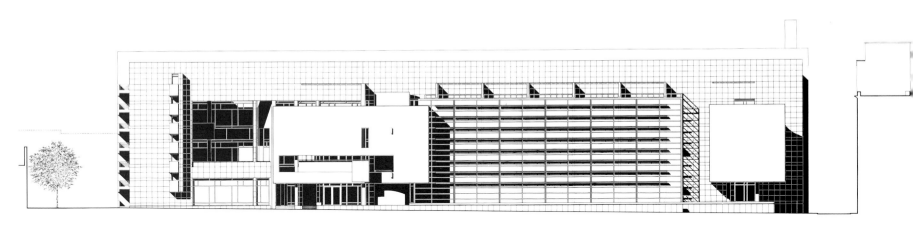

North elevation

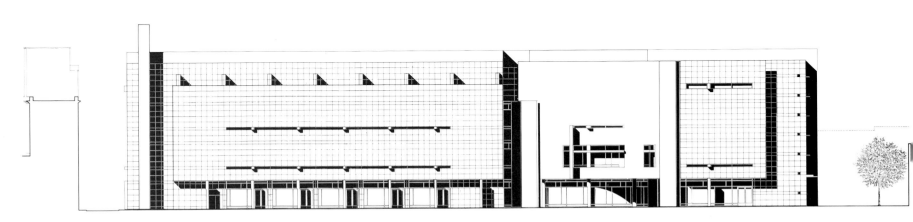

10 20   40   80

148

Section through rotunda

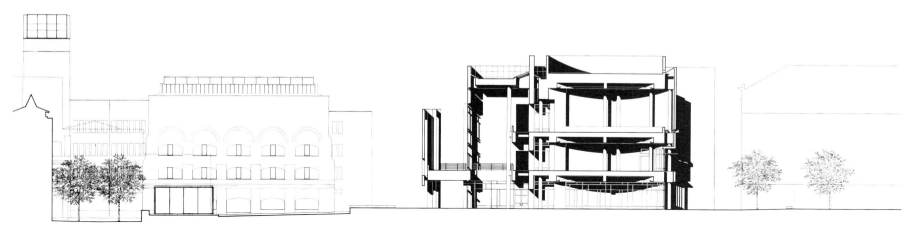

Section through typical galleries

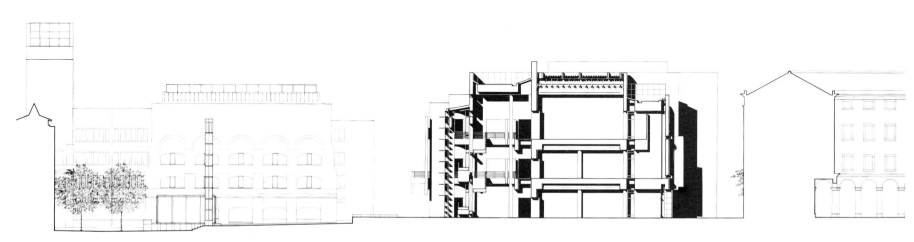

I began the design of the museum by looking closely at the possibilities offered by the site within this fabric of dense streets characterized by skewed inter-sections and ancient church domes. The compressed, low-scale mixture of commercial, institu-tional, and residential buildings offered few open spaces for pedestrian activity. There was no place where people could meet, talk, sit, read, watch children play, or walk their dogs. I wanted to create an open pedestrian plaza in front of the museum that would foster this type of activity.

Once inside the entry lobby, visitors ascend a ramp that unfolds within the triple-height hall. This transparent ramp-hall orients the visitor, offers broad views of the plaza and the city beyond, and mediates between the "old" of the surrounding context and the "new" of the art within the building. The light-filled, glass-walled volume also serves as a large public space for museum events. I felt that it was important to provide such a space, physically separate from the galleries but visually connected to both the art and the city beyond.

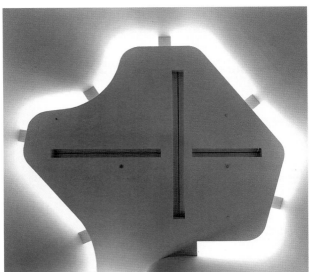

Canal+ Headquarters

Paris, France
1988–1992

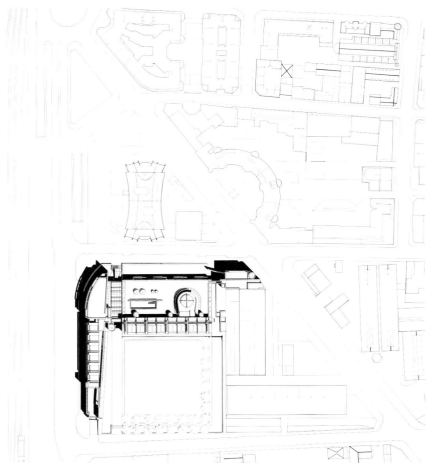

Located on the left bank of the Seine just west of the Pont Mirabeau and east of the Parc Citroën, this L-shaped television headquarters building borders two sides of a public park. On one side, an office slab varying from five to eight stories in height, tapering in plan, faces northwest over the Seine river. The other side consists of a four-story studio block facing northeast onto the rue de Cévennes, with a truncated, conical screening room punching up through it. The four television studios have been partially sunk into the ground to comply with zoning height limitations. Each studio may be accessed from its own separate street entrance or, alternatively, from an internal circulation spine. Between this opaque mass and the office slab is a glazed, dematerialized, three-story foyer with a canopy cantilevered over the street entrance. The opposite end of this foyer is intended to be accessed from the park, so the foyer can be used as a pedestrian right-of-way between the park and the rue de Cévennes. Aerial bridges spanning the foyer link the production and administration wings, encouraging internal communication.

Faced with white enameled-steel paneling, the exterior of the building is relieved by cantilevered terraces and by horizontal sun screens and vertical brise soleils that modulate the surface of both the street and the park elevations. Small, opaque glazed panels animate the louverless curved segment of the northwest river facade. The "urban window" cut out of this office slab was provided to comply with certain zoning requirements. The implicitly civic character of the complex is reinforced by its relationship to the park and by a monumental butterfly roof sailing over the offices facing the park.

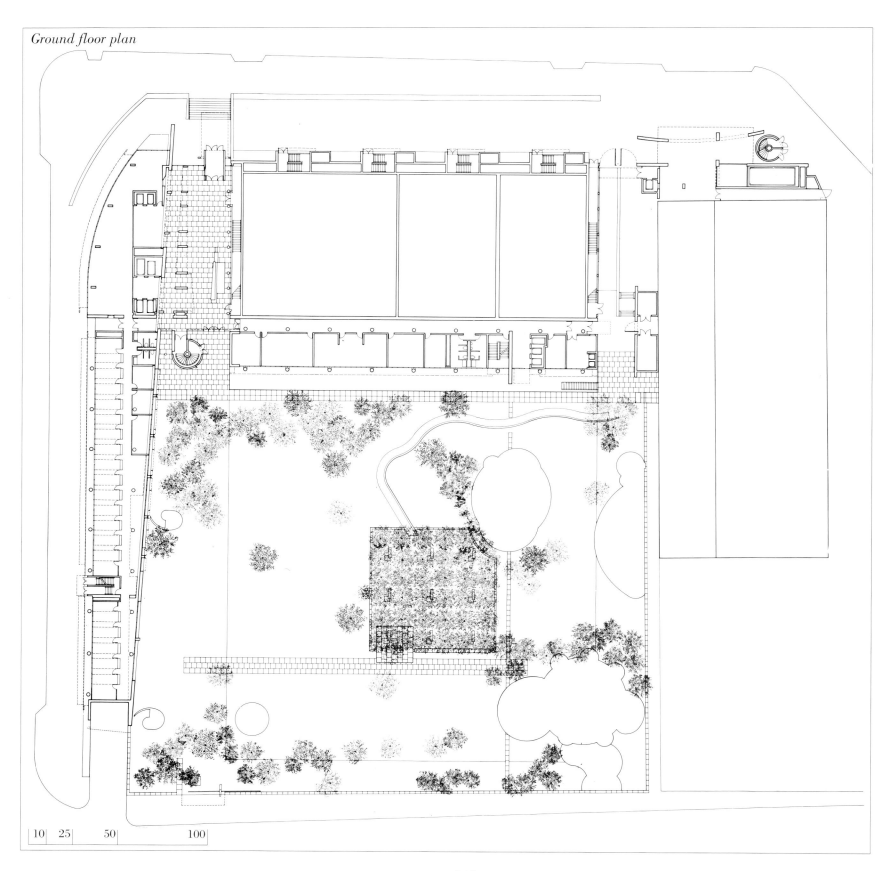

10 25 50 100

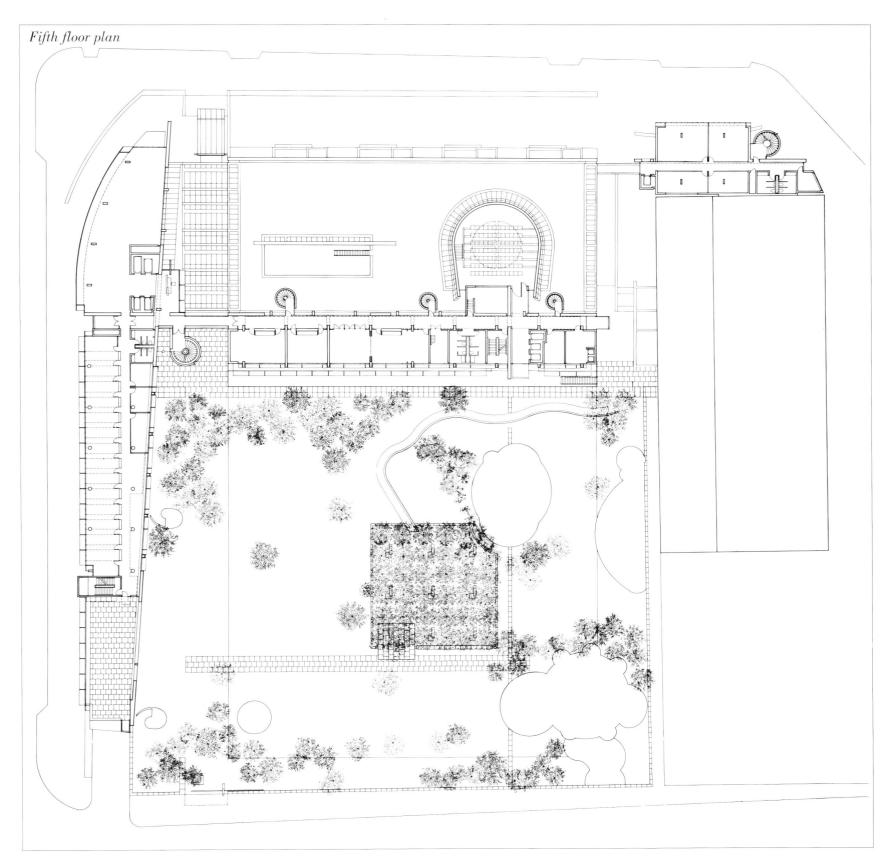

Fifth floor plan

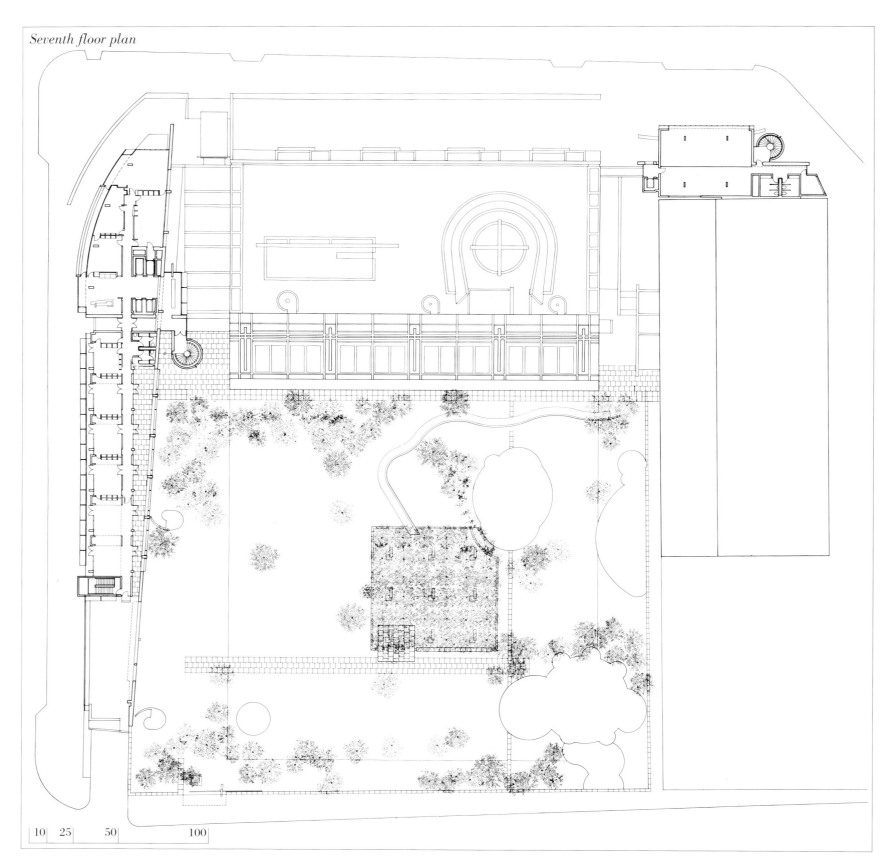

Seventh floor plan

10| 25| 50| 100|

162

Northwest elevation

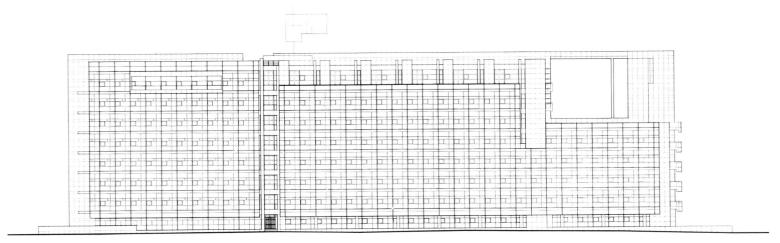

Southeast elevation

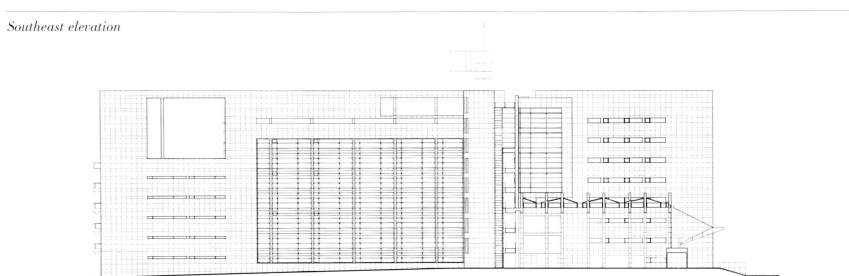

*Northeast
elevation*

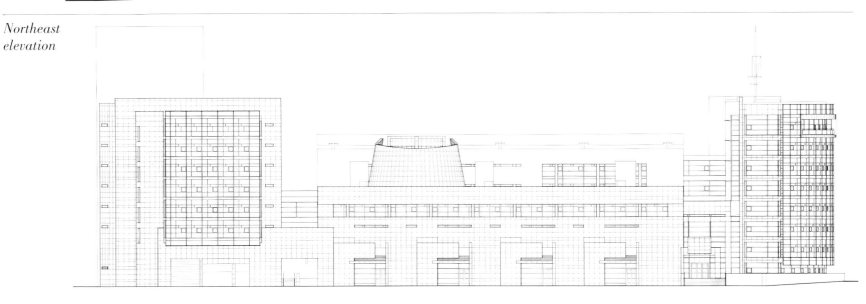

Sections looking west

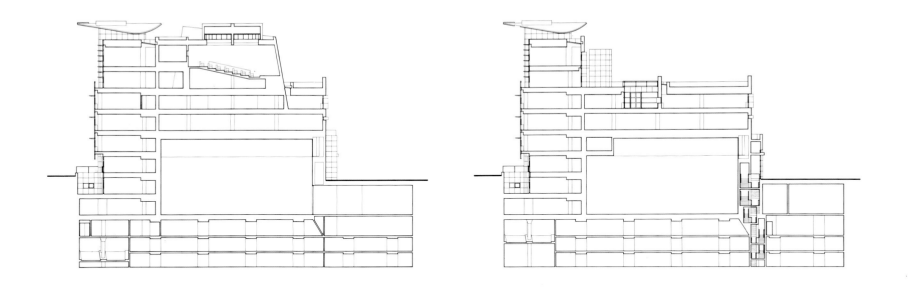

Longitudinal section

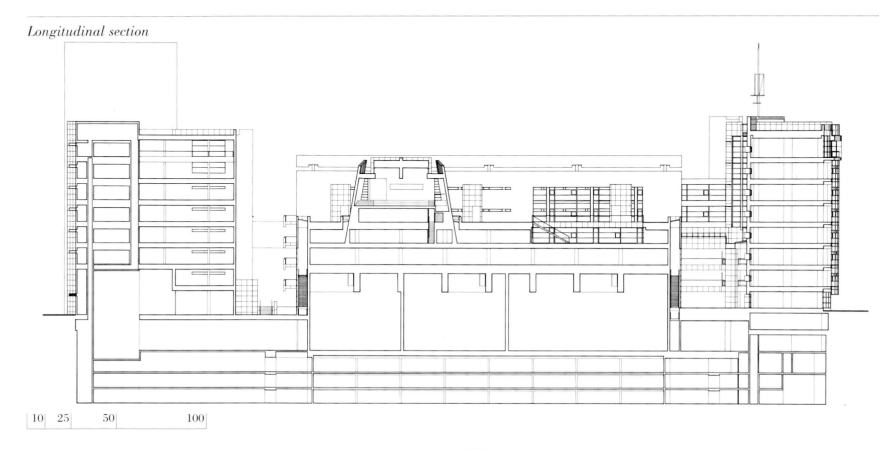

| 10 | 25 | 50 | 100 |

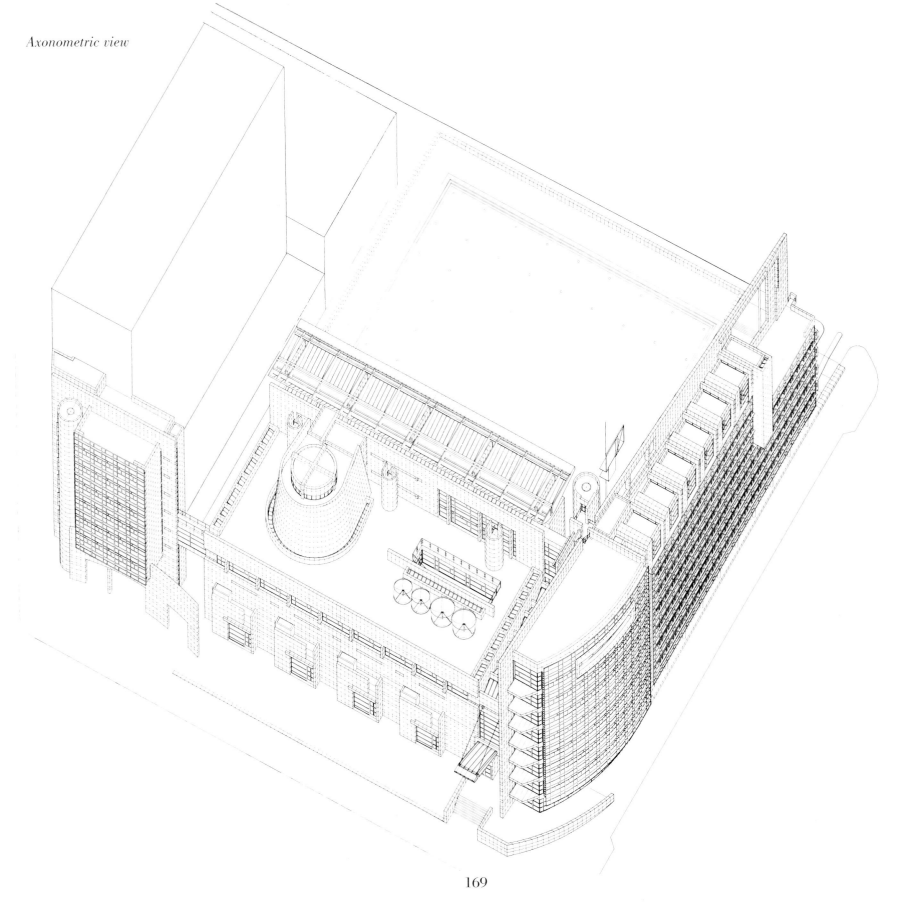

Axonometric view

169

Paris, the City of Light, the city of architecture and urban planning, the city in which public space is synonymous with almost all of les grands travaux *of the last two hundred years. The scale and quality of formal relationships in Paris are due in large part to maintaining the 28-meter height limit that unifies the urban fabric. In this instance, the aim was to integrate the building with the existing park to give a private television headquarters a civic face. The building was realized in record time under the patronage of André Rousselet, at that time the president of Canal+. It was built during the heyday of the Mitterand building boom, which was thought to represent a new reality in France. One never imagined for a moment that all too soon this boom would come to an end.*

Espace Pitôt

Montpellier, France
1988–1995

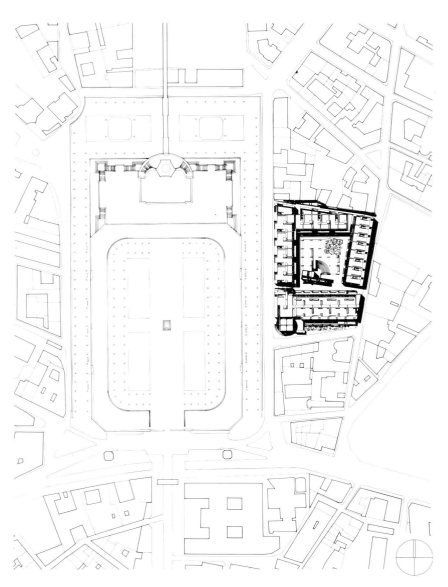

Located adjacent to the Place Royale du Peyron in Montpellier, the Espace Pitôt is a low-cost residential development that includes a hotel, law offices, and commercial frontage at the lower-grade level. The housing is essentially conceived as a perimeter block made up of a trapezoidal U-shaped element capped by a single orthogonal bar building; the two forms are unified by a cylindrical *bâtiment d'angle* located at the southwest corner of the site. This prominent feature houses the reception and entrance foyer to the hotel.

Due to the fact that one cannot build higher than a 49-meter datum above sea level, which is the level of the Place Royale, the entire three-story complex was dropped one complete floor below the adjacent street. This lower ground-floor level is treated as a paved plaza with an amphitheater and a steel loggia that jointly serve to animate the public area. These elements also separate this civic space from the shopping arcade that surrounds it on three sides. A prominent staircase and skylight in the plaza afford access and light to a public swimming pool in the basement.

The building is faced in coursed sandstone inside and out, providing a Mediterranean aura that is offset by the white modular brise-soleil that wraps around the interior of the court. A pine-tree cluster in the plaza and a rooftop garden on top of the perimeter block recall the formal planting of the nearby Place Royale, visible from the roof.

This work was the result of a competition organized by the mayor of Montpellier, George Freche, who saw it as an opportunity to build a demonstration project on a prestigious site in which a private developer would be required to work with the winning architect. On receiving first prize we began the joint evolution of the design in good faith, only to discover that as far as the developer was concerned, this was simply a marriage of convenience for which he had little sympathy. Despite this, we were able to realize the scheme largely in accordance with our original designs. Nevertheless, it was a head-to-head battle from start to finish.

179

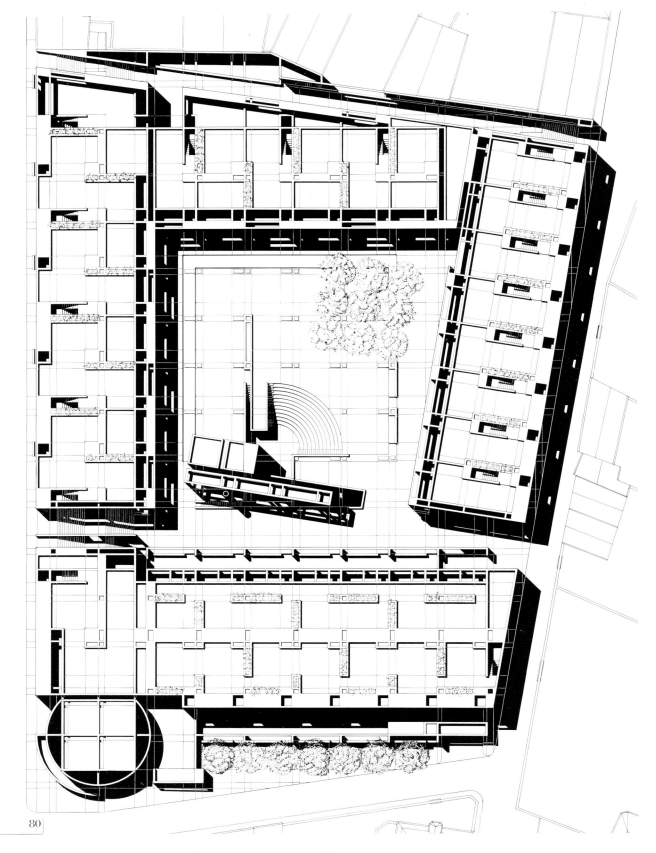

10 20   40   80

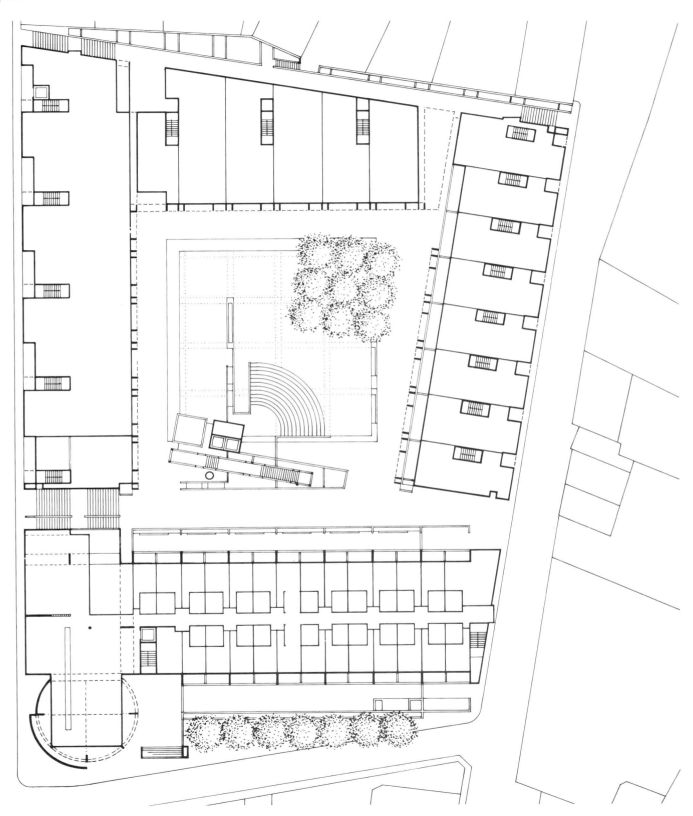

Hypolux Bank Building

Luxembourg
1989–1993

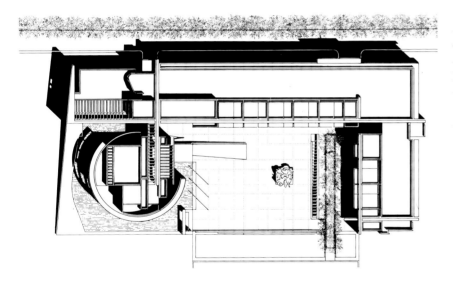

Located in a new office quarter on the main auto route between the airport and Luxembourg's historic urban center, this prestigious office complex comprises a cylindrical volume and an office slab elevated on a podium. Unlike the adjacent office buildings, which have been built mainly to occupy the entire block within the new urban grid, this structure encloses an open civic space. Within this space, the cylinder, which houses the main reception area and executive offices, announces the presence of the bank. A planted formal court with an ornamental pool both defines the surface of the podium and reflects the cylindrical wall screening the entry. Pedestrians access the bank via a gently sloped ramp over the pool.

The L-shaped office block parallels the rue Alphonse Weicker. The southeast end of this slab, adjacent to the cylinder, is devoted to bank functions that occupy the full height of the four-story atrium. At the opposite end, an independent podium entry and elevator core afford access to rental space above. The offices were planned as modules to provide a high degree of flexibility yet afford individuality to each space through proportional variation and window treatments.

The internal perimeter of the L-shaped office wing and the end walls are clad in dark gray stone, while its external face is modulated by brises soleils in enameled-metal paneling. The double-square geometry determining the rhythmic proportion of the plan also controls the organization of the plaza. Within this space, a monumental sculpture by Frank Stella reinforces the entry sequence.

Geometry

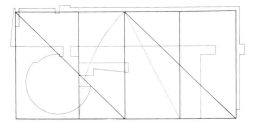

Structure

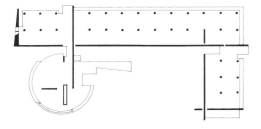

Circulation

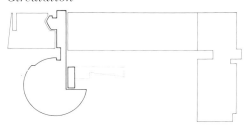

Entry

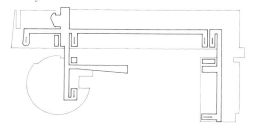

Public/private

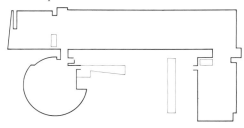

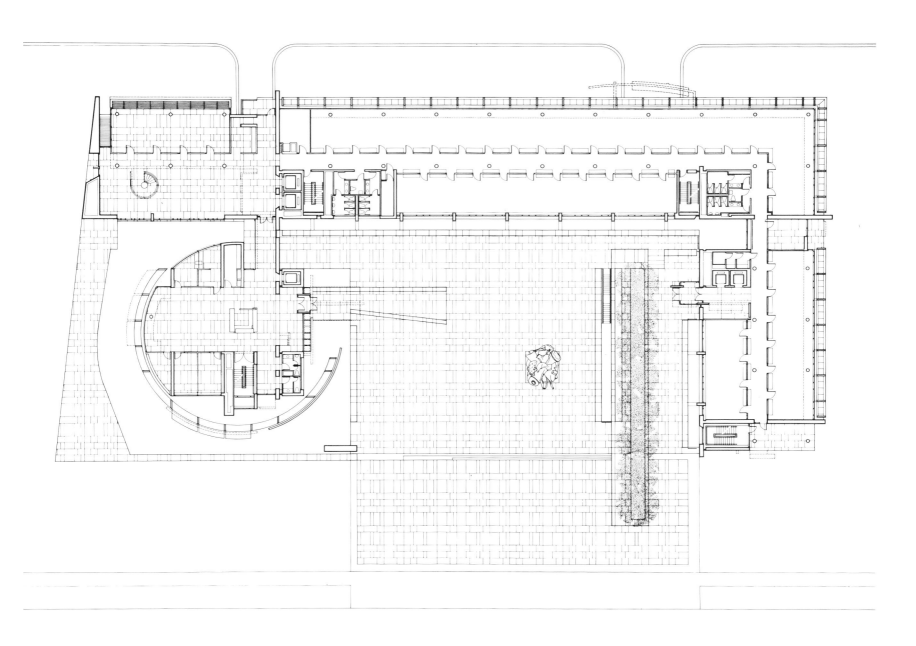

10 20 40   80

At first glance this building seems free from all the usual constraints of urban contextuality. Indeed, the flat rectangular site is a part of a no-man's-land just outside the historic city where a large number of banks and corporations have relocated. Since this is neither a pedestrian nor a residential area but rather a satellite zone without historic precedent or distinctive natural features, most of the buildings constructed in this district to date have tended to turn inward.

Rather than exploit the full block delineated under the building ordinance, this ensemble, with its spacious plaza serving as a civilized oasis within a commercial desert, creates an exception to the norm.

Third floor plan

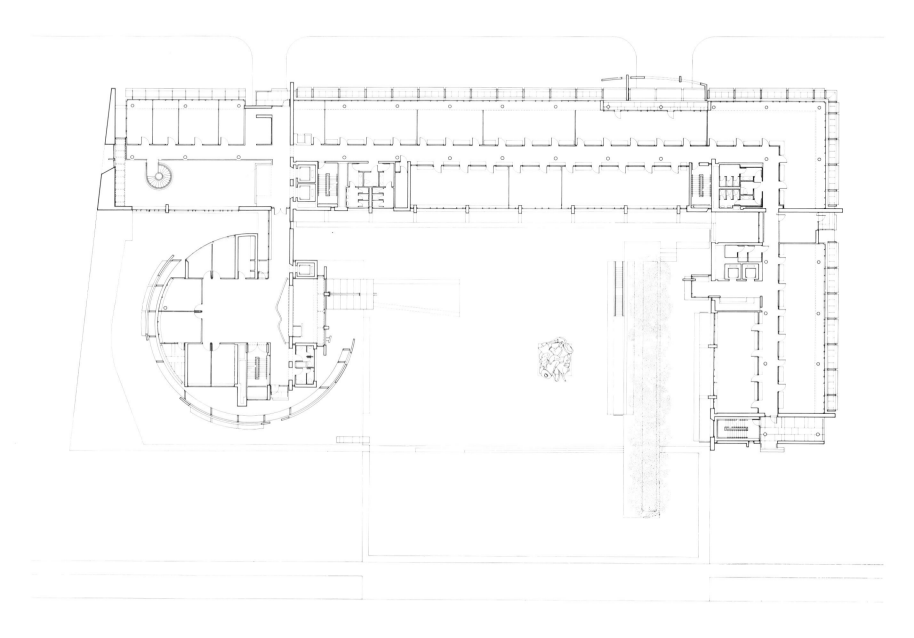

10 20 40 80

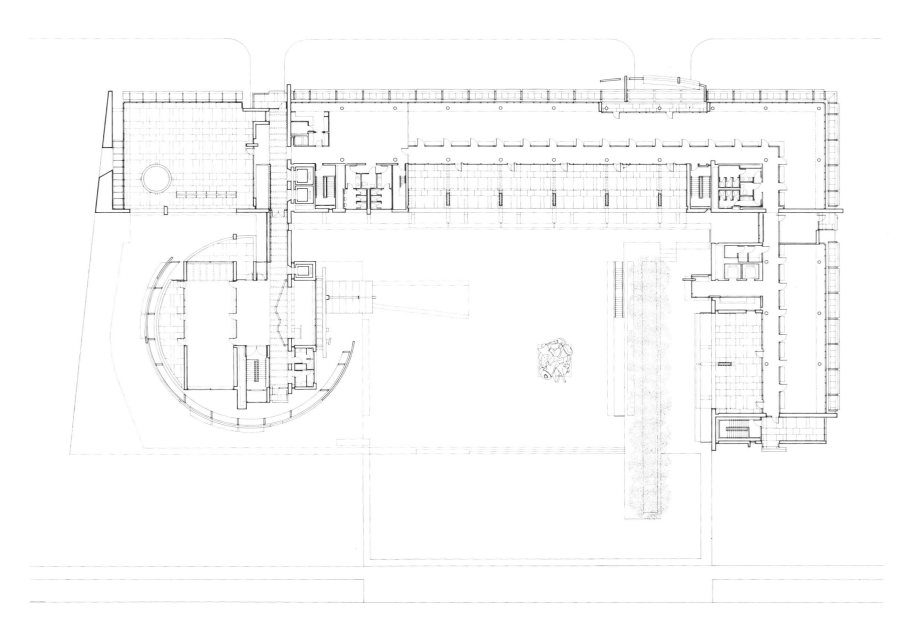

The freestanding, spread-eagle form of Frank Stella's sculpture has its own structure and inherent logic. Its non-geometric, formal organization acts as a welcome foil to the geometry of the architecture that embraces it.

There is an inherent challenge to building in Europe, apart from the obvious differences in language and culture. It was often difficult for us to find contractors who had experience with buildings that demanded as much or as little tolerance for detail as ours did. In the end, though, I think that those who worked with us found it a rewarding experience in spite of the challenges, and were proud of the quality of their accomplishments.

Daimler-Benz Research Center

Ulm, Germany
1989–1992

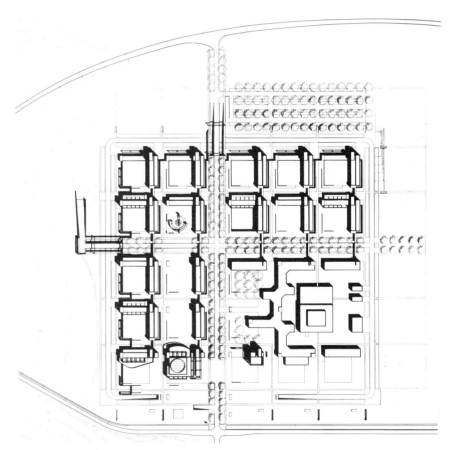

These laboratory/research facilities for Daimler-Benz in Ulm are the partial realization of a master plan for a larger research campus. The campus is organized as a repetitive grid of L-shaped office/laboratory units on either side of a central greensward. Within this space is a semipublic building housing a cafeteria/restaurant on the ground floor and meeting rooms and a library on the second floor. This building serves as the sociocultural core of the complex. At present, this somewhat Jeffersonian plan is flanked by three new office laboratory units to the west and by a preexisting brick-faced research complex to the east.

The L-shaped office/lab module establishes a basic rhythm that may be varied slightly to accommodate atypical local conditions. In general, the offices occupy the external perimeter of the L-shaped module, while the laboratories line the interior and overlook the inner grass-covered court. The two research modules built in the first phase share a large, open basement workshop for the fabrication of oversized components. This space is lit by skylights in the turf-covered roofs that span the factory/laboratory space below. A depressed ring road serves this lower industrial level, thus preserving unobstructed views from the laboratories over the city of Ulm to the south and southeast and over the open country to the north and northwest. While security clearance is required throughout, all circulation is primarily pedestrian, with employees and visitors entering the compound via a central parking area to the north of the present phase. A single internal access road bounds the southeastern edge of the greensward.

Site program

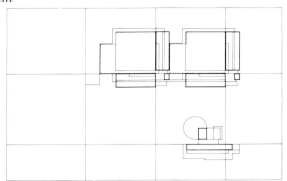

Site geometry

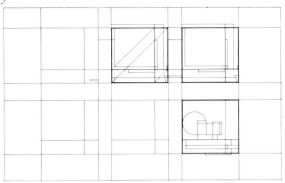

Site structure

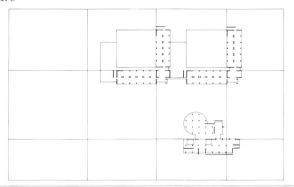

Site circulation

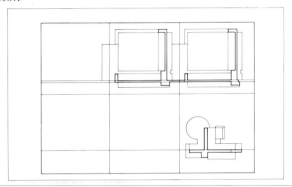

Cafeteria program

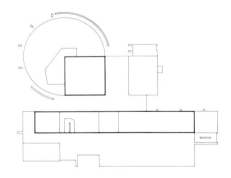

Cafeteria geometry

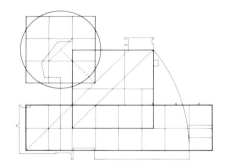

Cafeteria structure

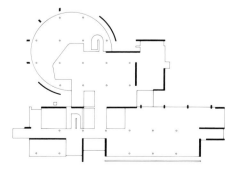

Cafeteria circulation

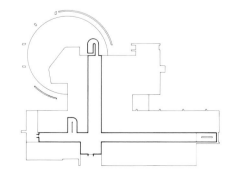

198

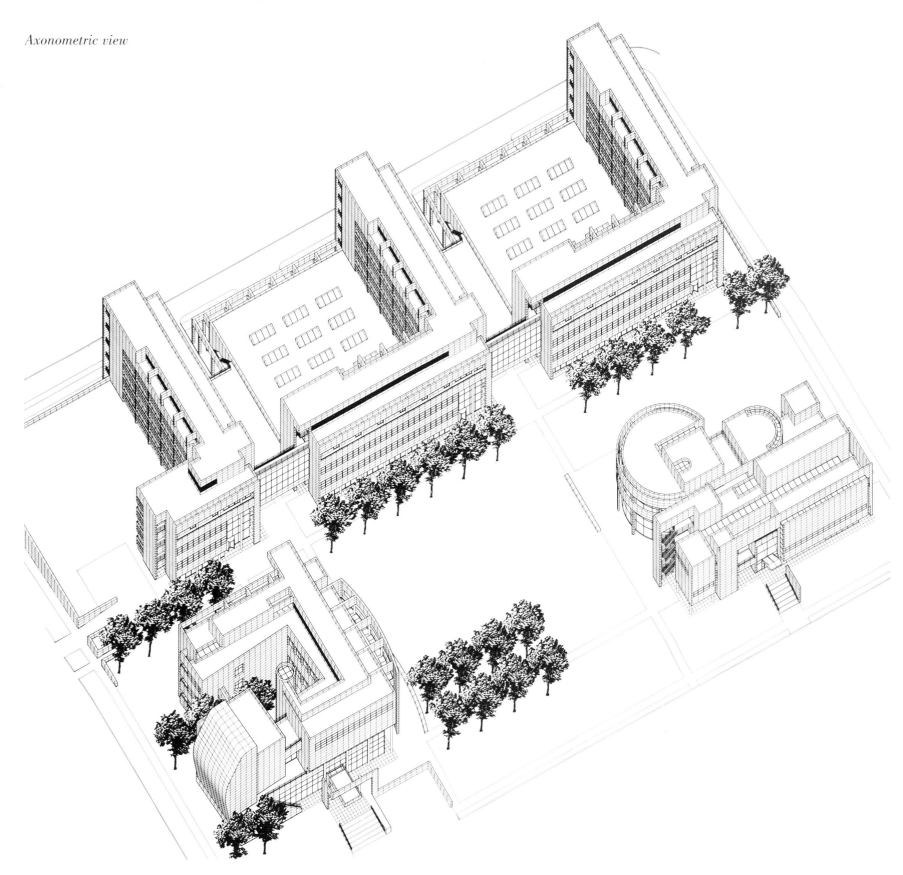

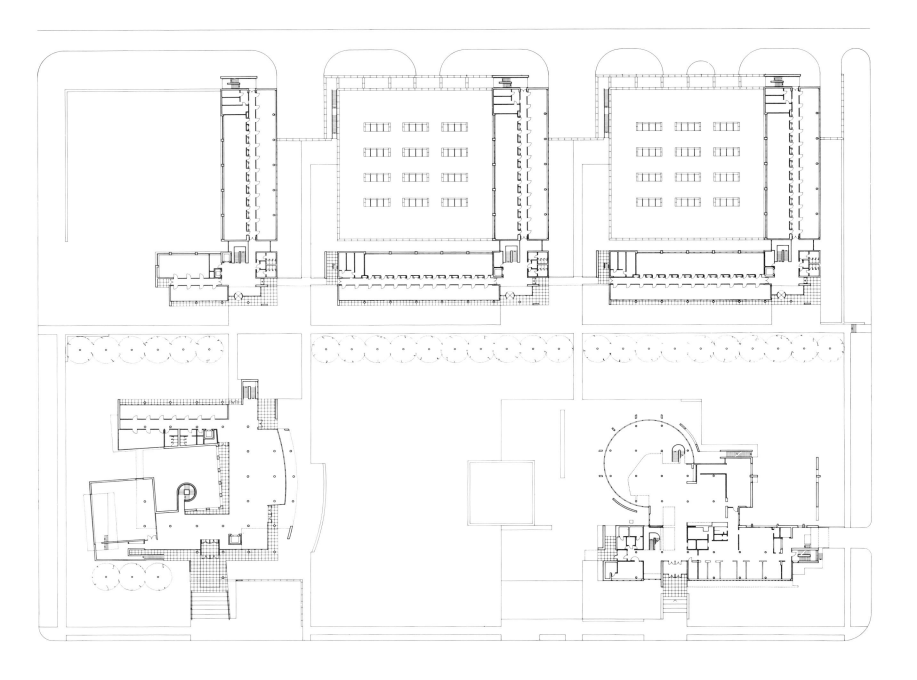

25 50   100   200

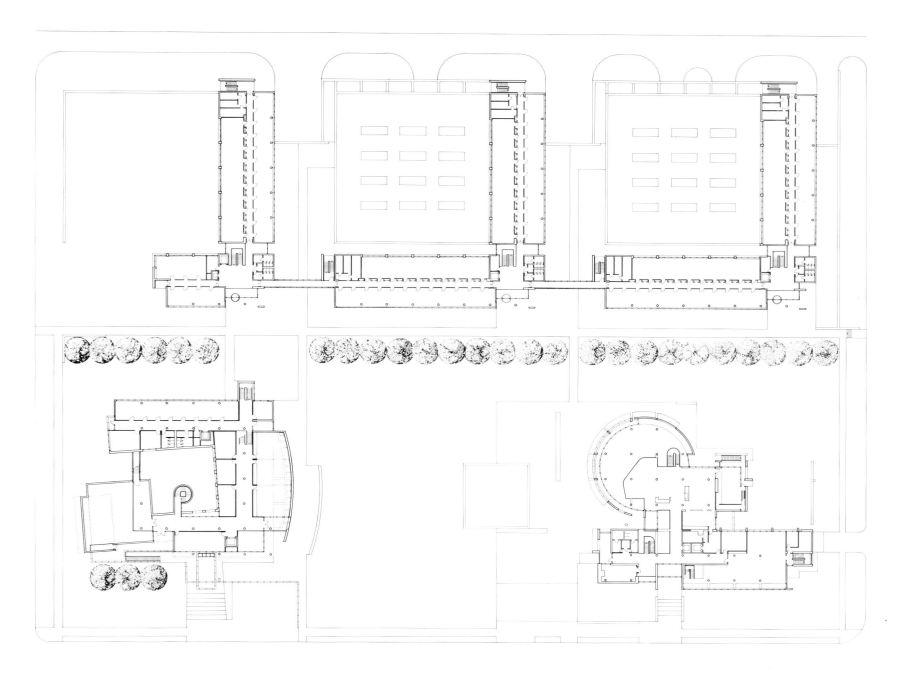

As the master plan of the complex indicates, the prototypical laboratory units and the atypical refectory-cum-social building were conceived originally as an integral part of a much larger research campus, one that would have comprised some nineteen laboratory blocks plus extensive communal facilities around a central greensward. Regrettably, it has not been possible to complete the overall plan.

Camden Medical Center

Singapore
1990–1999

The Camden Medical Center is located at an interface between commercial and residential areas of Singapore. The 18-story building was designed to house medical suites or offices in addition to retail space on the ground floor. Its cylindrical profile celebrates the culmination of Orchard Street, which links the commercial center at the water's edge to the residential district above.

The cylindrical, multilayered metal shell wrapped around the body of the building is also a consequence of equatorial conditions, where all exposures require solar protection. A combination of structural brises soleil and horizontal fretted sun screens integrated into the facade provides protection from the sun and adds a human scale that relates to the rhythm of the residential towers to the east and southeast of the site. The circular plan is subdivided orthogonally, and the cylinder is serviced by a rectangular core. The cut-away portion of the cylindrical mass is occupied by an opaque, free-standing cylindrical escape stair pierced at intervals by slot windows.

Natural stone covers the ground-level retaining walls and elevator cores. This finish creates a strong contrast to the lightweight metallic walls of the tower. The building footprint was reduced to the minimum to allow for landscaped open space at grade.

The vehicle drop-off and turnaround is slightly depressed from the street and takes advantage of the site's sloping topography in order to provide privacy for the main entrance. Pedestrian access is along a covered walkway that weaves through the ground floor of the building and permits the required covered connection to neighboring commercial buildings. This building offers an alternative model for development within the overbuilt urban core, where more often than not structures rise to 60 stories.

Ground floor plan

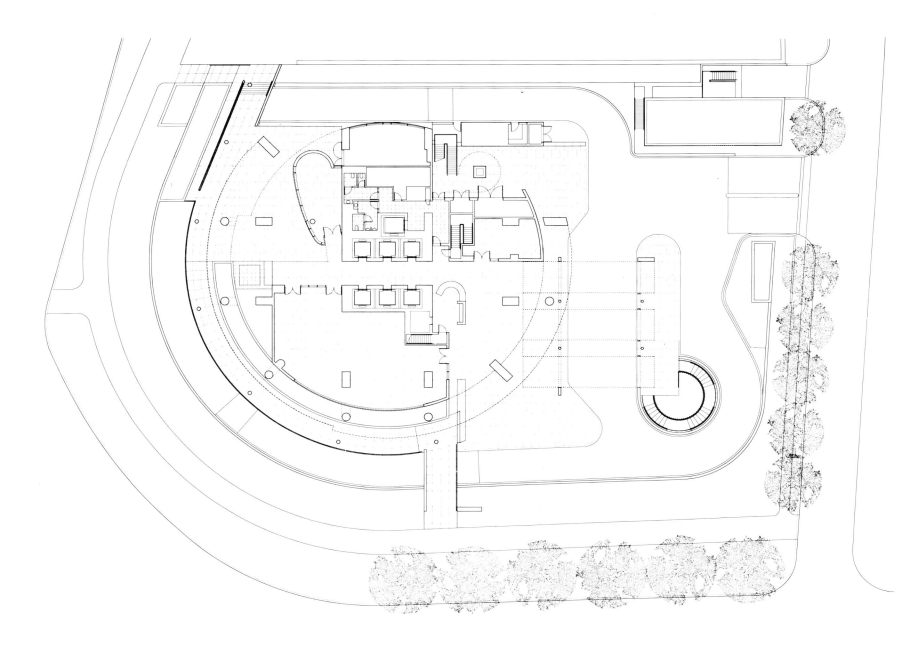

10 20   40   80

Eighth floor plan

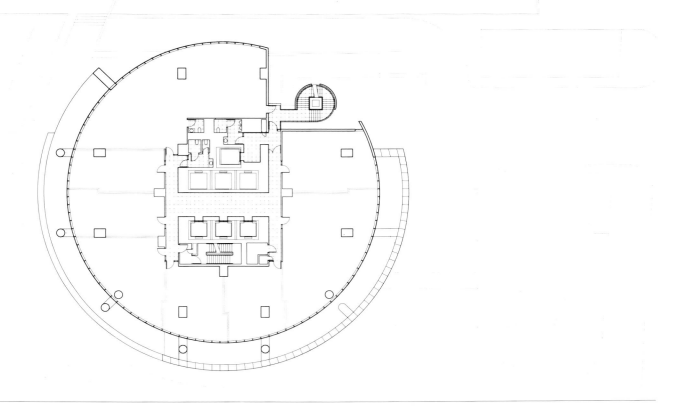

Fourteenth floor plan

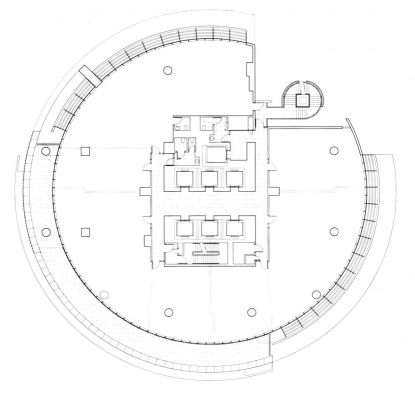

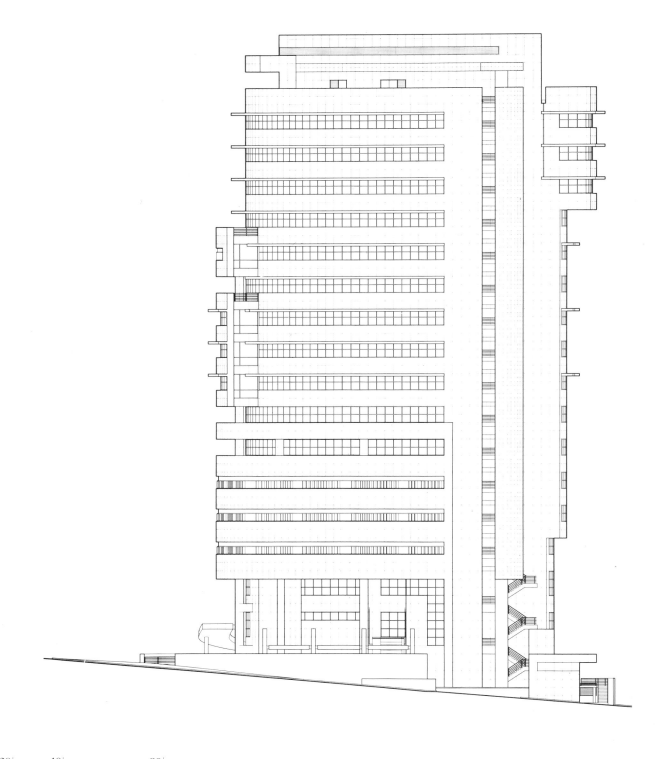

10 20   40   80

While the Southeast Asian building boom of the past decade has created an unprecedented opportunity for architects worldwide, overheated economic and political conditions generally have failed to give rise to any serious thought to the broader urban implications of such instant high-rise development. Invariably, each site and each building complex has been conceived on its own terms, with little if any consideration for the way in which its height and mass relate to the preexisting urban fabric or even to the pattern of the emerging metropolis. In this instance we attempted to break down the scale of an 18-story development so it would relate in some way to the relatively low-rise buildings that surround it.

Euregio Office Building

Basel, Switzerland
1990–1998

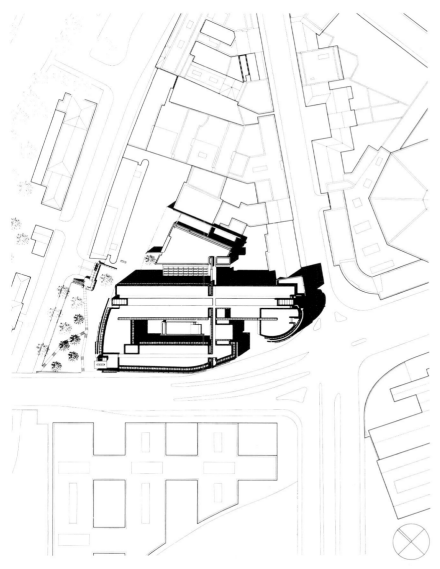

Originally commissioned as a bank headquarters and subsequently developed as an office building with commercial space on the ground floor, this complex structure was realized on an extraordinarily difficult site with severe zoning restrictions. Located near Basel's central railway station, at the intersection of Viadukstrasse and Innere Margarethenstrasse, the building responds to the dome of the nearby market hall with its cylindrical corner. The lower two floors are based on an opposition between context and program and were originally conceived as a double-height banking hall; something of this space still remains. The main entrance is between this volume and a rectilinear complex consisting of offices on three sides of a central light court.

The remainder of the frontage on Viadukstrasse affords direct access to the commercial space on the ground and lower ground floors. Since there is a drop in grade at the western end of the site, organizing the four subterranean parking levels and servicing facilities became one of the most challenging aspects of the project.

The building is located between the city center and outer districts, and these two urban scales are reflected in the different facades. The south facade along Viadukstrasse is a layered curtain wall with projecting blades in white glass that shield the offices from direct sunlight. The north facade, where continuous strip windows are set into a solid metal panel wall, responds to the more traditional character of the adjacent buildings.

217

Given this irregular, heavily contoured infill site typical of contemporary Swiss city development, height limits, and a complex program, we attempted to provide as much public open space as possible in the form of an interior and exterior courtyard. Long, sweeping lines of fenestration and sun screens sustain the unity of the building along the main street facade.

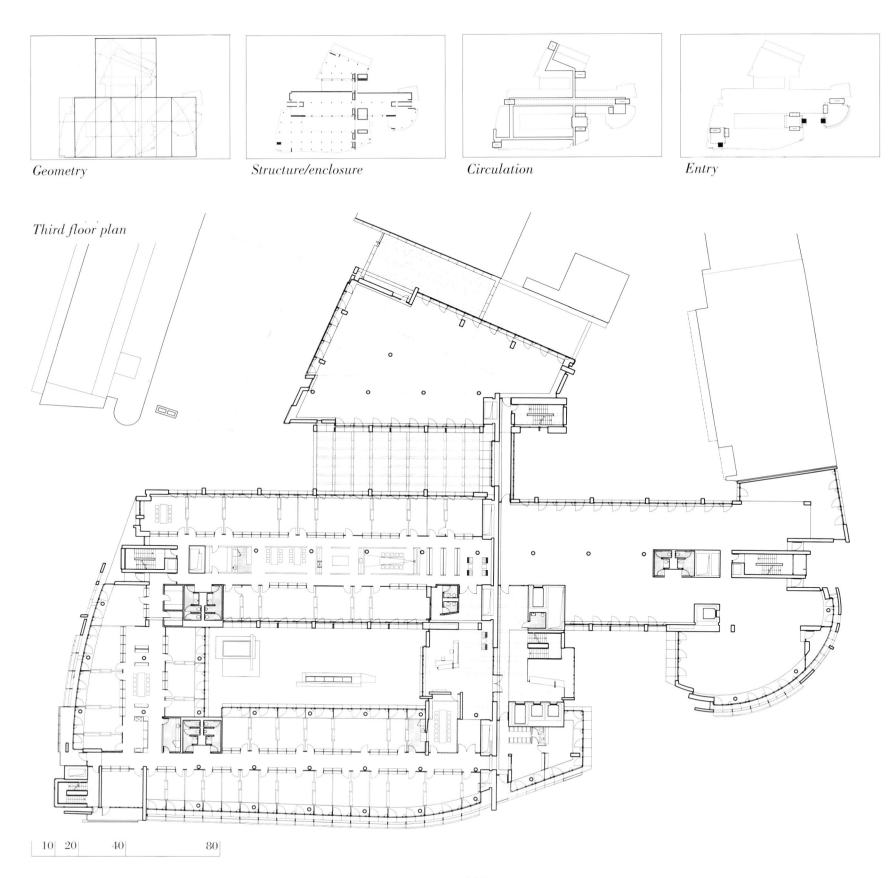

Geometry

Structure/enclosure

Circulation

Entry

Third floor plan

10 20 40 80

220

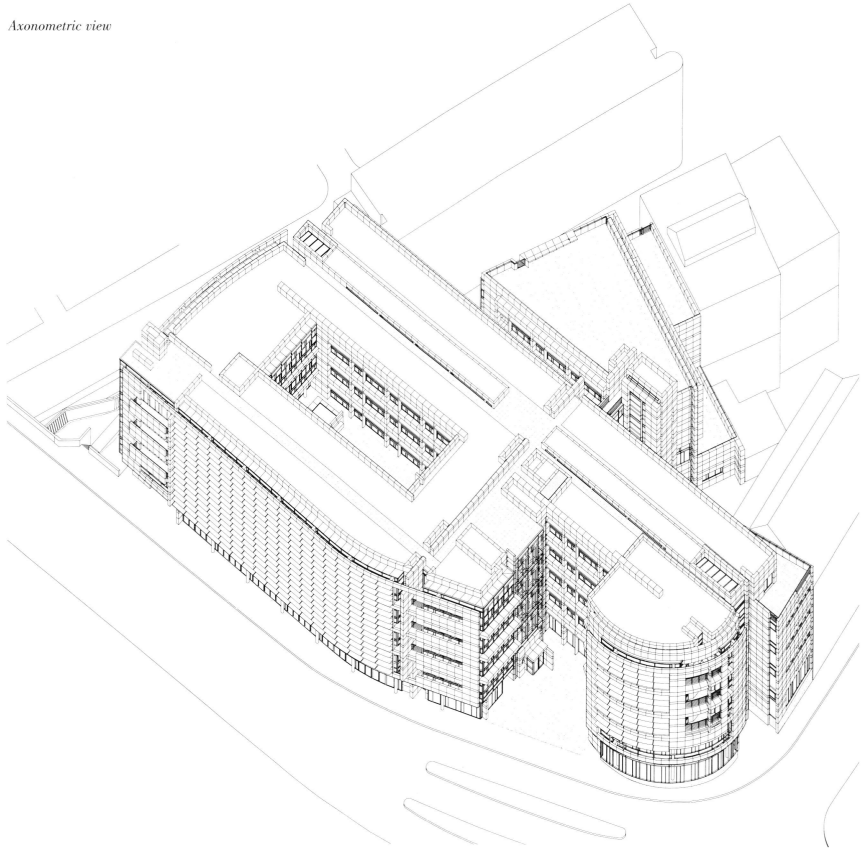

West elevation

South elevation

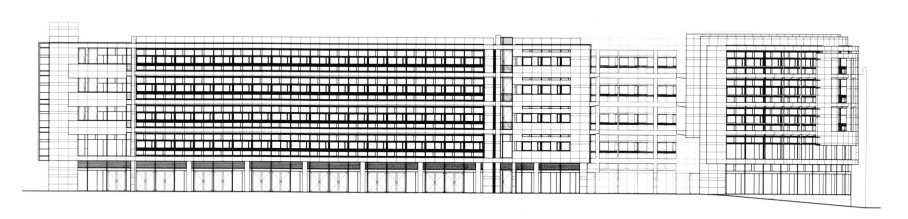

10 20   40   80

Section through loading dock looking south

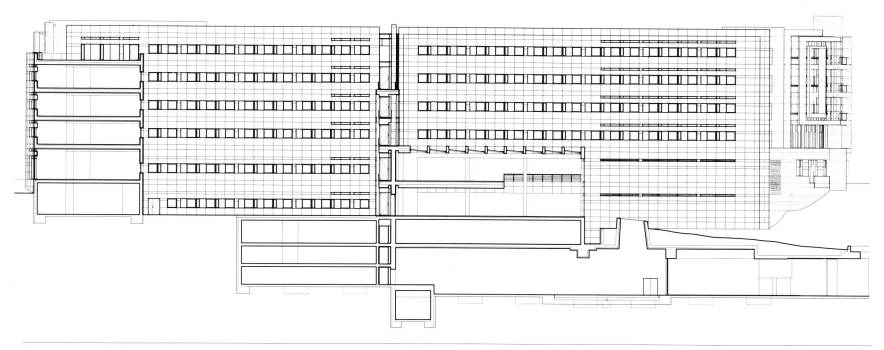

Cross section looking east

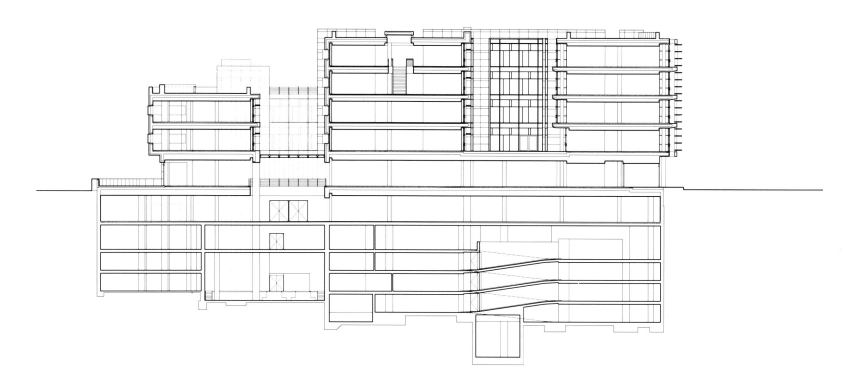

Hans Arp Museum

Rolandseck, Germany
1991–2000

Poised on a hill some forty meters above the main railroad station between Bonn and Koblenz, this museum commands spectacular views over the Rhine River valley. The Arp Foundation originated as a long-established cultural center incorporated into an underused railroad station. The new building was conceived as an extension of a local communications hub uniting bus routes, a railway, and a ferry.

The museum was designed to house a unique collection of work by Hans Arp and Sophie Taeuber-Arp and their friends. Although a large part of the collection is sculpture, it includes a wide variety of objects—drawings, paintings, and textile designs—that require an equally wide variety of spaces and lighting conditions.

The 4-story, 65-meter-long, sculpture-like building is connected to the railway station via two elevated walkways. Visitors enter the main level either on foot from the station via an elevated bridge or by automobile from the southern approach road. The basic orthogonal volume is overlaid with gently curved forms in plan and section. A walkway and brise soleil expand into a terrace on the first floor, while at roof level, curved longitudinal beams support light baffles above the top-lit sculpture gallery. Similar outdoor terraces on every floor afford views over the Rhine. A short covered walkway connects the main level to a detached, two-story, top-lit gallery conceived as an honorific chamber for the exhibition of selected works. Amoeba-shaped in plan and canted in section, this symbolic gallery may also be used as temporary exhibition space.

229

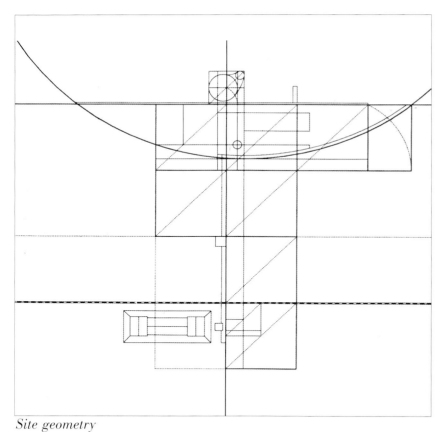

Site geometry

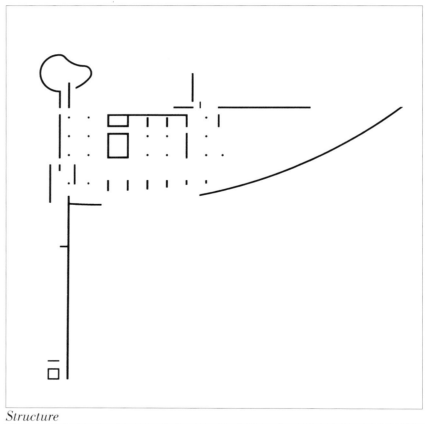

Structure

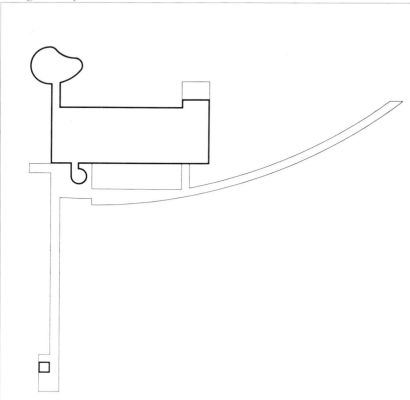

Enclosure

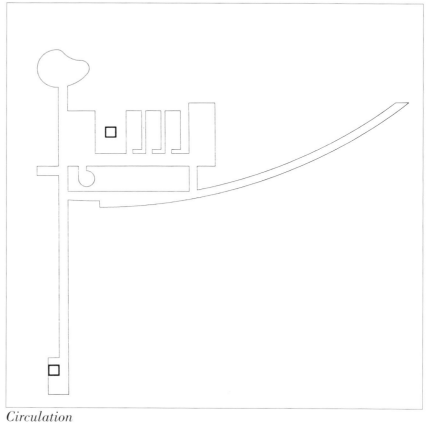

Circulation

230

Site plan

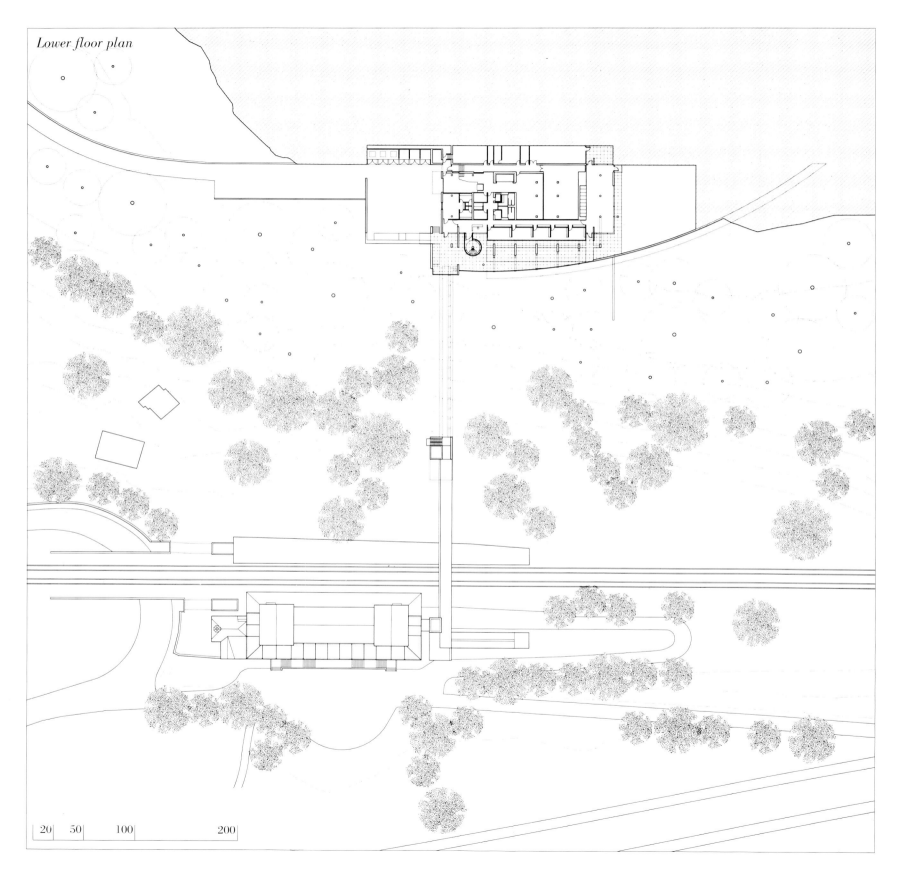

Lower floor plan

20 50   100   200

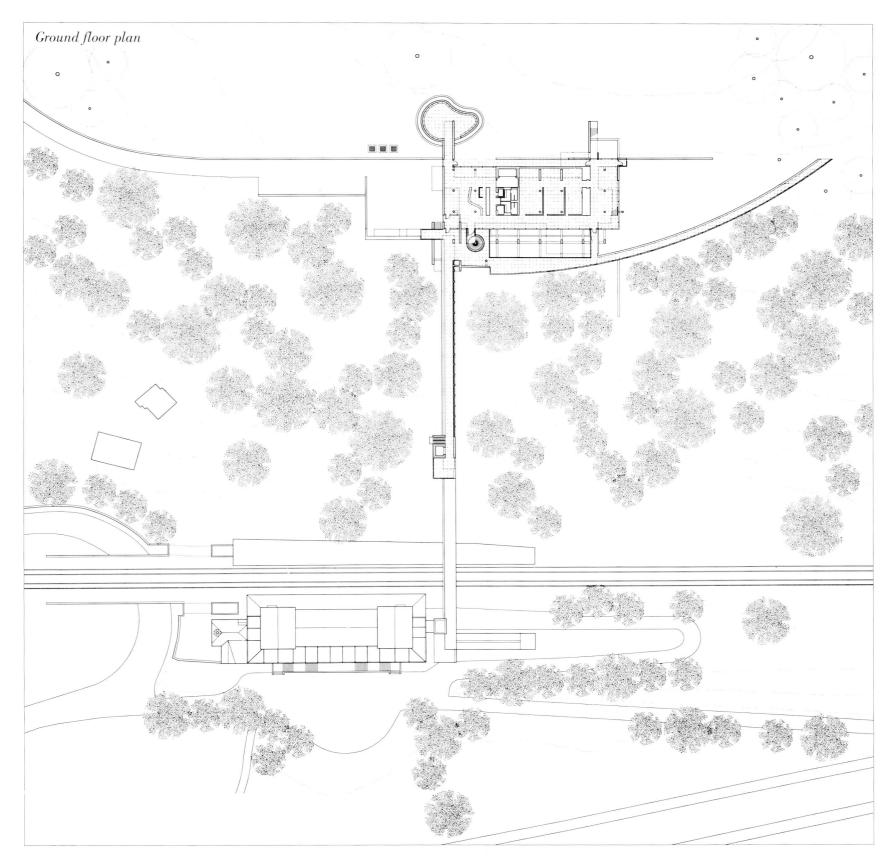

Ground floor plan

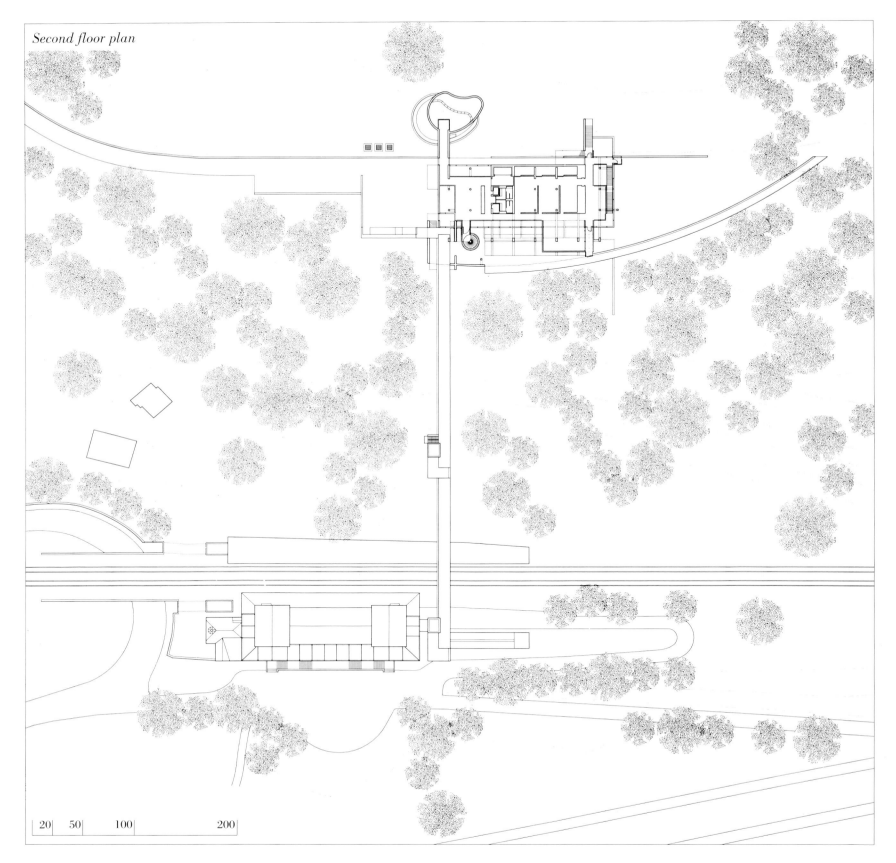

Second floor plan

Penthouse plan

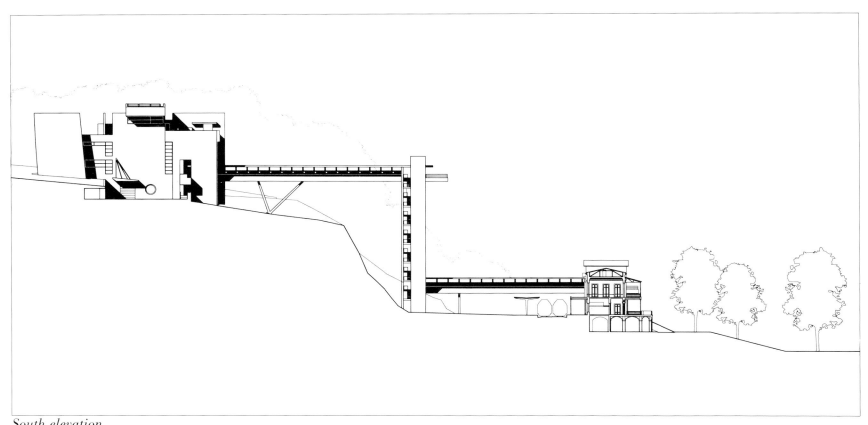

South elevation

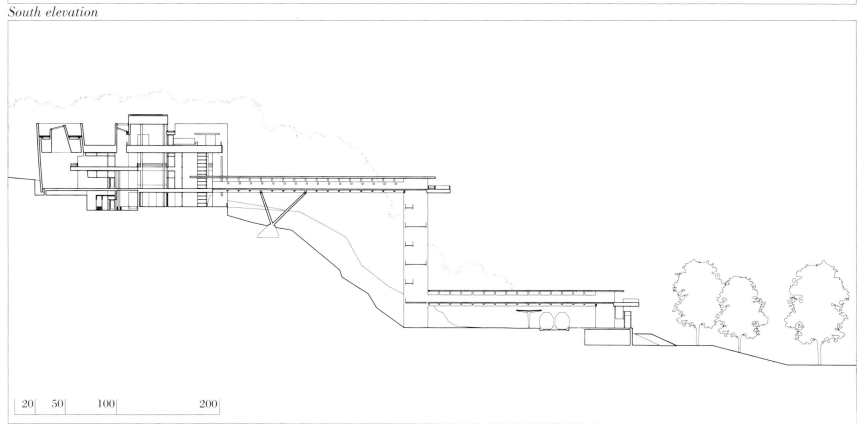

| 20 | 50 | 100 | 200 |

Cross section through bridge

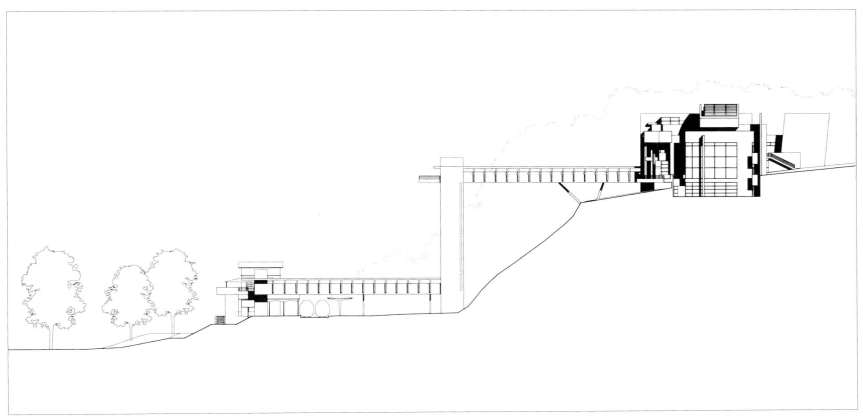

North elevation

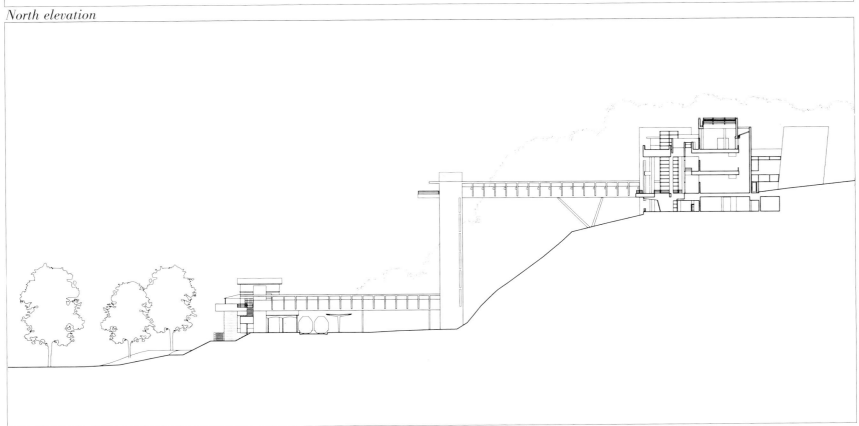

Cross section through galleries

Swissair North American Headquarters

Melville, New York
1991–1995

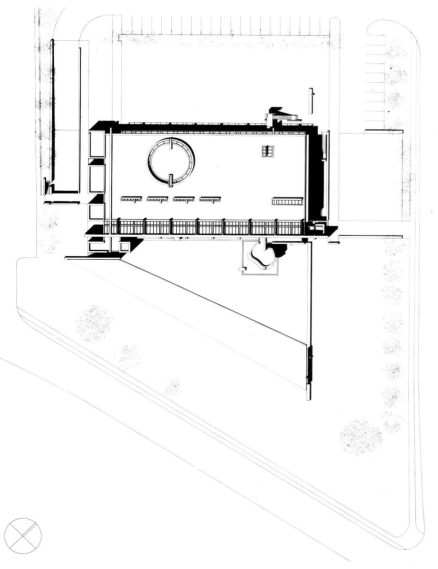

The Swissair headquarters was conceived as a distinctive formal element that would stand in contrast to the nondescript suburban environment surrounding an adjacent intersection. A number of factors led to the decision to recess the building into the ground, thereby creating a lower ground floor. One of these was the need to meet local zoning and height restrictions while accommodating the requirements of the program. The recessed lower floor enabled us to provide an outdoor recreation patio on the sunny side of the building for lunchtime use by the staff. Another was the necessity to create privacy and to shield the building acoustically from the nearby Long Island Expressway. A substantial berm to the east and south also shields the forecourt from noise and exterior views.

The orthogonal circulation, open-plan workspace (designed on a module for flexible subdivision), and location of the cafeteria on the lower ground floor promote efficiency without sacrificing environmental quality or access to light, air, and surrounding views. The southeast elevation facing the highway is closed in order to isolate the offices from the noise of the expressway. Its internal circulation space is lit by a roof light, and a long window in the facade permits distant views.

The northeast end of the building overlooks a narrow sunken patio, while the southwest end accommodates services, the elevator, and lavatories, which are housed in three solid prisms separated by full-height glazing. The double-height, glazed northwest elevation faces a parking lot with demarcated bays that is treated as a parterre. This building may be seen as an emergent exurban office type that has been given a particular identity in keeping with the client's prestige.

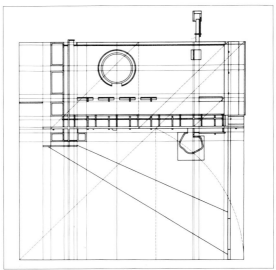

Regulating lines and proportional grid

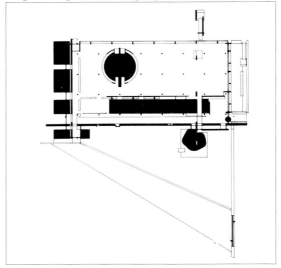

Figure ground/solids vs. voids

Program

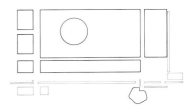

Geometry

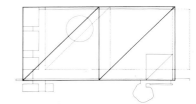

Structure

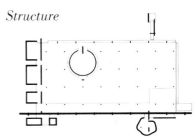

Circulation

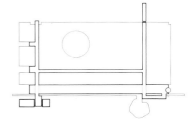

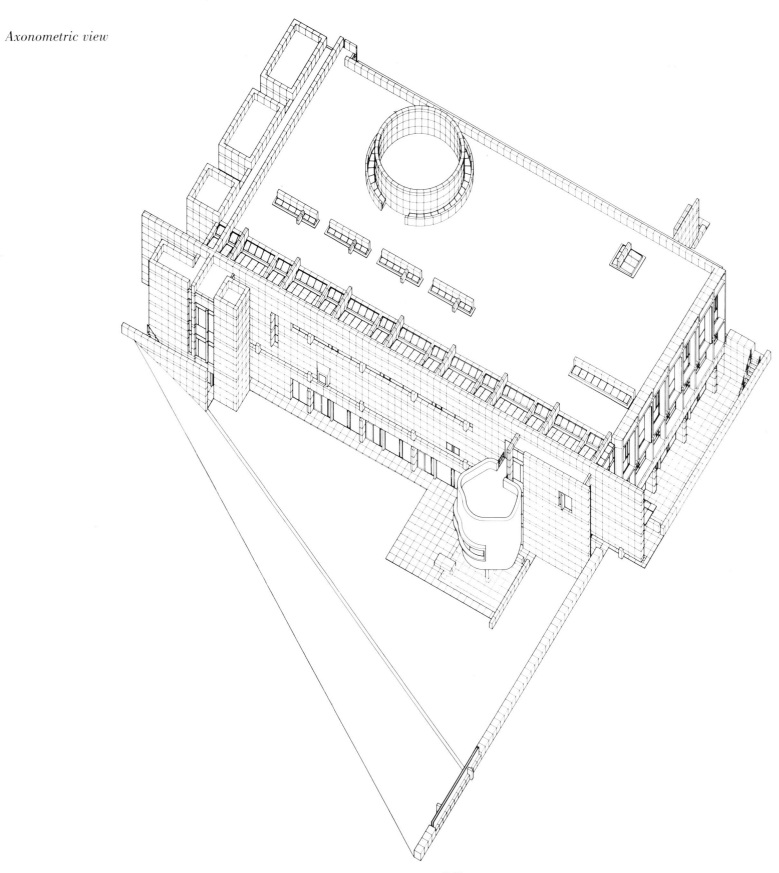

Ground floor plan

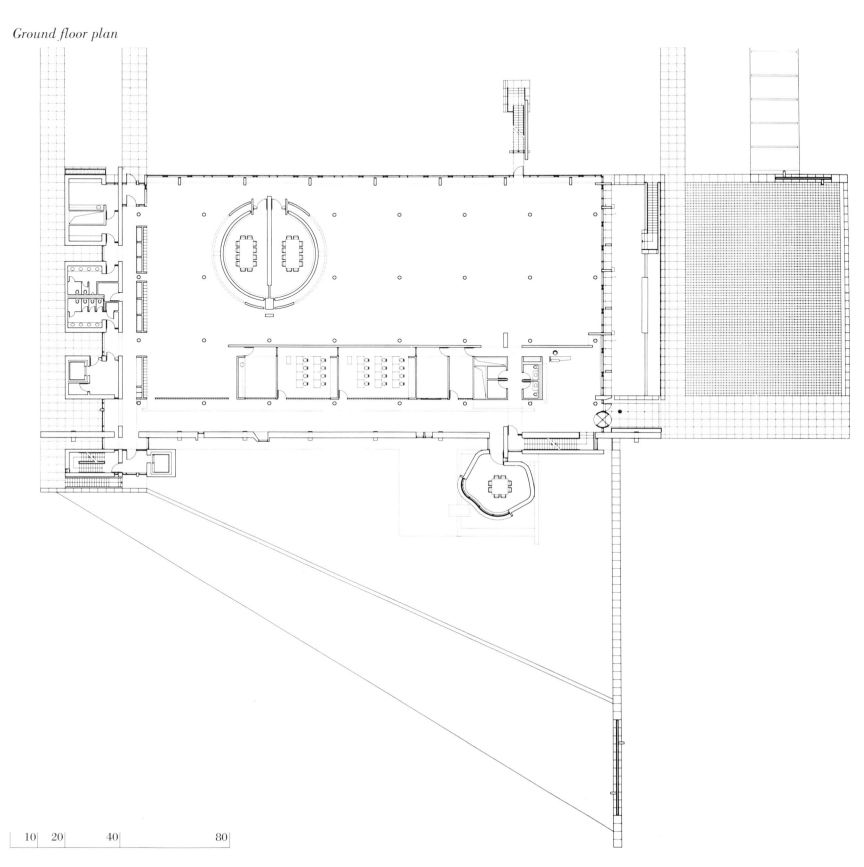

10 20 40 80

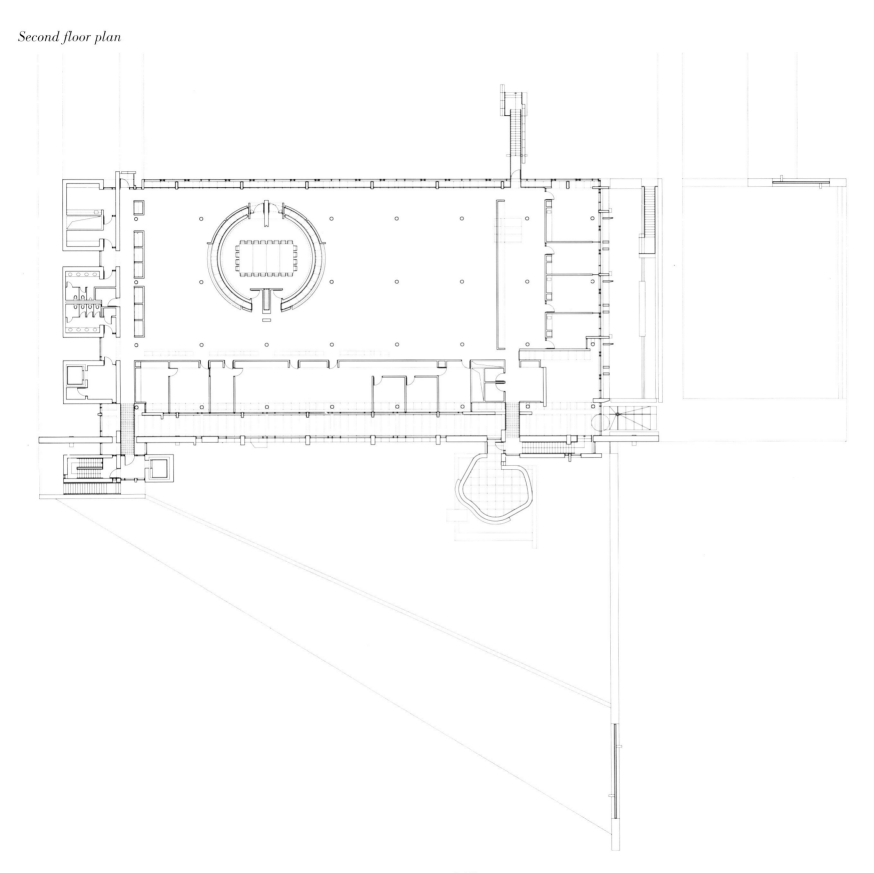

Once one is out of the five boroughs of New York City, one enters into that infinite expanse where there is hardly any architecture for miles and miles. In this demoralizing regard, Long Island is typical of the country as a whole. This new airline headquarters—shifted from Kennedy Airport to reduce commute time—offered an opportunity to place a building of distinction in an otherwise nondescript landscape of careening freeways and scattered, rather mediocre suburban development.

South elevation

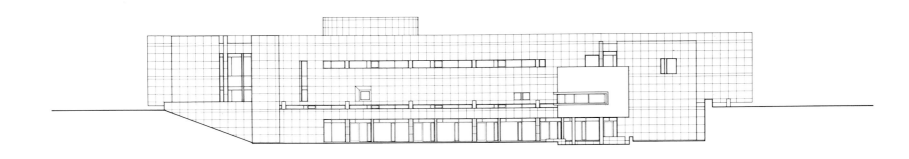

North elevation

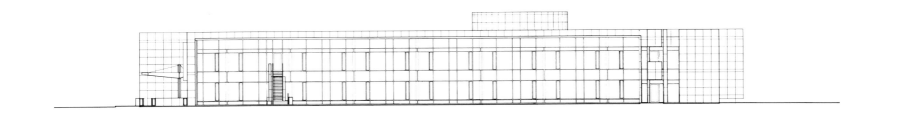

East elevation

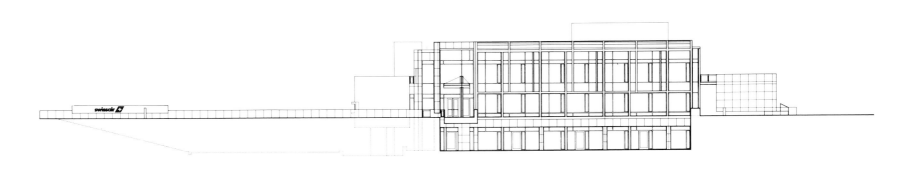

| 10 | 20 | | 40 | | | 80 | |

West elevation

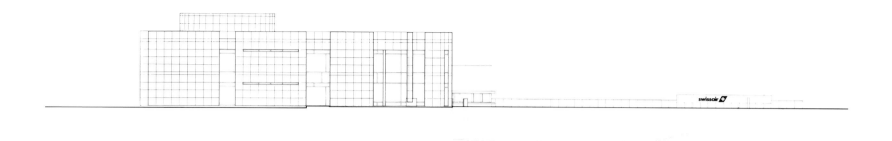

Section through atrium and conference room

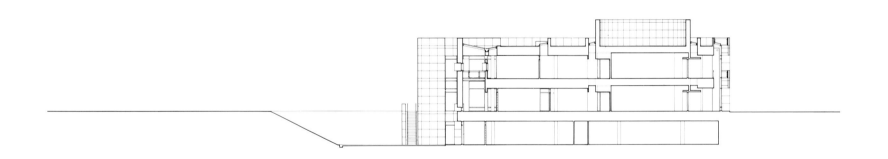

Section through atrium

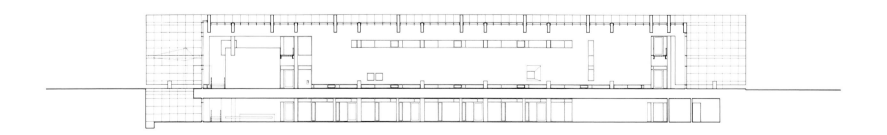

Natural light is highly important to me and my work. Its change-ability is what makes it all the more interesting. In architecture, light reinforces certain structural ideas in a building. Light must support, accentuate, and open up existing surfaces and spaces. Natural light gives mood to space; as it changes throughout the day and according to the seasons of the year it modifies and articulates space—space that is calm yet brimming with life.

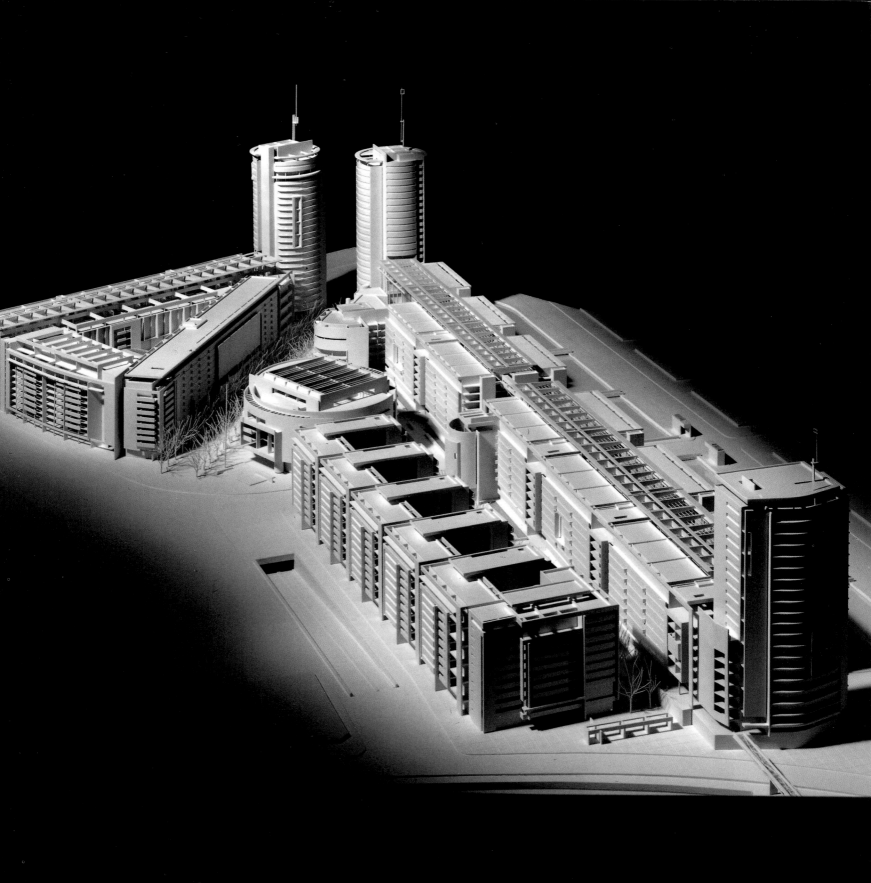

Potsdamer Platz Master Plan

Berlin, Germany
1992

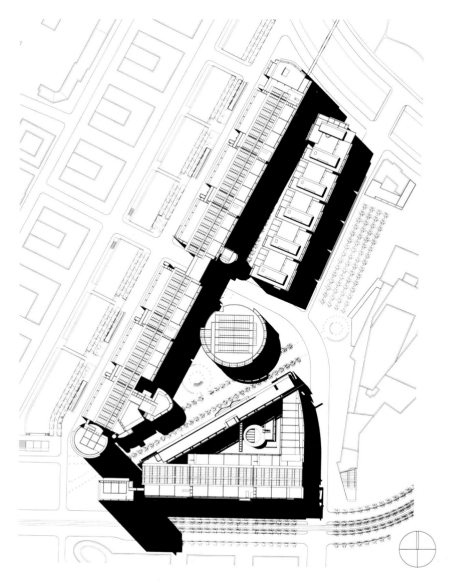

The site for this master plan is adjacent to Berlin's historic Potsdamer Platz, which was destroyed in the Second World War. The competition brief called for the development of office and commercial space adjacent to the hexagonal Leipzigerplatz and close to the postwar Staatsbibliotek designed by Hans Scharoun, which stands at the eastern edge of the so-called Cultural Forum. Four schemes were instrumental in determining the overall parti for this overdeveloped site: (1) a more or less continuous, 11-story infill block capped at its northern and southern extremities by office towers from 15 to 25 stories in height; (2) a five-block, top-lit, 11-story galleria running parallel to Linkstrasse and evenly subdivided by streets according to a grid established for the area by Hilmer and Sätler; (3) a pedestrian walkway, flanked by trees, running diagonally between the Staatsbibliotek and the Postdamer Platz (this diagonal echoes a similar radial street flanking the northeastern edge of the adjacent site); and (4) rows of trees used at certain points throughout the scheme as either buffers to traffic arteries or devices for focusing pedestrian movement on certain civic institutions such as the Staatsbibliotek or the proposed theater at the effective center of the site.

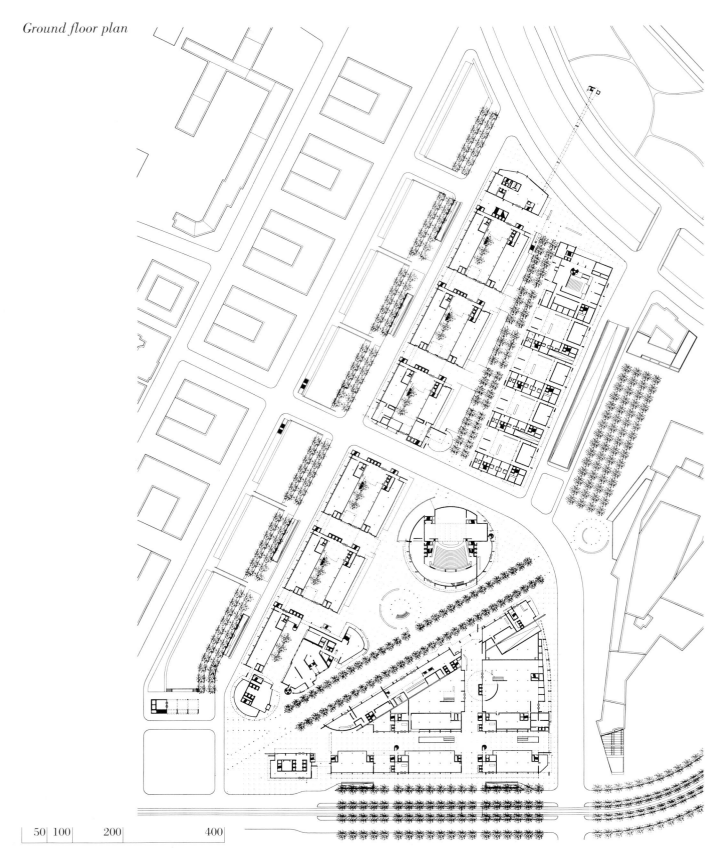

50 | 100 | 200 | 400

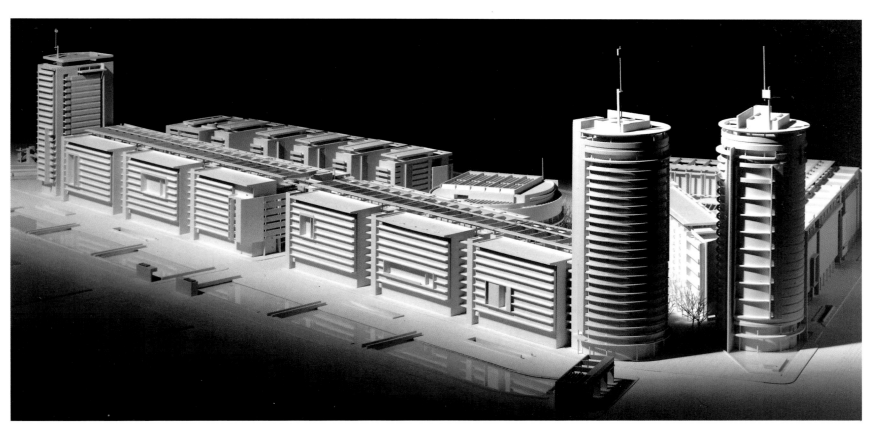

Federal Building and United States Courthouse

Islip, New York
1993–1999

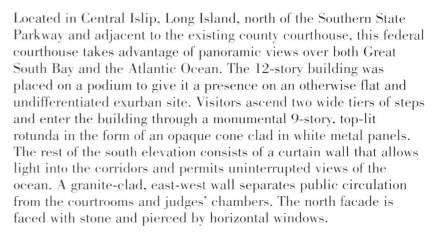

Located in Central Islip, Long Island, north of the Southern State Parkway and adjacent to the existing county courthouse, this federal courthouse takes advantage of panoramic views over both Great South Bay and the Atlantic Ocean. The 12-story building was placed on a podium to give it a presence on an otherwise flat and undifferentiated exurban site. Visitors ascend two wide tiers of steps and enter the building through a monumental 9-story, top-lit rotunda in the form of an opaque cone clad in white metal panels. The rest of the south elevation consists of a curtain wall that allows light into the corridors and permits uninterrupted views of the ocean. A granite-clad, east-west wall separates public circulation from the courtrooms and judges' chambers. The north facade is faced with stone and pierced by horizontal windows.

The west wing of the building houses four district courts per floor, while two bankruptcy courts are located on each floor in the east wing. Both wings connect to a central, top-lit, 12-story atrium with public foyer spaces at each courtroom level that link with the adjacent cone. In response to functional and security requirements, distinct circulation zones for the public, judicial staff, and detainees were provided via a careful sequencing of layered public areas, courtrooms, and judges' chambers.

This building reinterprets the courthouse type to enable it to function as a new kind of civic institution, receptive to public events as well as to the formalities of the judicial process. The rational, gridded plan allows for some modification of the circulation and provides for internal expansion of court facilities over a 30-year period.

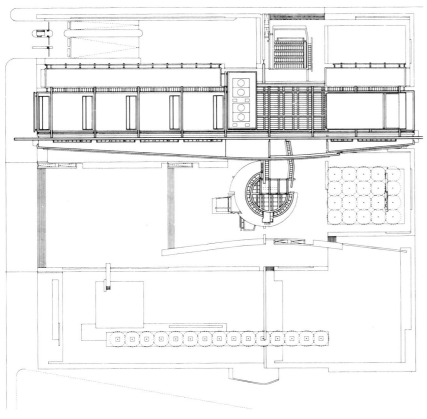

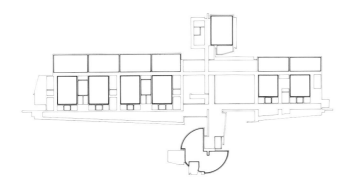

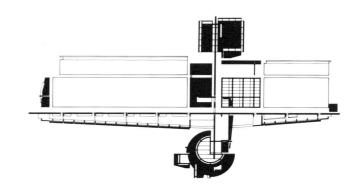

Geometry

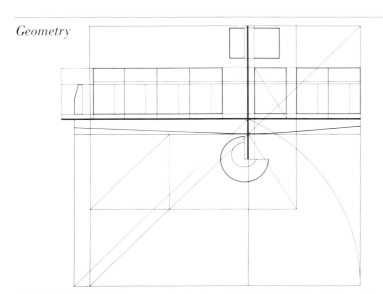

Structure

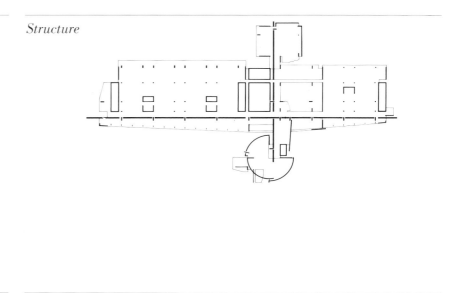

Circulation

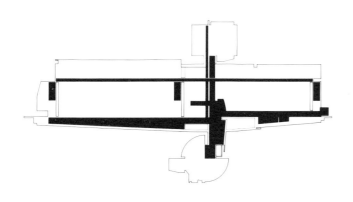

Figure/ground

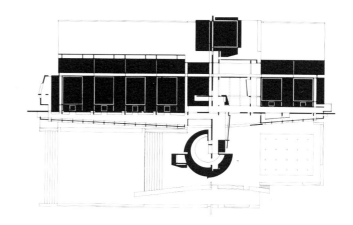

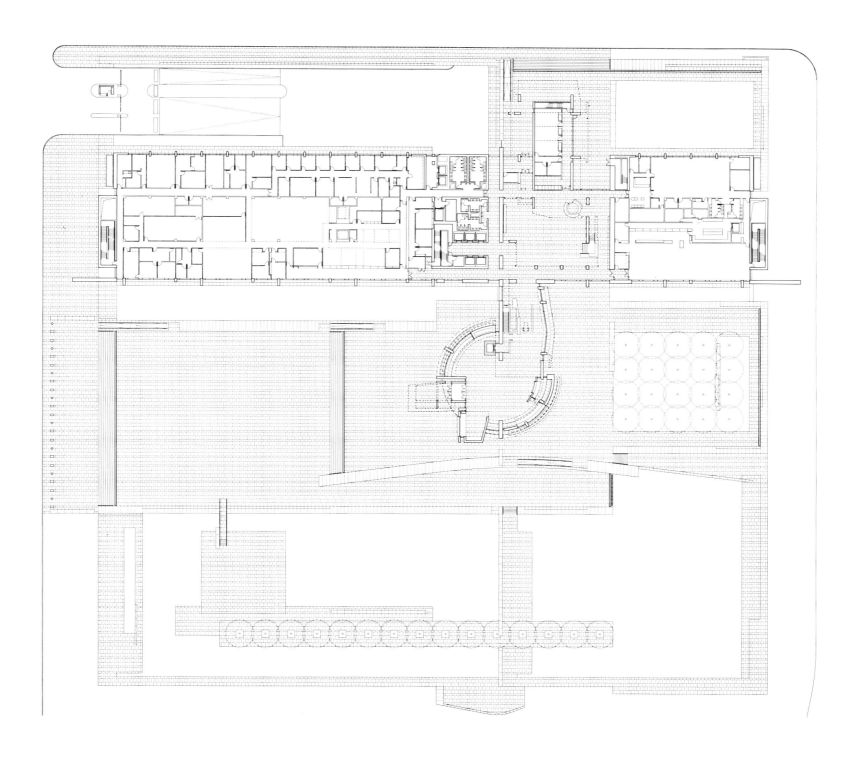

25 50   100   200

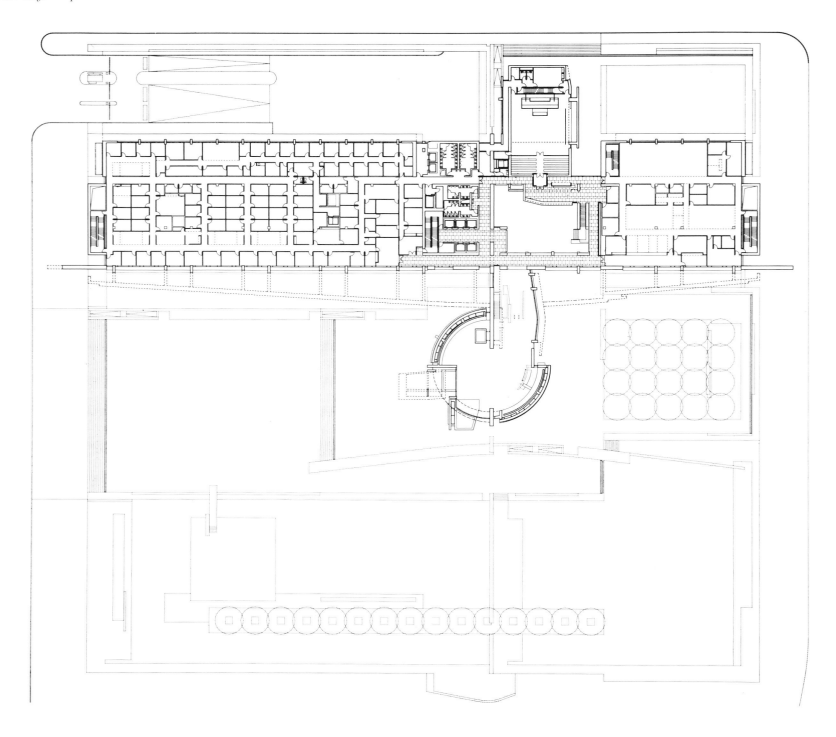

25 50   100   200

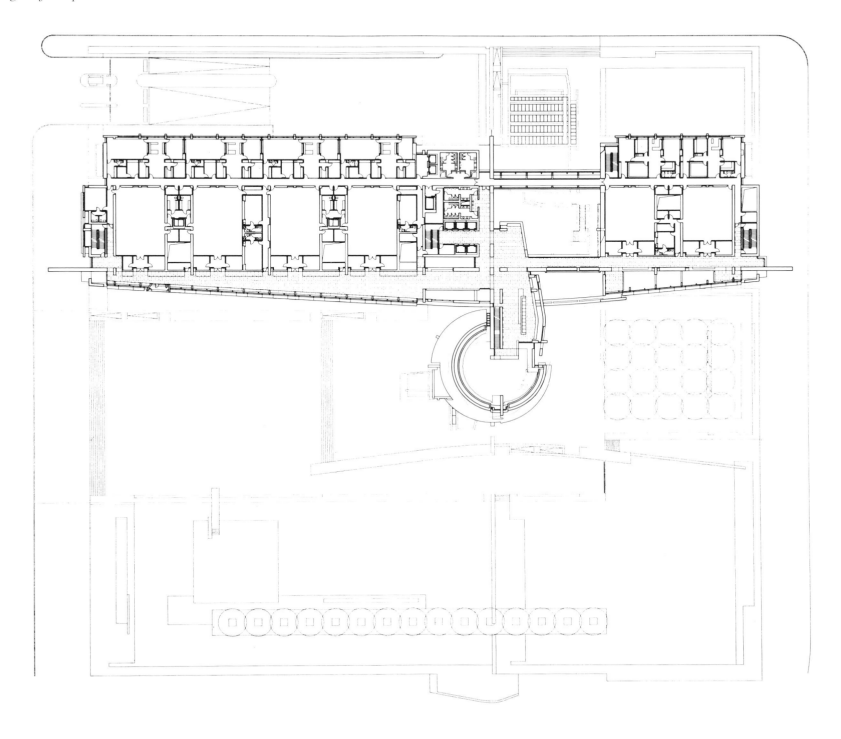

South elevation

North elevation

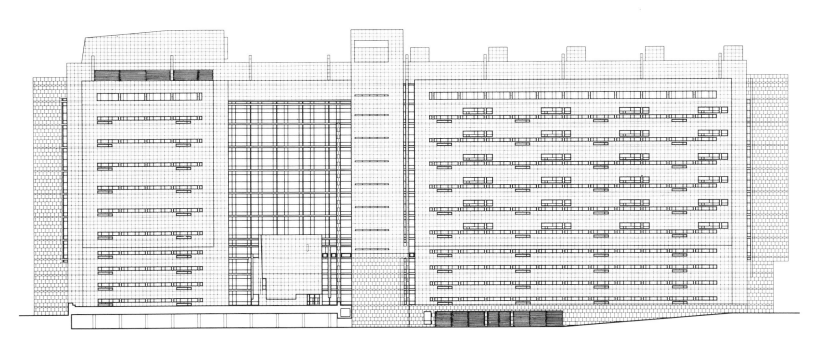

25 50 100 200

West elevation

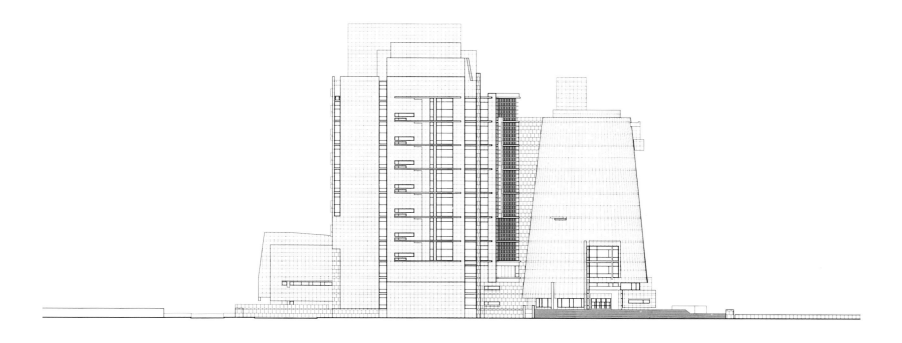

Section through rotunda

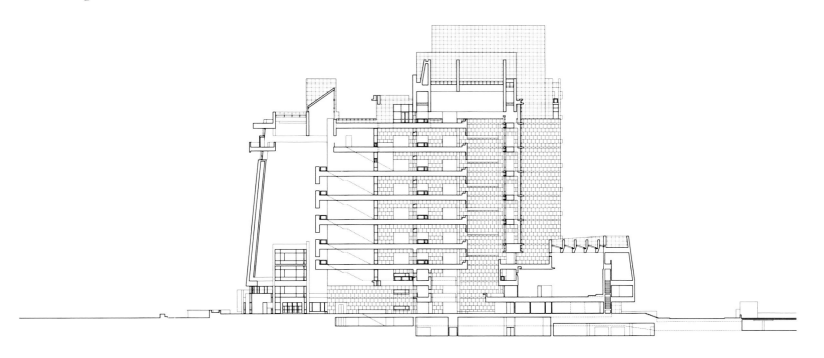

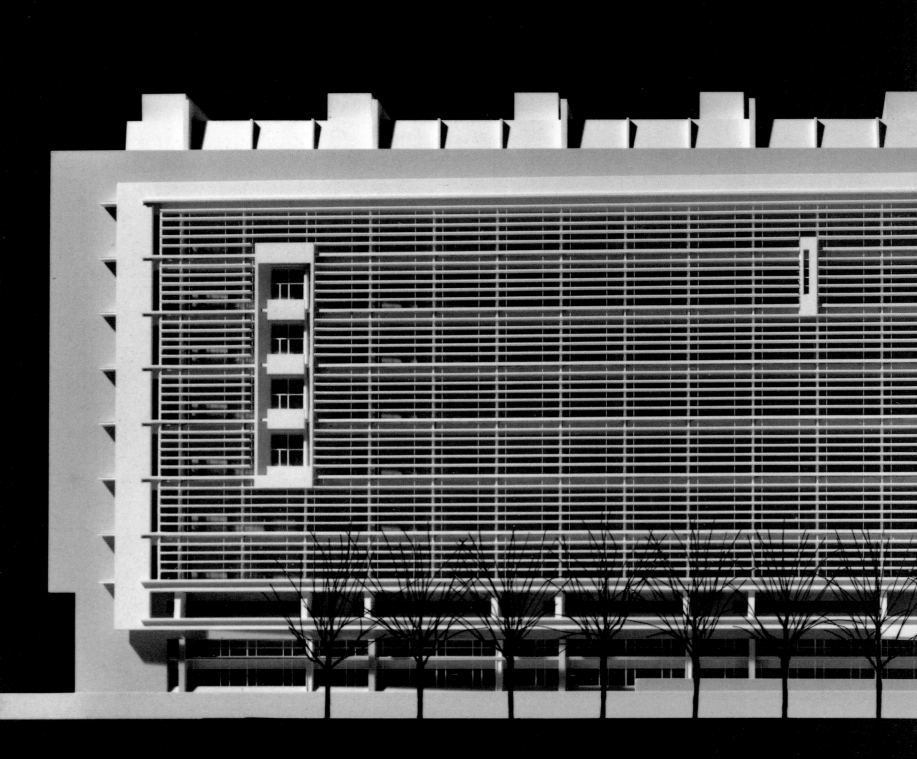

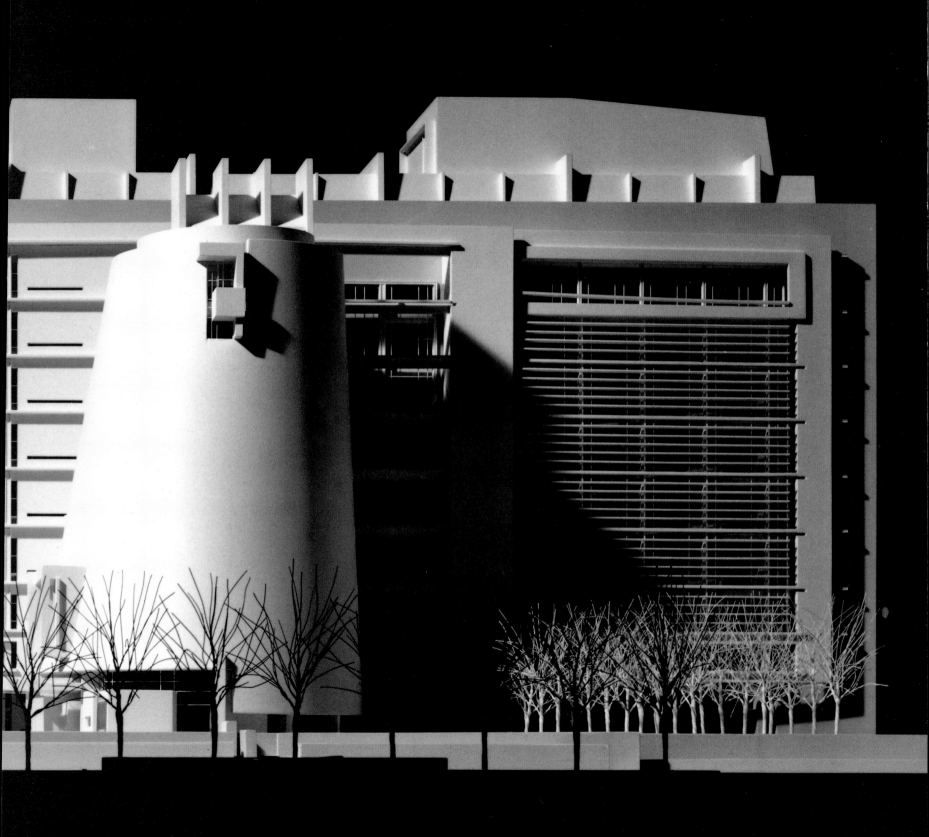

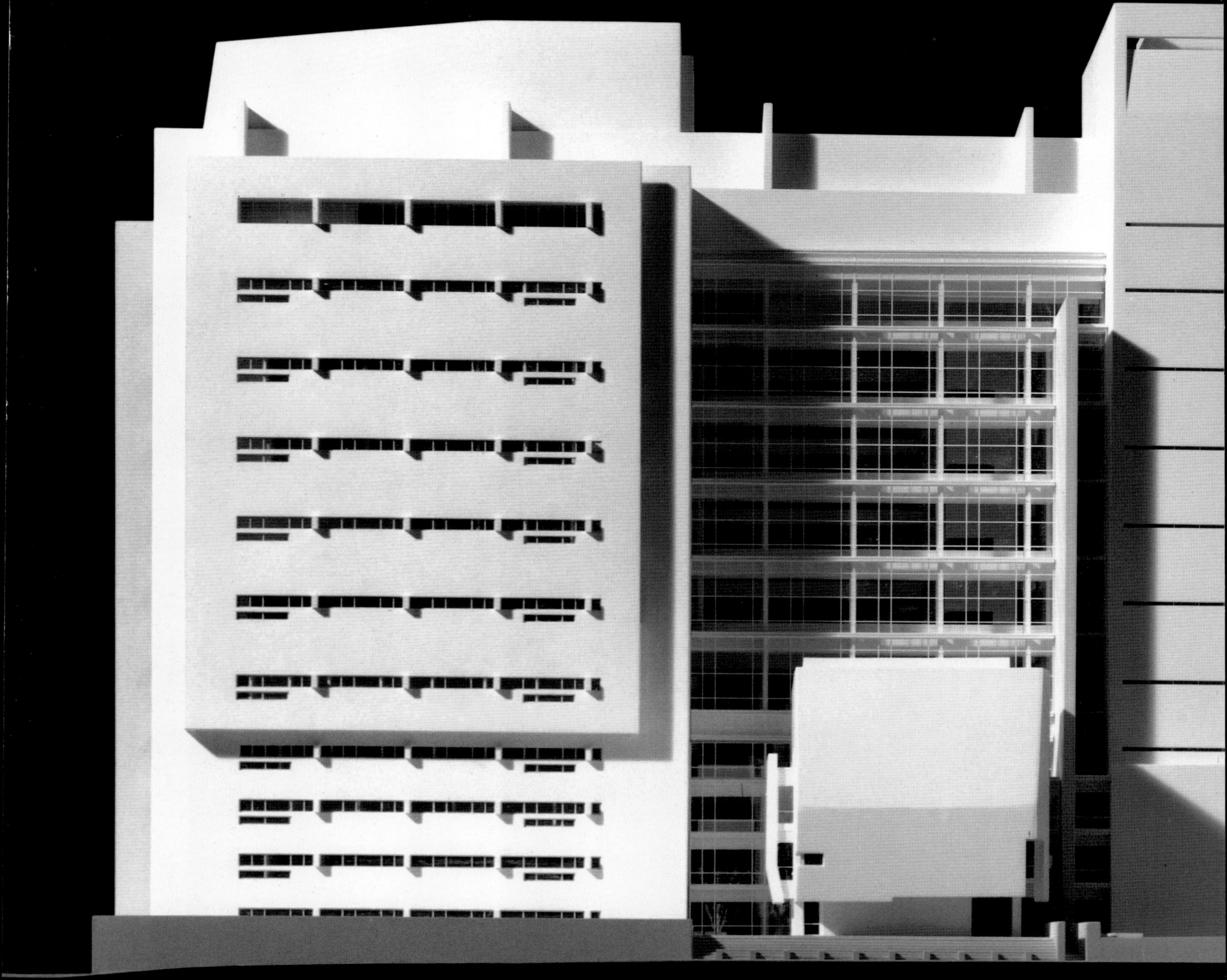

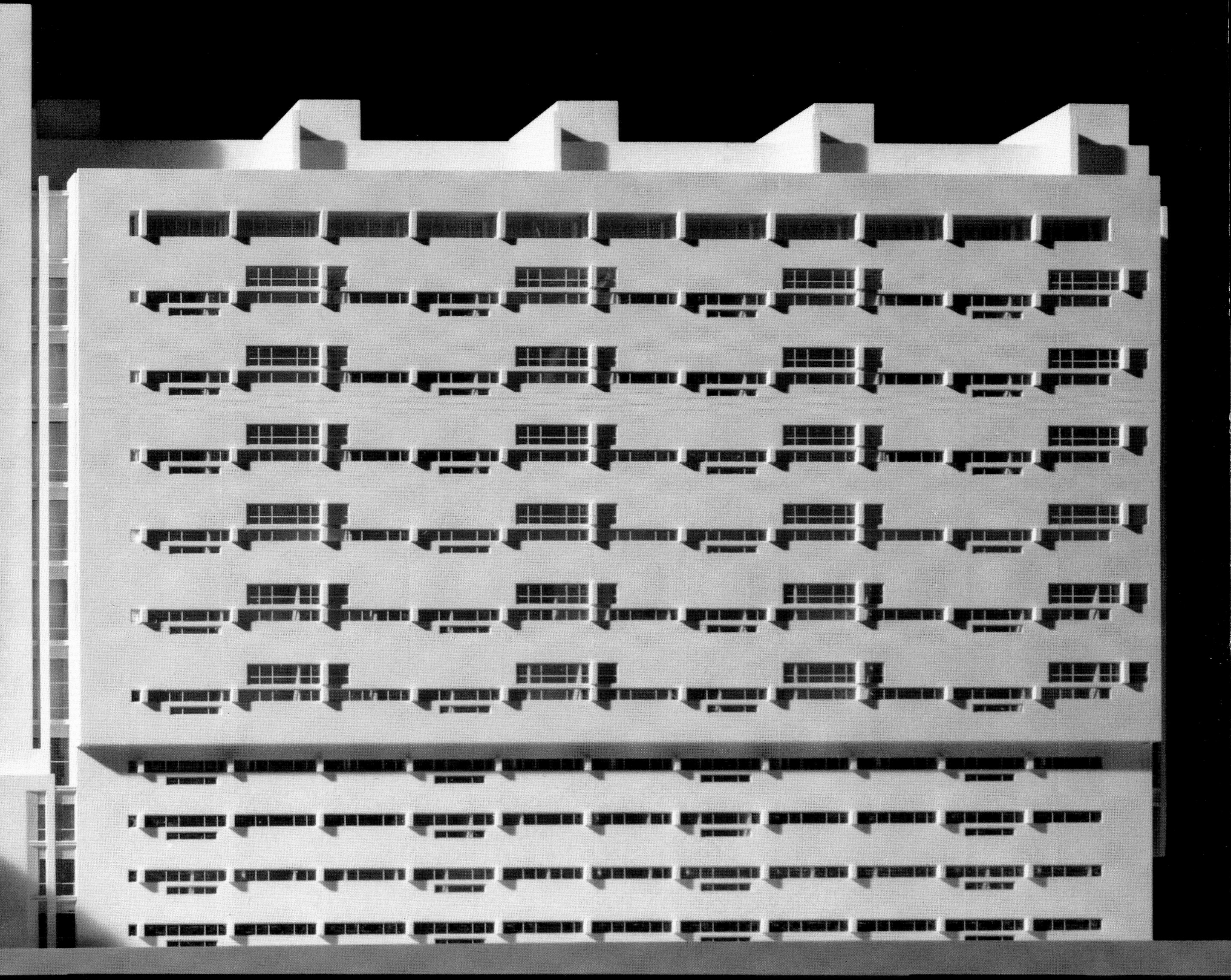

Museum of Television & Radio

Beverly Hills, California
1994–1996

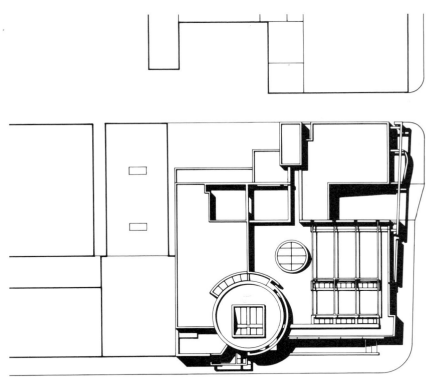

The Museum of Television & Radio in Beverly Hills is located prominently at the corner of North Beverly Drive and Little Santa Monica Boulevard. Flooded with natural light and open to the street, this two-story building is the result of the remodel and rearrangement of an existing structure. Set between two newly glazed planes, one for each public facade, the main volume is highly visible from the sidewalk, and vice versa.

The North Beverly Drive entrance is set back from the property line in order to create a threshold at the entrance, a top-lit cylindrical lobby that is the symbolic center of the museum. The lobby affords access to the gallery, the 150-seat theater, the Radio Studio, and the Listening Room. The information desk, the museum shop, and a multipurpose education room are on the ground floor, off the lobby. Visitors reach the second floor via a stepped ramp that penetrates the rotunda and overlooks the exhibition space, providing views of the streetscapes beyond. Here the movement system is inseparable from the viewing system as the stair culminates in the reading room on the second floor. The less public spaces are located on the third floor: the trustees room and the roof garden with views into the rotunda. Access to this level is by elevator or by a circumferential stair inside the top-lit space.

Program

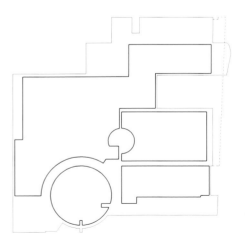

Geometry

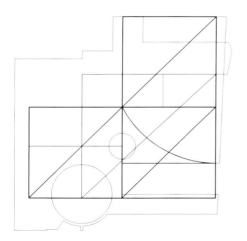

Structure

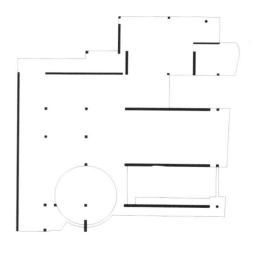

Enclosure

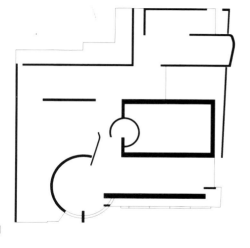

Circulation

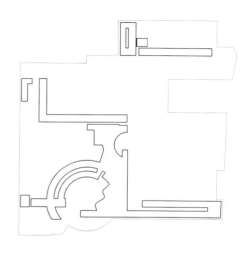

Figure/ground

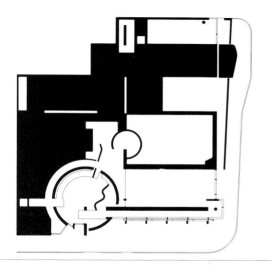

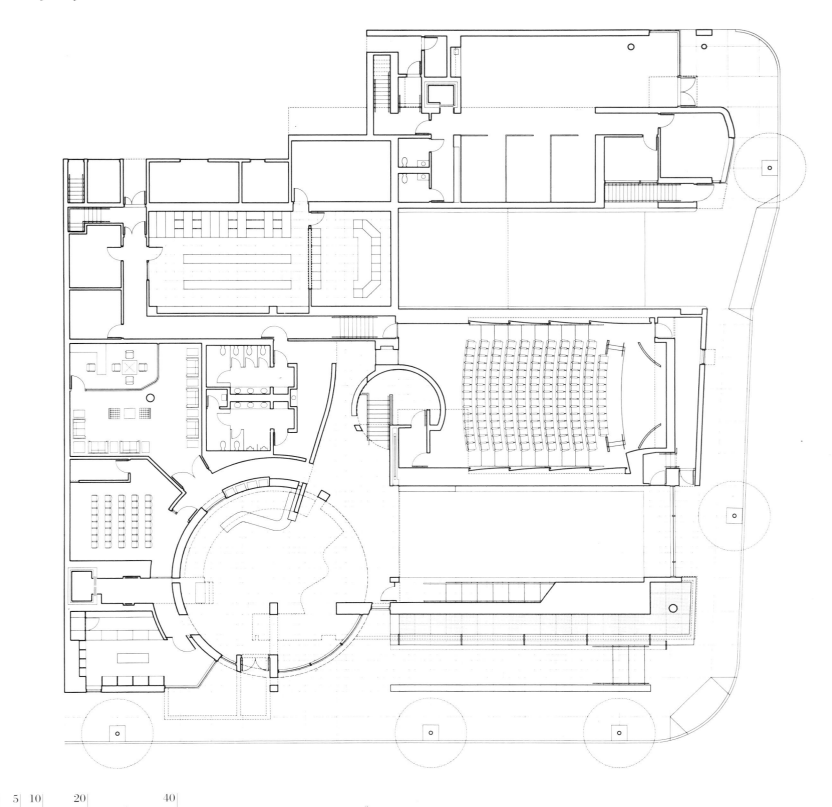

5 10   20   40

Even if it does not use the architectural language of Richard Neutra and Rudolph Schindler, this building surely approaches the progressive humanism of the Southern California school of the first half of this century, thanks to the freewheeling, consumerist, exclusively Hollywood vision of Los Angeles that was popularized by Reyner Banham. It is ironic, to say the least, that this should happen to be a media museum.

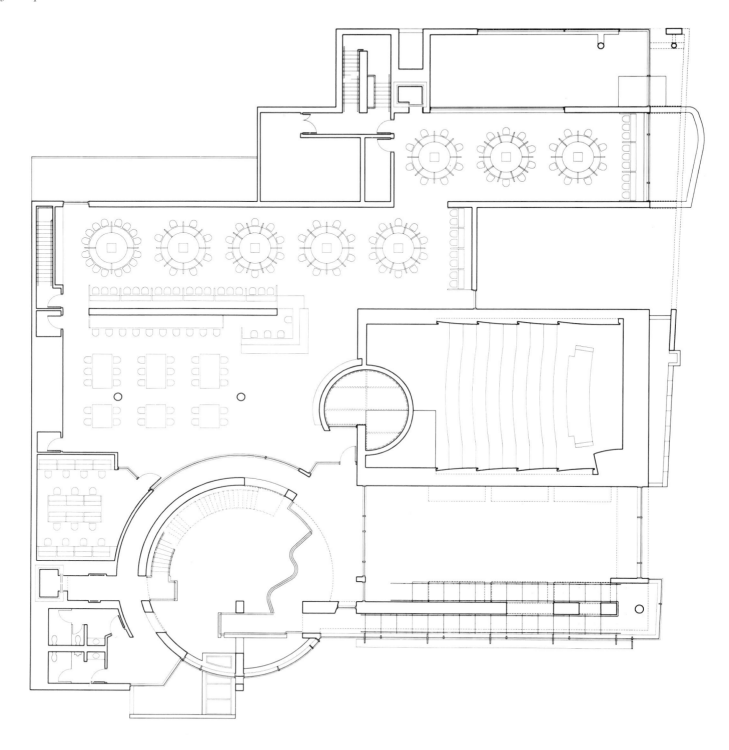

5 10 20 40

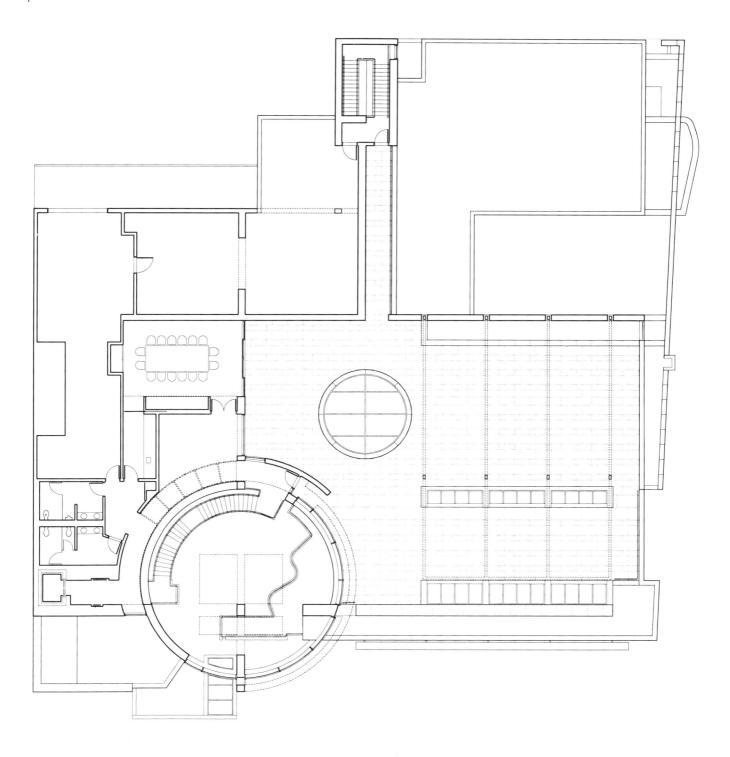

East elevation

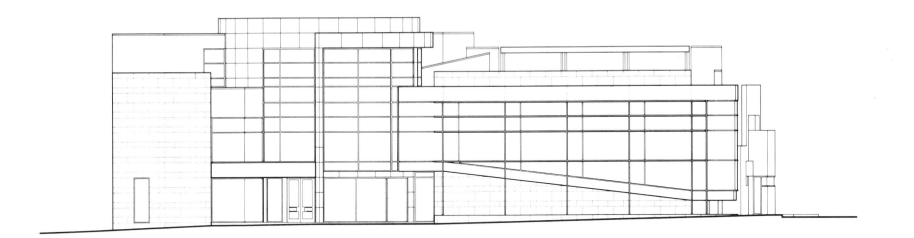

North elevation

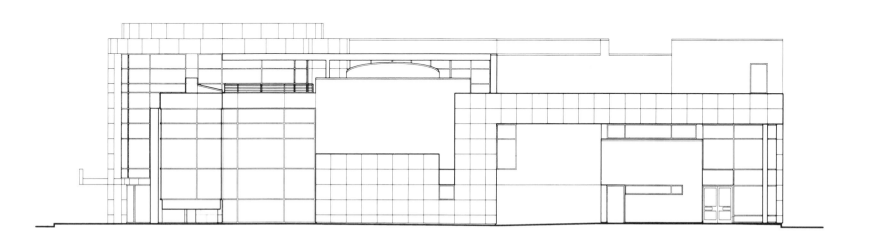

5 10 20 40

Section through theater

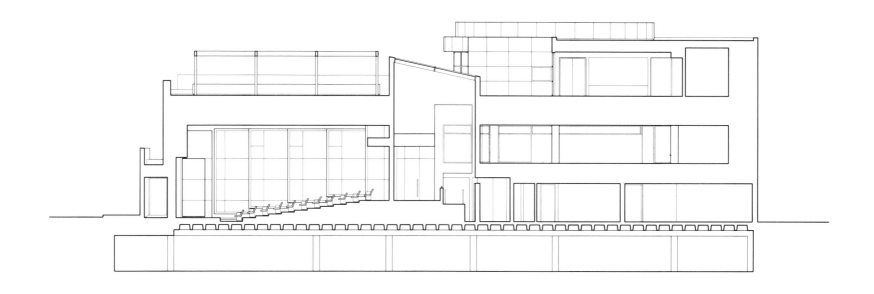

Section through gallery

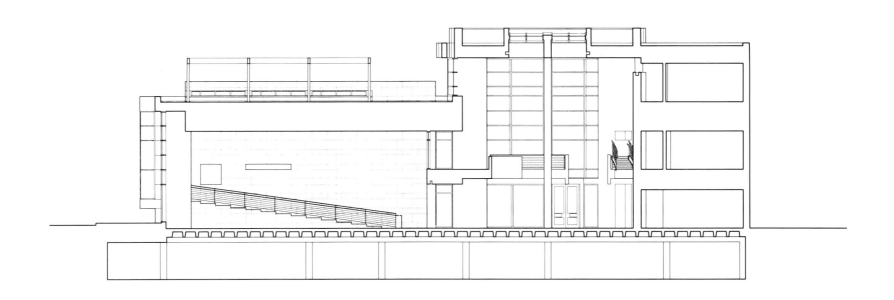

This project was originally designed during a weekend charrette. The client invited a few architects to participate in a 48-hour weekend design competition. Michael Palladino, my partner, and I sat together in our office in Los Angeles to analyze the program and the site; then we drew it up together. The museum was on a very tight schedule and a limited budget, so the design developed quickly, true to our original concept. What we drew that weekend is basically the design that we built.

Federal Building and United States Courthouse

Phoenix, Arizona
1994–2000

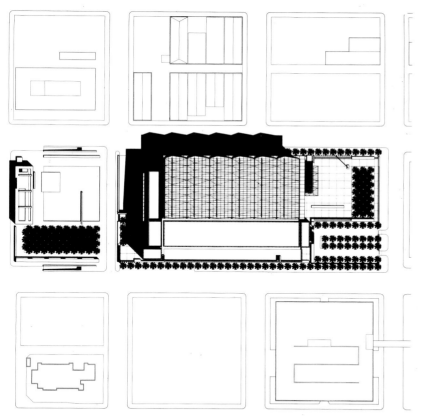

The courthouse, irrespective of its size and constituency, has always been the one building type that has sustained the communal and public values of the U.S. Constitution. Traditionally located in the center of the city, it represented all three branches of government while remaining the one monument and public space to which citizens gravitated. Despite today's sophisticated technology, it is still necessary to maintain the appropriate physical relationship between judge, jury, and spectators. Light plays a critically symbolic role in the reading of this structure, which is enlightened by reason during the day and by the equally radiant glow of artificial light at night.

The courthouse's main public space, a 350-by-150-foot covered atrium, is orientated toward the city center and situated on an axis with the state capitol some five blocks to the west. The atrium extends on its eastern and western ends into paved plazas that are furnished with shade trees, pools, and fountains. These areas serve as transitional zones between the harsh desert climate and the atrium itself, which is cooled by evaporation and natural convection. Hot air escapes through vents in the roof, drawing fresh air across the atrium, where it is cooled by water from a misting system before dropping to the floor.

Nineteen district courtrooms and four magistrate courts occupy the top four floors of the building. This functional arrangement is complemented by a three-story, cylindrical special proceedings courtroom at podium level, a symbolic space that serves as the focus of the atrium.

Glazed throughout in shaded clear glass and ceramic fritted low-e glass, the high-tech character of the atrium stems from its trussed tubular-steel roof structure, which is carried on steel columns integrated with the louvered fenestration of the north and east elevations.

291

Program

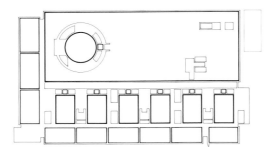

Geometry

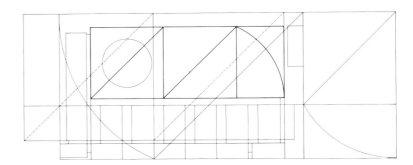

Structure

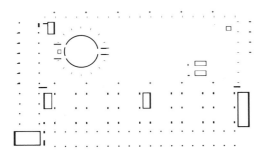

Enclosure

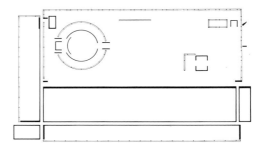

Circulation

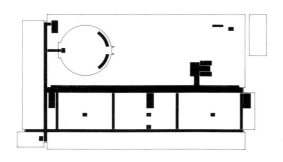

Figure/ground

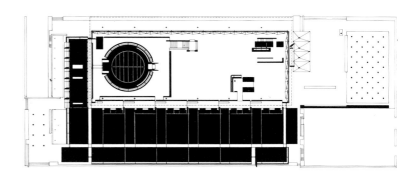

Ground floor plan

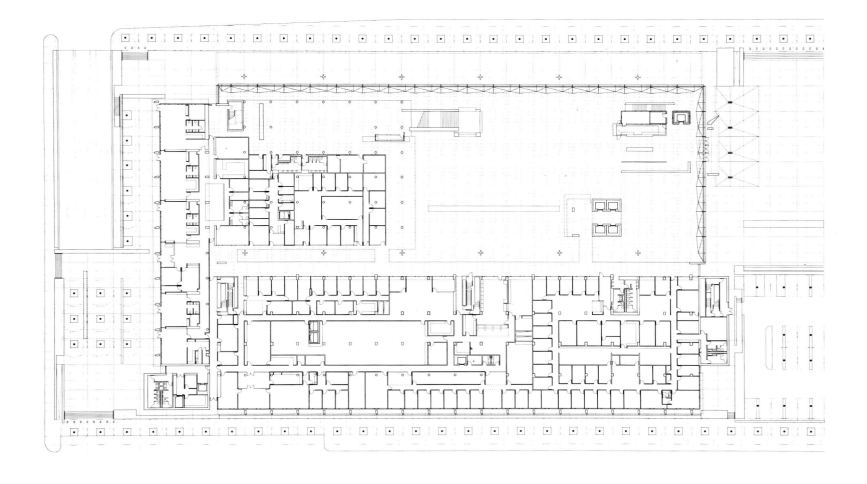

| 25 | 50 | 100 | 200 |

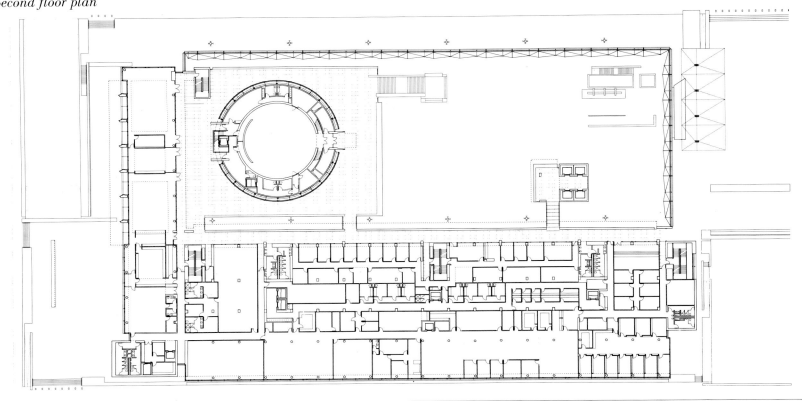

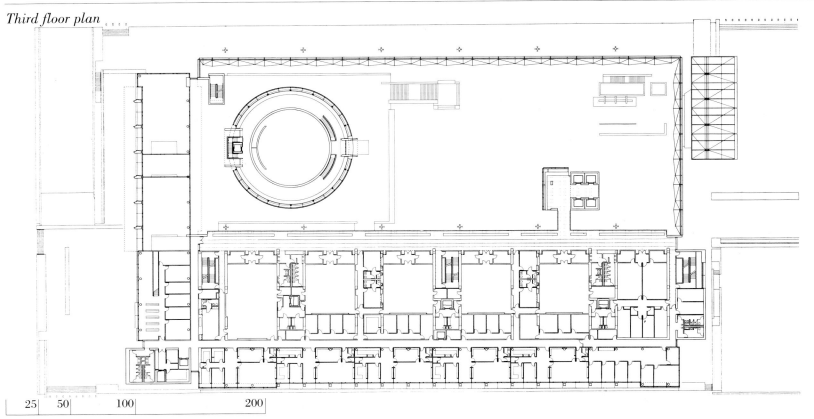

25 50 100 200

Fourth floor plan

Fifth floor plan

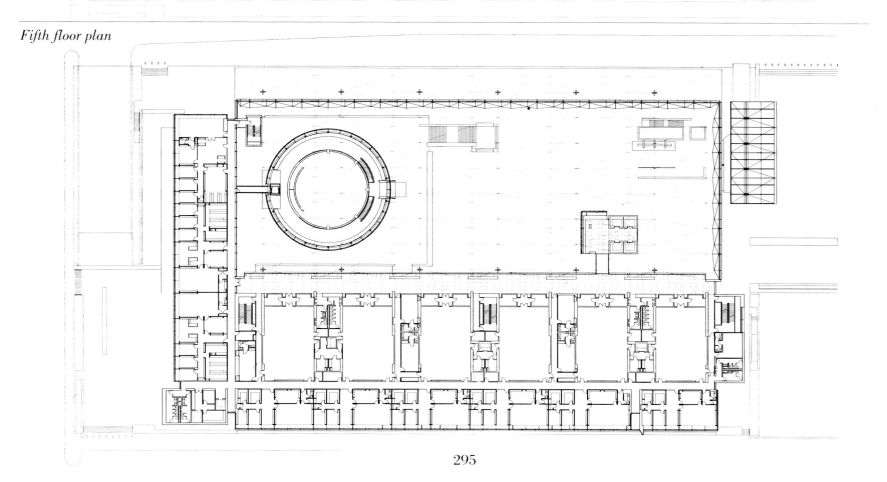

North elevation

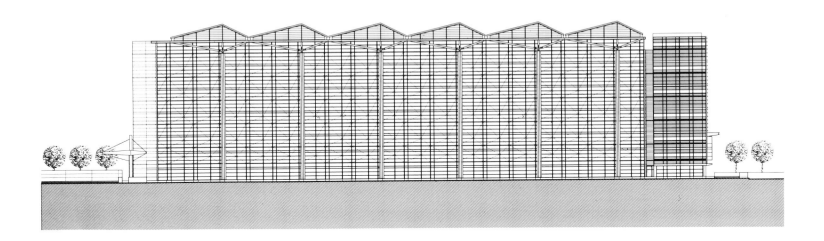

South elevation

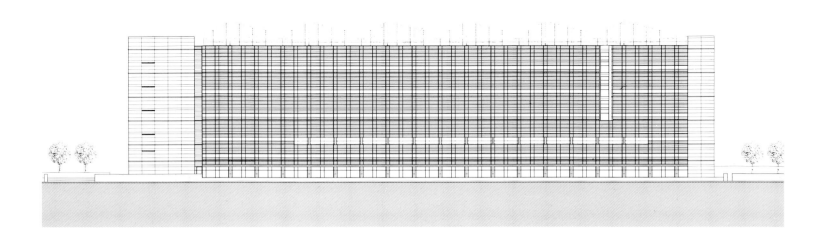

25 50 100 200

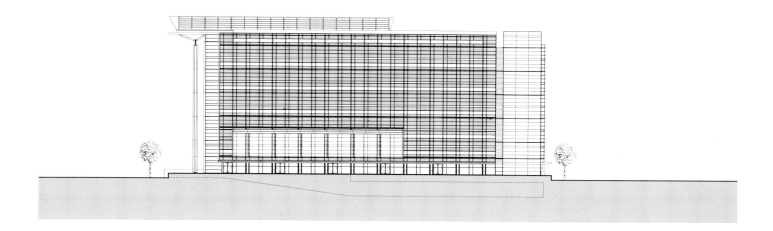

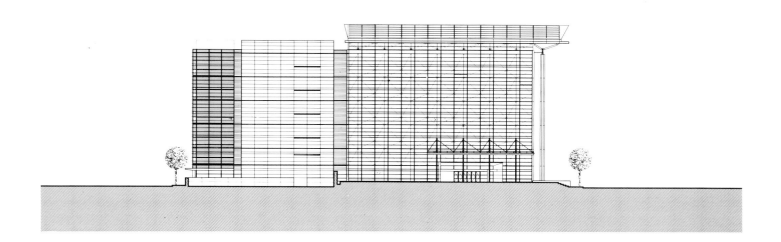

Section facing south

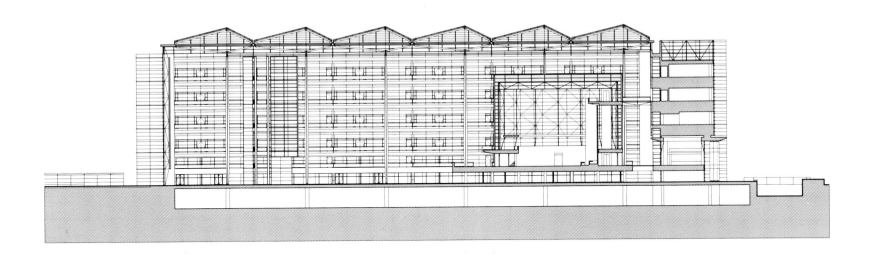

Section facing west

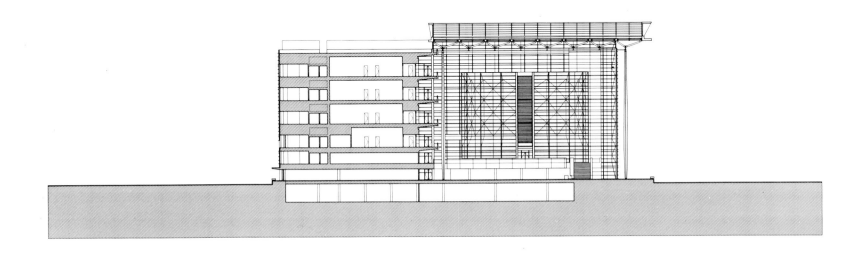

25 50   100   200

Building in an arid region where the temperature can easily reach 110-120°F during the summer, I opted for creating a large, livable public foyer, an intermediary space between the air-conditioned courtrooms and the raw desert climate. The hall is cooled passively in part by exhausting hot air through the roof and in part by providing misted air that descends from outlets around inner perimeters.

Gagosian Gallery

Beverly Hills, California
1994–1995

In a city where the automobile is king and architectural "differences" must be writ large in order to attract the attention of drivers and passengers moving at 60 mph, the Gagosian Gallery projects an insistent but subtle authority. Its high, white wing and the sharply articulated play of layered transparencies and shadows draw attention to a work that is otherwise a fairly minimal transformation of a preexisting storefront. The street elevation is composed of an overhead-glazed door and an expanse of clear and frosted glass held in place by a lattice of aluminum mullions and white sun-screening blades. Just visible above the roofline is a gently pitched monitor light with an airfoil profile carefully designed to admit indirect natural light into the interior. The glazed aluminum door can be raised from sidewalk level so artworks can be seen from the street during al fresco events or openings. This provision, dependent upon the California climate, amounts to an arresting, provocative gesture, particularly for gallery-goers who are more accustomed to the hermetic formal character of the enclosed private gallery.

Visitors entering the gallery first see a blank, full-height wall that opens to the main volume when you least expect it. The main gallery is a soaring space top-lit by clerestory windows at the north and south ends of a bowed ceiling. Sunlight is beautifully diffused through this surface and varies over the course of the day, from warm on one side to cold on the other. Visitors' circulation is controlled from an elliptical reception desk that also monitors access to the secluded upper-floor viewing room and the adjacent office space. A second, smaller gallery on the ground floor also receives light through the roof. Throughout the gallery track lighting partially suspended from a double-cruciform, steel-stanchioned grid beneath the main monitor light complements the natural light.

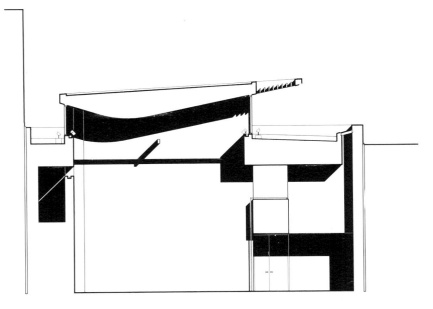

The gallery was designed to capture and diffuse the Southern California light. Its whiteness lends a certain neutrality to the space, thereby intensifying one's appreciation of works by Rubens, Picasso, Stella, Clemente, Salle, or Newman. Since I knew Larry Gagosian in New York and experienced the extraordinary exhibits he has organized, I was pleased to have the opportunity to design this gallery, albeit within a very short time frame. It was a small project but a highly satisfying California experience.

Ara Pacis Museum

Rome, Italy
1995–2000

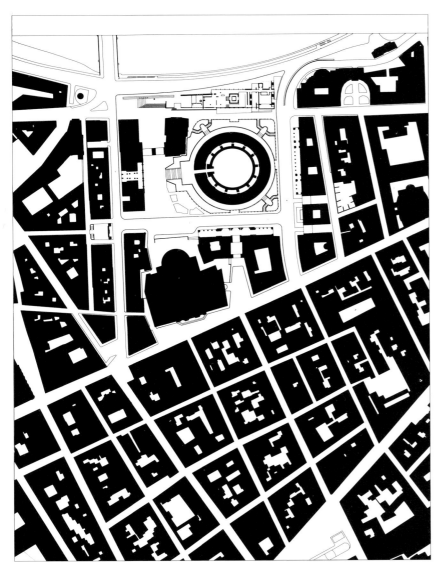

This small museum on the bank of the Tiber river has been designed as a renewed setting for the Ara Pacis, a sacrificial altar built in 9 A.D. and now located on the western edge of the Piazza Augusto Imperatore. Planned as part of an effort to protect Rome's cultural legacy, the new structure replaces the monument's present enclosure, which is in a state of advanced decay. The proposal consists of a long, single-story, glazed loggia elevated above a shallow podium. This structure provides a transparent barrier between the embankment of the Tiber and the existing, circular perimeter of the Mausoleum of Augustus. In addition to protecting and displaying the altar, the new pavilion will accommodate a small exhibition space, a museum shop, and a 150-seat auditorium.

The altar was removed from the Campo Marzio in 1938 during the Mussolini era. In order to relate the altar's present position to its original site, we applied a system of regulating lines to the new project. Bisecting the distance between the present center of the mausoleum and its original site yielded a four-square urban grid that was used as a proportional frame to reorganize the piazza and its surroundings. An artificial obelisk is used as a historical reference on the north-south axis through the altar. The space housing the altar is top-lit by adjustable monitor lighting, while the loggia-pavilion is faced in stone and steel-framed plate glass. The overall syntax refers discreetly to the Italian Rationalist architecture of the 1930s.

The design for the new Ara Pacis Museum complex will be an integral part of a master plan for the Augustan area. The area will be converted to a pedestrian zone, and traffic circulation surrounding the mausoleum and the Ara Pacis will be modified appropriately.

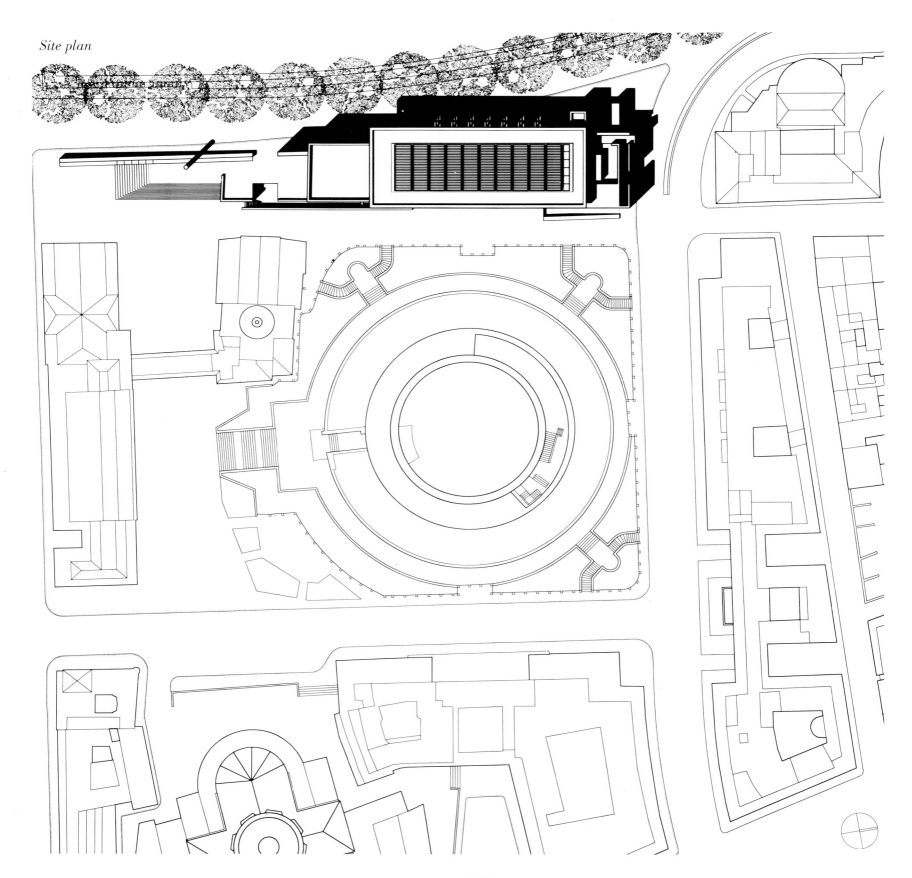

Site plan

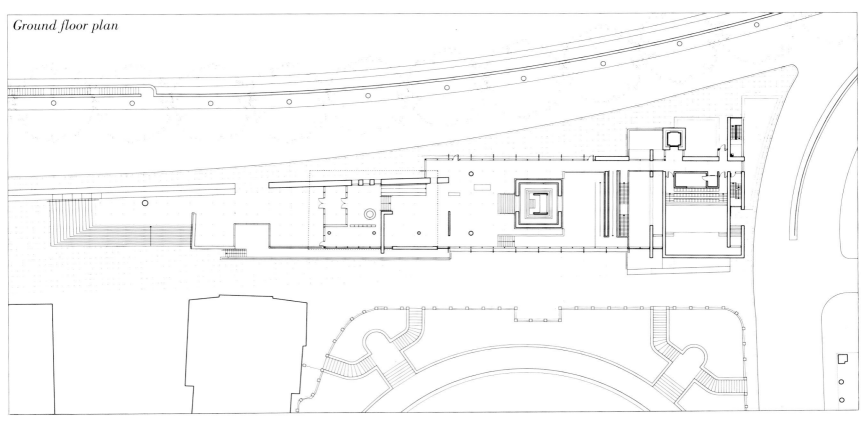

Ground floor plan

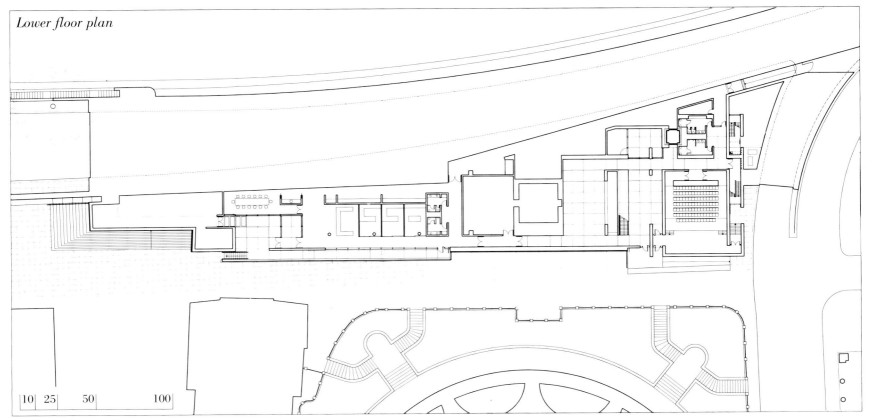

Lower floor plan

10 25 50 100

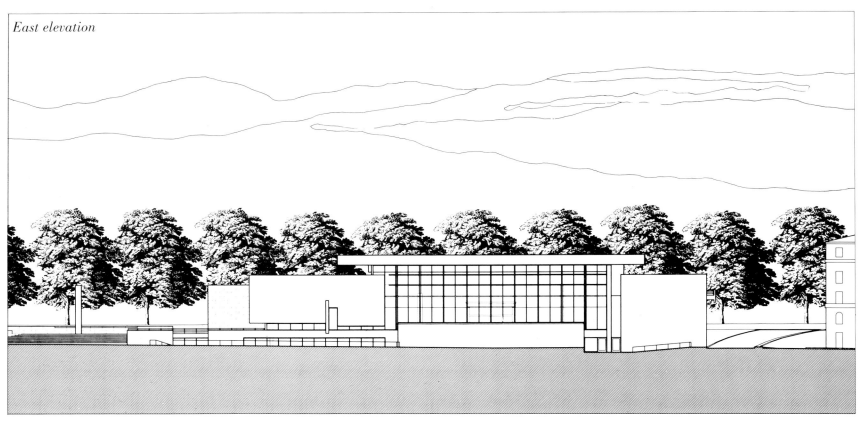

East elevation

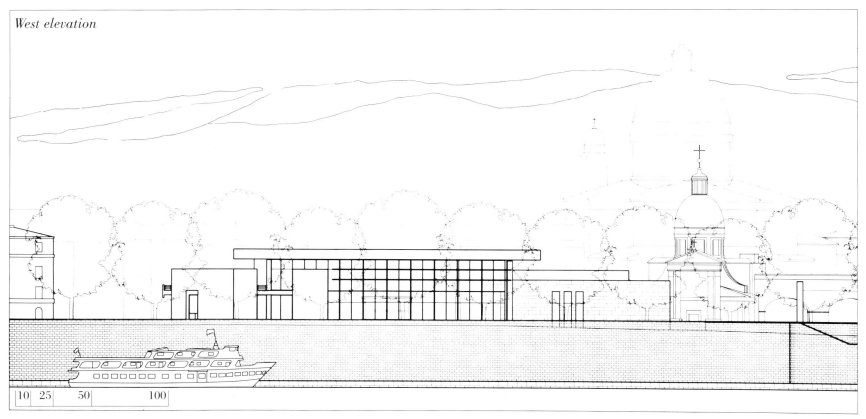

West elevation

|10| |25| |50| |100|

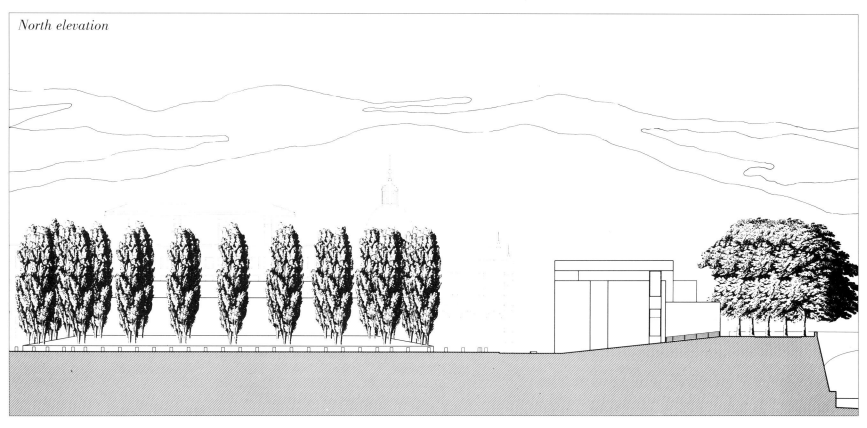

North elevation

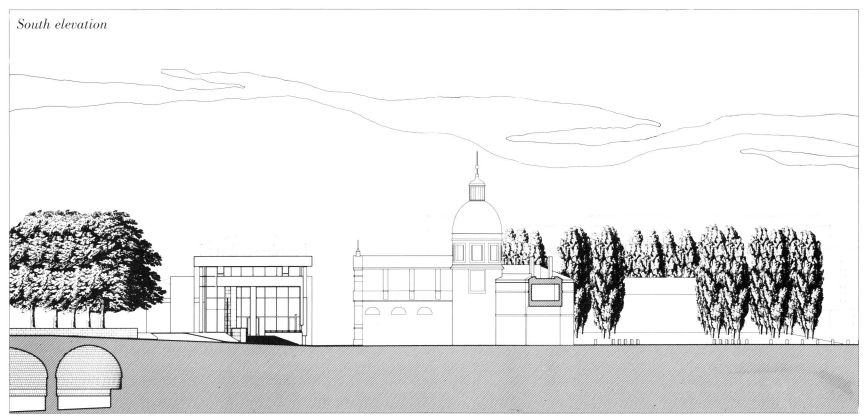

South elevation

The Getty Center

Los Angeles, California
1984–1997

The Getty Center occupies a chaparral-covered hilltop that stretches along the San Diego Freeway, then juts south from the Santa Monica Mountains into the residential neighborhood of Brentwood. Severe zoning restrictions limited the extent and height of the buildable volume under the terms of a conditional-use permit. Within these limitations the layout of the complex was largely determined by the contours of the elevated site, which affords spectacular views over the city, the mountains, and the distant ocean. Most of the buildings are arranged along the two natural ridges that form the southern end of the 110-acre site. Axes through these ridges meet at an angle of 22.5 degrees in plan, which corresponds to the inflection of the San Diego Freeway as it bends north out of Los Angeles to traverse Sepulveda Pass. The layout is based on an interplay between this angle of intersection and the Los Angeles grid, together with a number of curvilinear forms derived from the specific topography.

An underground parking garage and a tram station were established close to the freeway (some three-quarters of a mile to the north), well below the main complex. Whether one comes by car, taxi, bus, or on foot, one enters under the freeway overpass through the same propylaeum. The majority of visitors reaching the site by automobile park in the subterranean garage. Everyone takes a five-minute ride on the tram to the top of the site. The winding route affords magnificent views of the diverse surrounding topography and glimpses of the complex.

The route terminates at the arrival plaza, where visitors may orient themselves to the site as a whole. Here one immediately encounters the 450-seat auditorium that, together with the J. Paul Getty Trust offices and the Getty Information Institute, constitutes the North Building. Immediately to the east is the Getty Conservation Institute, the Education Institute for the Arts, and the Getty Grant Program, buildings that for the most part are not open to the general public. The museum itself extends south along one of the ridges, while the Restaurant/Café and the Research Institute for the History of Art and the Humanities occupy strategic positions along the other ridge extending to the southwest. Due to the conditional-use permit, much of the complex remains below the hilltop datum of 896 feet above sea level and, as a result, much of the facility is underground.

On arrival visitors are invited to choose between entering the museum immediately or exploring the site at their leisure. Those who opt to see the collection approach the museum lobby via a wide esplanade of steps. They enter the museum through a three-story cylindrical lobby that opens directly onto the museum court and the various galleries beyond. The pavilion structure of the gallery itinerary modulates the scale of what would otherwise be an overwhelmingly large institution. The pause spaces between the various pavilions, both closed and open, provide for panoramic views of the surrounding landscape.

The exhibition sequence is organized chronologically and according to artistic medium. Making a clockwise circuit around the perimeter of the courtyard affords a chronological experience of the collection, while the different media are divided between the upper and lower levels of the galleries. The painting galleries occupy the upper level of every cluster. Due to the climate and the unique system of monitor top-lighting, paintings may be viewed during the day without artificial light. Natural light is filtered differently according to the character of the collection. Decorative arts, manuscripts, photographs, and works on paper are housed on the ground level to protect them from damaging ultraviolet light. By moving from one level to the next within each cluster, visitors experience different media from the same period, or, if they prefer, they may follow the evolution of one medium through time by remaining on one level. Several special exhibition spaces—including a larger one for mid-

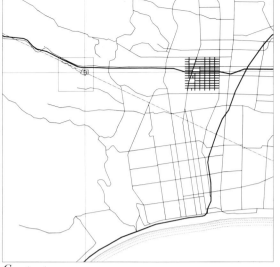

Context

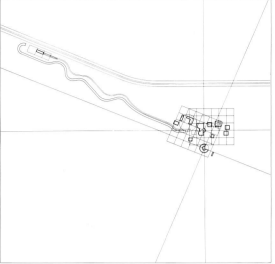

Geometry

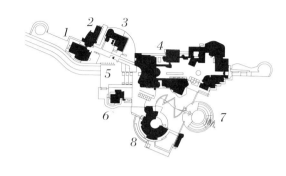

1. Auditorium
2. The Getty Information Institute/
   The J. Paul Getty Trust
3. The Getty Conservation Institute/
   The Getty Education Institute for the Arts/
   The Getty Grant Program
4. The J. Paul Getty Museum
5. Arrival Plaza
6. Restaurant/Café
7. Central Garden
8. The Getty Research Institute for
   the History of Art and the Humanities

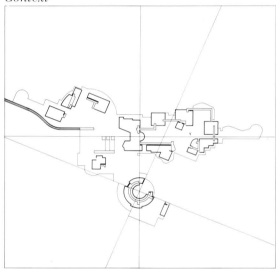

Structure

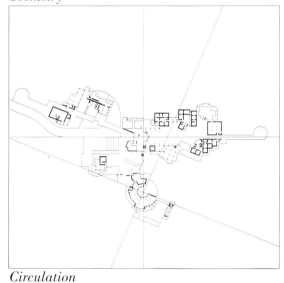

Circulation

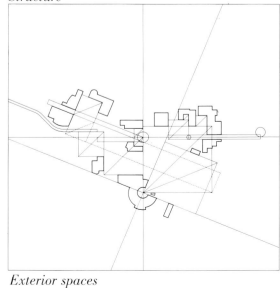

Exterior spaces

Landscape

316

size traveling exhibits—offer relief from this sequence. Visitors who wish to view a certain part of the collection are encouraged to take a secondary route, thereby bypassing the chronological sequence.

Although the museum is the most public program of the Getty Trust, its galleries are only a part of the entire complex. Other programs of the Trust employ an even greater number of people, and the structures they occupy may be of interest to the casual visitor. The Restaurant/Café, with its two categories of food service, will inevitably be a part of the overall attraction. Situated close to the central plaza, it is easily reached from most parts of the complex and its windows and terraces afford outstanding views of the mountains to the north and the ocean to the west. On the other side of the plaza lies the auditorium, a popular venue for lectures, concerts, and other cultural events.

The Getty Research Institute for the History of Art and the Humanities is situated on the more secluded western ridge and completes the complex. The cylindrical building houses a one-million-volume library, reading rooms, study carrels, a small exhibition space, and offices for staff and scholars. This vast reference requirement is organized more or less radially within the structure. The information is not centralized, however, but organized into a series of smaller sub-libraries. The plan is designed to encourage scholars to explore incidental areas in open stacks in the process of searching for specific material. At the same time, the building's cylindrical form expresses the Research Institute's essentially introspective nature.

The staff members who catalogue and maintain the collection retrieve their material from the closed stacks below grade, while visitors and scholars gain access to the same material in the reading room and carrel spaces above. Scholars have the option of taking this material back to their offices for further study. Some of these offices are arranged around the top floor, while an additional fourteen offices are located in the Scholar's Tower to the south of the central complex, facing the city and the ocean.

Throughout the site, landscaping integrates the complex into the topography via heavily planted terraces that extend beyond the built volumes. Water also plays an essential role in enlivening the various sequences, with fountains and channels draining into the central gardens between the two prominent ridges.

Various types of cladding not only tie the complex to the site but also represent the status of its various institutions. Since the museum is the most public element, it is clad honorifically in split travertine. This facing imparts a feeling of permanence and constitutes an appropriate transition to the ridge on which the museum stands. All the major buildings are provided with stone-faced earth-works that appear to flow uninterruptedly into the various retaining walls deployed throughout the site. In less prominent places, stucco and other traditional earthen materials face incidental retaining walls.

Since the Research Institute, East Building, Auditorium, Restaurant/Café, and North Building are all curvilinear in form, they are largely faced in metal panels with large areas of fenestration. While almost as permanent as stone, the matte metal paneling reflects light and gives a sense of dematerialized translucence without being shiny. At the same time, this material, combined with stone and the lush vegetation, harmonizes with the Southern California landscape.

The Getty Center is dedicated to the preservation and assimilation of our cultural memory by way of making its collections available to the public for future enjoyment and use. Given this mandate, the complex was designed to combine symmetrical organization with asymmetrical form, thereby suggesting a balance between the humanism of geometry and the spontaneity of its organic assembly. Opened in December 1997, this institution has become the major cultural center in the Los Angeles Basin and a major attraction for U.S. and international visitors.

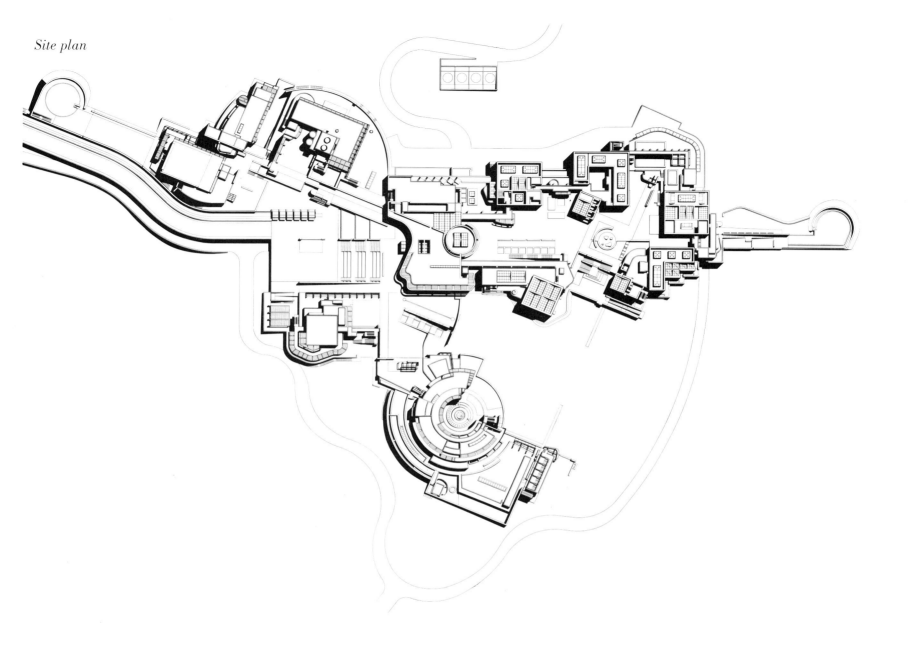

50 100   200   400

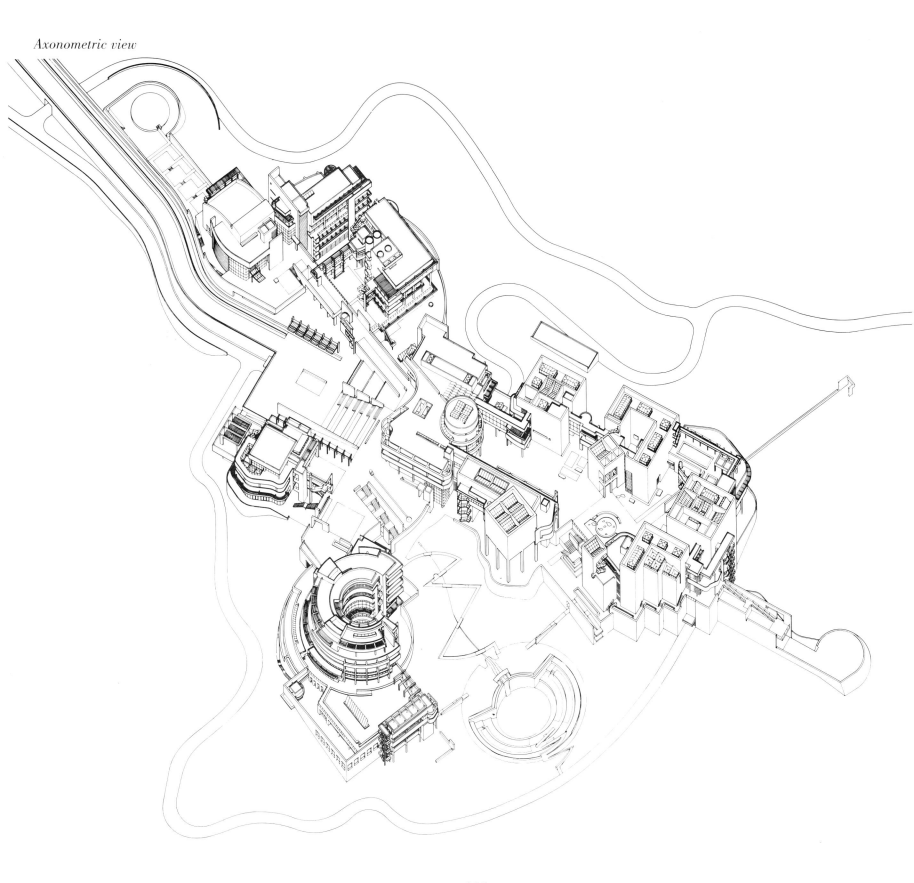

Axonometric view

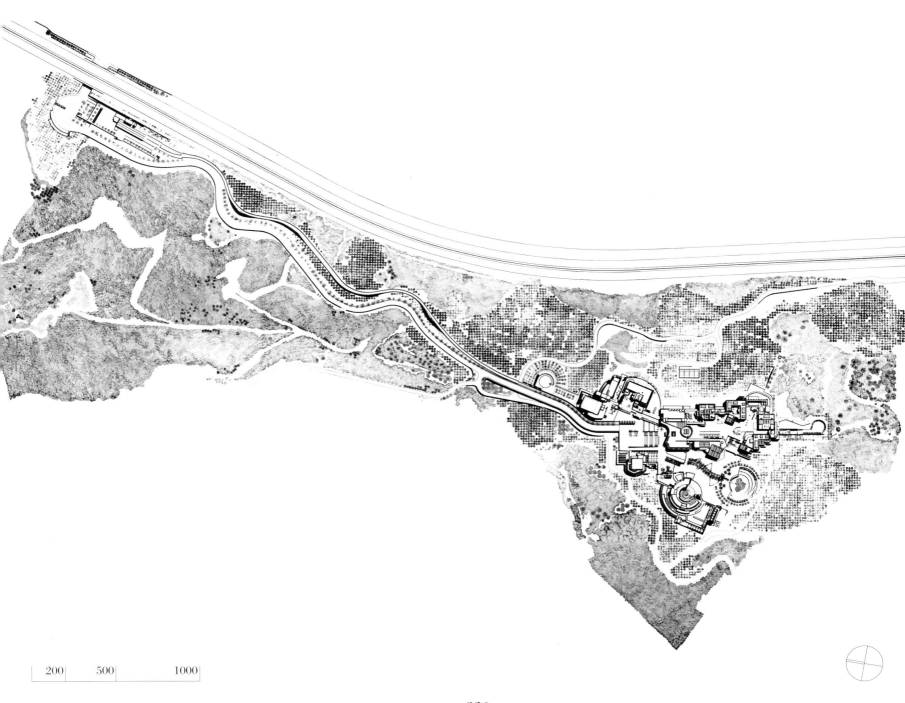

200   500   1000

The Getty Center is both in the city and removed from it. It therefore has to evoke simultaneously a sense of urbanity and remote contemplation. This dual nature is partly expressed by the organization of the complex along the axes of two hilltop ridges that meet at an angle of 22.5 degrees, which corresponds to the angle of the adjacent freeway as it bends out of Los Angeles through Sepulveda Pass. When you get off the tram you already sense these twin axes. At the museum, you find that the pavilions housing the permanent collection are on the street grid line, while the pavilion for changing exhibitions is aligned with the angle of Sepulveda Pass.

The J. Paul Getty Trust offices, Auditorium, Conservation Institute, and Restaurant
Entry floor plan

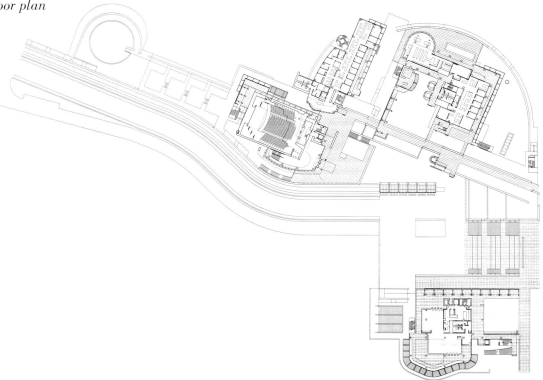

The J. Paul Getty Trust offices, Auditorium, Conservation Institute, and Restaurant
Upper floor plan

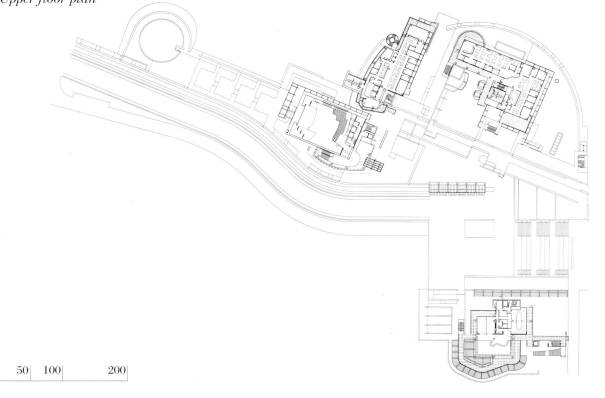

50   100| 200|

Although my vision of the building follows an American predisposition toward openness, warmth, flexibility, and invention, it has as much to do with European ideals such as permanence, specificity, and history. The materials used reaffirm this image of solidity, of a permanent presence in the landscape. Architecture at its best integrates human scale with civic grandeur, decorative simplicity with material richness, and technical innovation with a respect for historical precedent.

From the San Diego Freeway
you see a more or less continuous
string of buildings, but once you
are within the complex you
realize that there is really a lot of
open space. In fact, gardens,
courtyards, and terraces are an
essential part of the experience.
I have stood on the site and
directed the crane operator,
locating the trees one by one
to give them an architectural
density, so the landscaping
modulates the space between
the buildings. This relationship
between landscape and architecture is now beginning to come
alive, and visitors to the site
are discovering how important
the exterior spaces are to
experiencing The Getty Center.

Apart from topography, the most powerful aspect of the Getty site is the quality of the natural light, which is astonishingly beautiful, the clear, golden California light that is so intoxicating to an Easterner. As soon as I saw the site I longed to make walls flooded with light, walls that would cast crisp shadows. I wanted to set the structure against the brilliant blue sky of Southern California.

I imagined it as a light metal fabric combined with stone in such a way as to provide a solid, rocklike appearance, thereby opening a dialogue between massive enclosure and an open, lightweight transparency.

Most of the cues for the design came from the light and the landscape. Perhaps the most important initial decision was to work with the configuration of the land. We did not want to bulldoze the place, which is what a developer would have done—you make a flat plain and build up from there. That did not seem to be appropriate for this wonderful site. Why come up on this magnificent hill and turn it into a plain? Instead, we dug into the natural topography and then rebuilt it. With the completion of The Getty Center, the original, natural form of the hilltop is in fact clearer than ever. That is important for two reasons: first, we preserved something that is beautiful in itself; second, the topography provided an essential key for the organization of the complex.

Los Angeles has two cultures, the second of which is too often hidden behind stereotypical images. People think of L.A. as a city of traffic, movie sets, and false fronts, all in constant motion—all of which is true. But Los Angeles was also the city of Rudolph Schindler, Richard Neutra, and Frank Lloyd Wright, a city that became a second home to Thomas Mann and Arnold Schoenberg. I believe people from all over Southern California—and from all over the world—who visit The Getty Center recognize that it belongs to the cultural tradition of Los Angeles. They come away saying, "That was a terrific day," even though it is obvious that this place has not been built for entertainment value.

*We undertook an exhaustive
search to find the right stone, at
the right price—and even then
we were lucky, because we easily
could have come up empty-
handed. But then we found just
what we had been looking for, a
cleft-cut travertine quarried in
Bagni di Tivoli, just an hour
north of Rome. It is probably one
of the least expensive stones in
the world, since there is an endless supply in the quarries, but it
has exactly the warm color
and rough texture we wanted.*

Stone at the Getty is used as the traditional material for public architecture. Its presence is immediately reassuring to visitors, for they realize that despite the site's openness, they are in a public place. Beyond this civic character, the stone also expresses certain qualities that *The Getty Center* celebrates: permanence, solidity, simplicity, warmth, craftsmanship. Finally, it is a rough-cut stone that looks substantial, not like a wallpaper veneer. It offers a tactile connection to the landscape that no other material can provide.

When I first saw the hilltop, I thought it was the most beautiful site I had ever been invited to build on. Having this vast, open space, with magnificent views in all directions, right in the heart of Los Angeles, so easily accessible to everyone—this was an extraordinary situation. Some people criticize The Getty Center for being on top of a hill. They say it makes the place seem remote, imperious, elitist. But I do not believe it is necessarily elitist to put works of art above the city. Yes, The Getty Center is proposing that art can be something elevated, set a little apart from daily life. But in the same gesture, the Getty is also making Los Angeles accessible to people in a new way.

While designing the Getty I kept recalling Rome, particularly Hadrian's Villa and Caprarola for their thick-walled presence and figurative spatial order in which building and landscape lock into each other. At the same time, I felt that the Getty's materiality must derive not only from history but also from the regional ambience of Southern California, its colors and textures, its openness, warmth, and ease.

The J. Paul Getty Museum
Entry floor plan

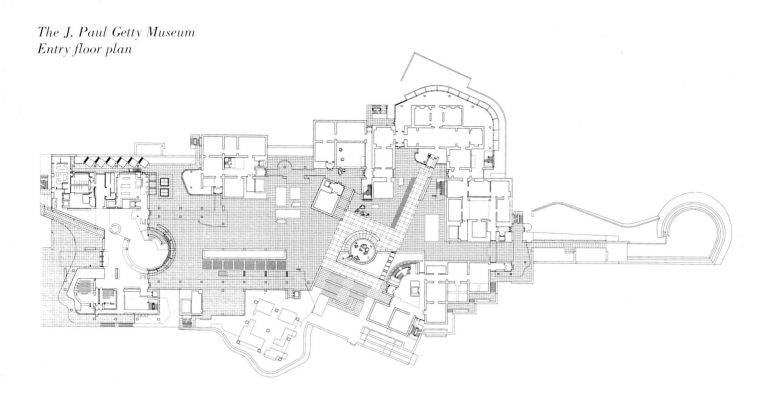

The J. Paul Getty Museum
Upper floor plan

50 | 100 | 200

The museum sequence begins with a large, light-filled rotunda that opens onto the central courtyard. Once inside this open lobby the visitor becomes aware that the museum consists of five distinct, two-story pavilions. At this point one may either proceed clockwise, through the peripheral pavilion sequence, or start at the upper level on the right-hand side of the courtyard with the pavilion for temporary exhibitions. Alternately, one might decide to see photographs, or nineteenth-century sculpture, or baroque painting, and at this junction the visitor is free to go directly to whatever gallery interests him or her.

From the outset the director of the museum felt that the new museum should be similar to the J. Paul Getty Museum in Malibu—not in terms of appearance, but rather in the sense of offering visitors the possibility to move freely inside and outside, to walk from garden to gallery and from gallery to garden. We decided jointly that the museum would not be hermetically sealed. Instead, it offers an ever-changing itinerary: one moment you are inside, focusing on works of art in the painting galleries; the next moment you are outside, enjoying a framed view of downtown Los Angeles or the San Gabriel Mountains, or looking west toward Santa Monica and the ocean. The museum allows intense moments of concentration on art, but while you are there, you are also always intensely aware of the city.

The Getty Research Institute for the History of Art and the Humanities
Lower floor plan

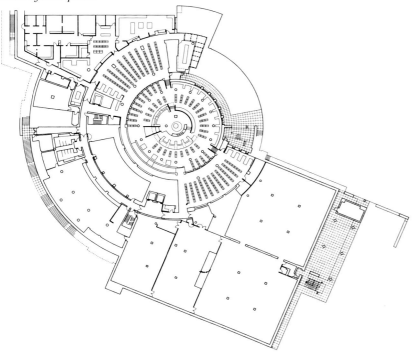

The Getty Research Institute for the History of Art and the Humanities
Entry floor plan

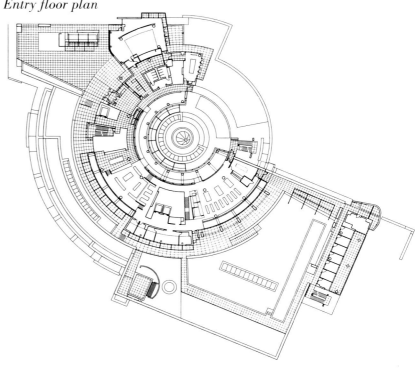

The Getty Research Institute for the History of Art and the Humanities
Courtyard floor plan

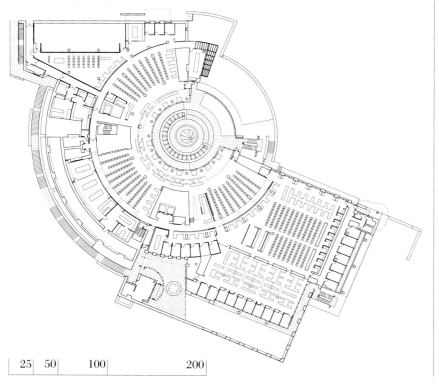

The Getty Research Institute for the History of Art and the Humanities
Upper floor plan

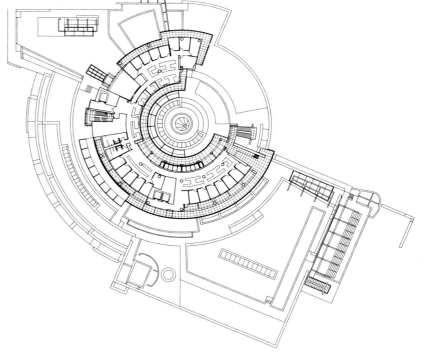

25 50 100 200

Despite the current cult of instant celebrity from which architects are not excepted, architecture still remains a largely anonymous practice. But, like the cinema—the ultimate media art form of our time—architecture remains a collective expression, requiring extensive time and manpower, just as it did in the Middle Ages. There can be no sole creator for any building larger than the average middle-class house, and this sobering fact distinguishes architecture from any other form of fine art. To put it differently, The Getty Center simply would not exist were it not for the innumerable architects, engineers, technicians, artisans, and builders who assisted me for thirteen long years. To all of them I owe an irredeemable debt of gratitude.

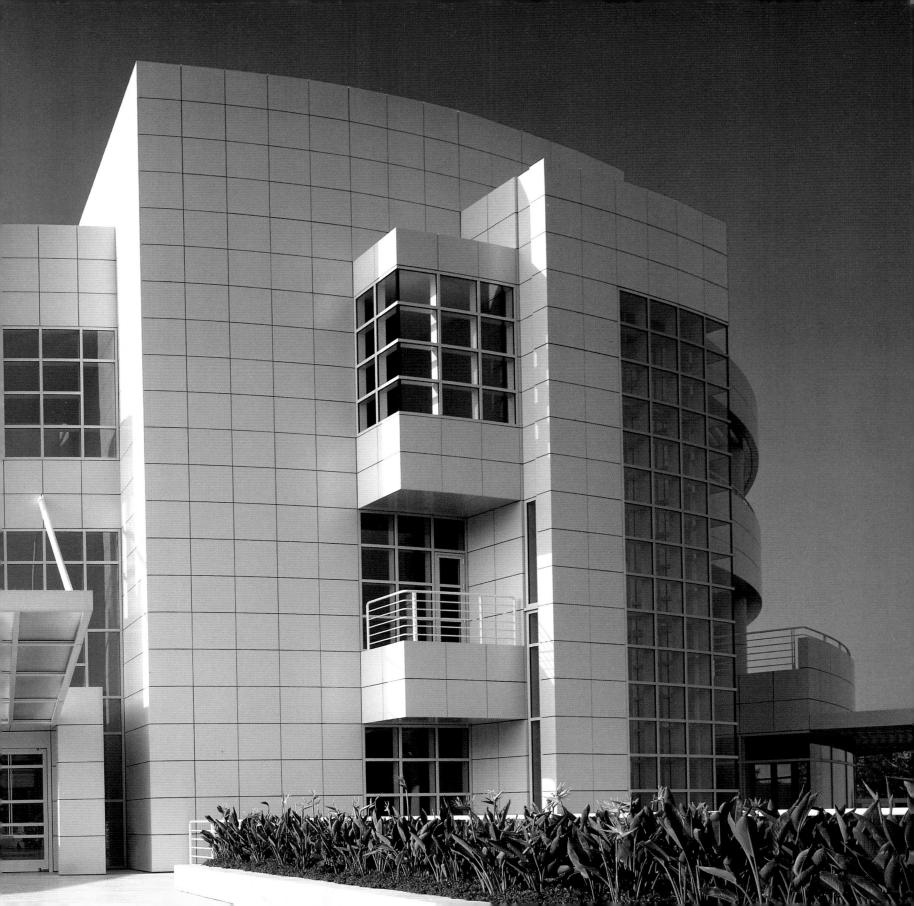

I recall standing on the plaza one Sunday afternoon in September 1997 and discovering that the buildings no longer needed me. It was a little like having to recognize that my children have grown up, only this time I would be the one leaving home. Every architect who has given his heart to a project knows the pangs of separation involved. Up to the point of completion, the project remains in your personal charge. The drawings may have long since determined the general outcome, but up to the last minute you are still adjusting minor details of the work. You want it to be right, and details become ever more important as the work nears completion. Yet, inevitably, there comes a moment when you must hand it over, and it becomes "theirs." As you leave, the building takes on a life of its own. You are no longer in control, and you have to face the fact that from now on you will be judged solely by what you leave behind.

Church of the Year 2000

Rome, Italy
1996–2000

Jubilee church

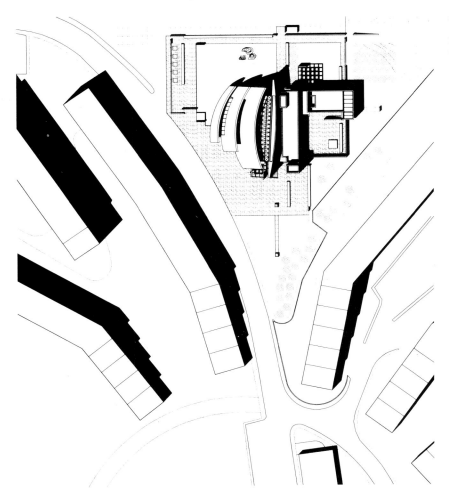

The parish church for the year 2000 was conceived as a new center for a somewhat isolated housing quarter on the outskirts of Rome. The triangular site is doubly articulated to divide the sacred realm to the south, where the nave is located, from the secular precinct to the north, and to separate the pedestrian approach from the east from the parking lot to the west.

The paved *sagrato* to the east of the church extends into the heart of the housing complex, providing an open plaza for public assembly. The northern half of the site is divided into two courts. The east court is sunk by a full story to provide light and access to the lowest floor of the community center. The elevated west court is separated from a meditation court behind the church by a paved walkway that leads to the parking area.

The proportional structure of the entire complex is based on a series of squares and four circles. Three circles of equal radius generate the profiles of the three concrete shells that, together with the spine wall, make up the body of the nave. The three shells imply the Holy Trinity, while the reflecting pool symbolizes the role played by water in the baptism ritual. The stone used in the portico, paving, wall cladding, and liturgical furniture has a dual significance: it alludes to the body of Christ's church and to the adjacent residential fabric.

Glazed skylights and side windows suspended between the shells diffuse natural light into the nave and throughout the interior of the church, which is enlivened by patterns of light and shadow that constantly change according to the hour, the weather, and the season.

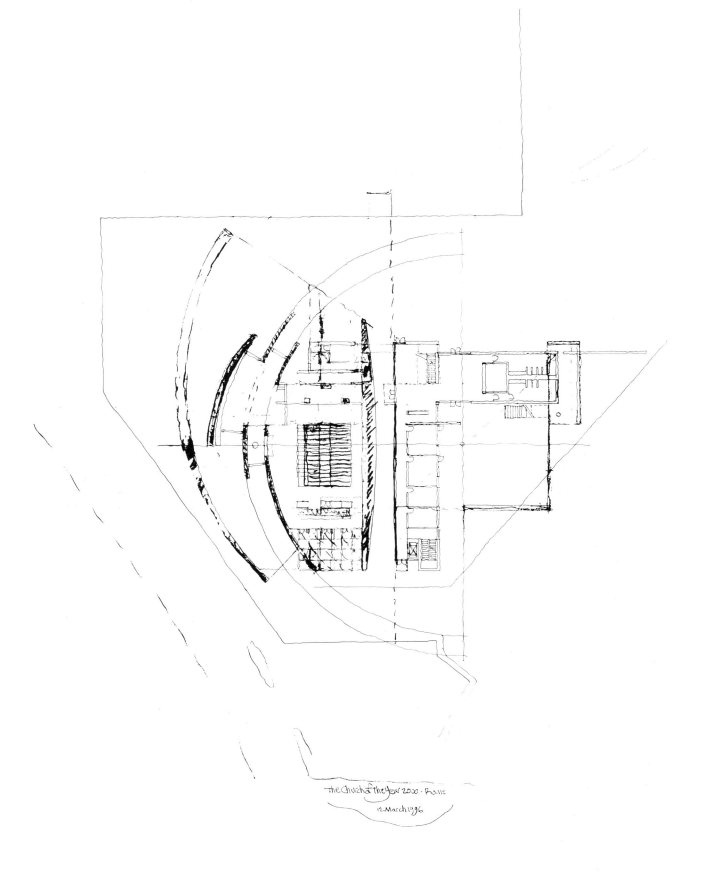

the Church of the Year 2000 · Rome

12 March 1996

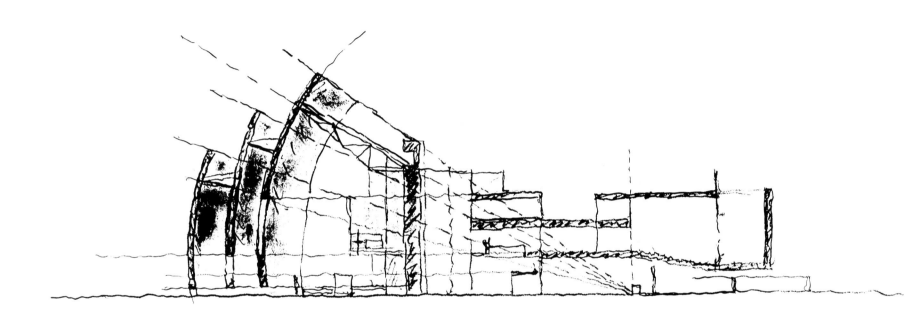

The Church of The Year 2000 Rome
Longitudinal Section
11 March 1996

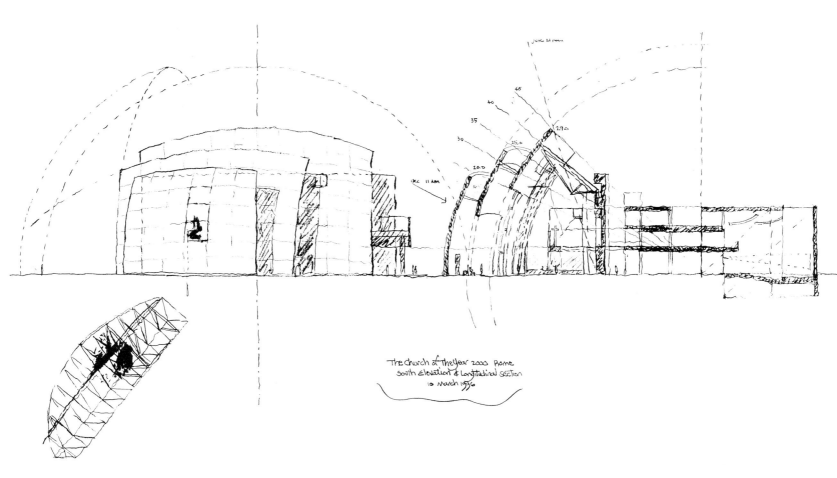

The Church of The Year 2000 Rome
South Elevation & Longitudinal Section
10 March 1996

DEC 11 AM

JUNE 21 noon

45
40
35
30
29.0
25.0
20.0

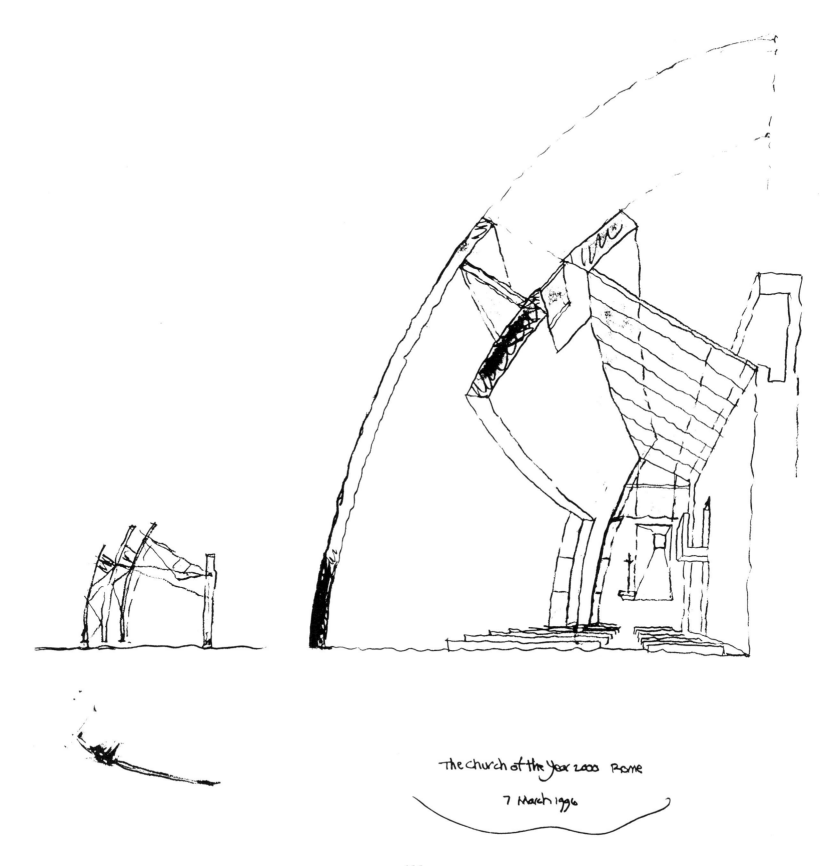

The church of the year 2000 Rome

7 March 1996

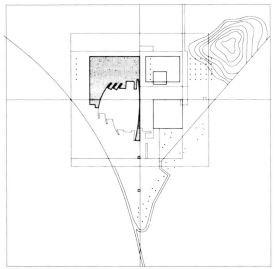

Site/landscape

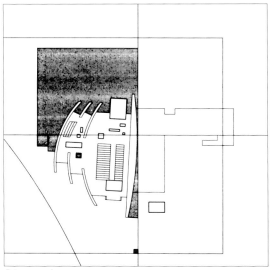

Liturgy/water

As these diagrams indicate, the church's design was initially based on a number of contingent factors: the triangular site, which juts down into existing housing nearby; the location of the peak of the nave to balance a nearby hill; the division of the church precinct into four quarters; the superimposition onto this quadripartite plan of four squares of progressively smaller proportions that generate the centers of three concentric circles; and finally, the symbolic division of the site on its north-south axis into water (sacred) and land (profane).

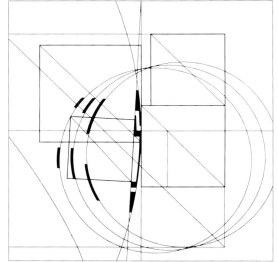

Geometry

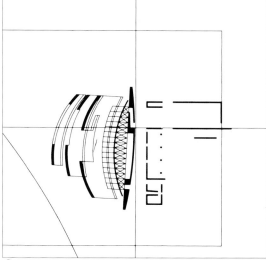

Structure

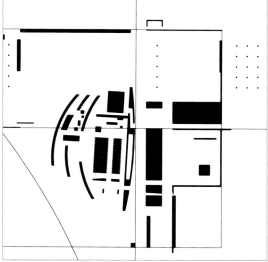

Figure/ground

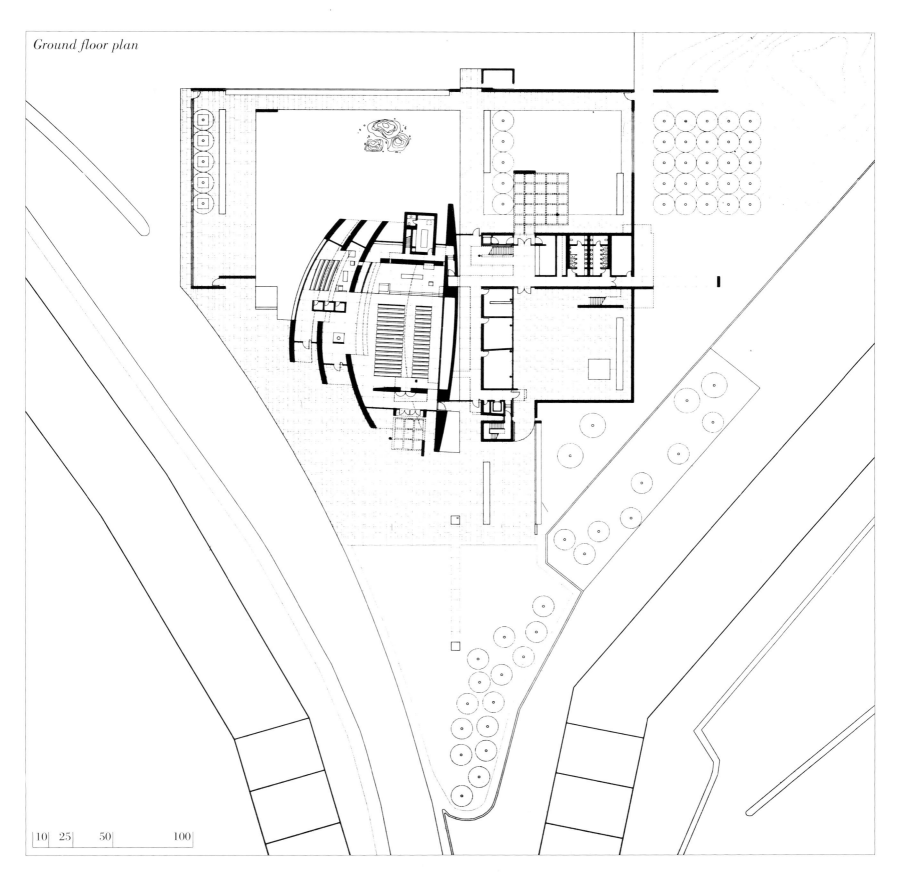

Ground floor plan

|10| 25| 50| 100|

413

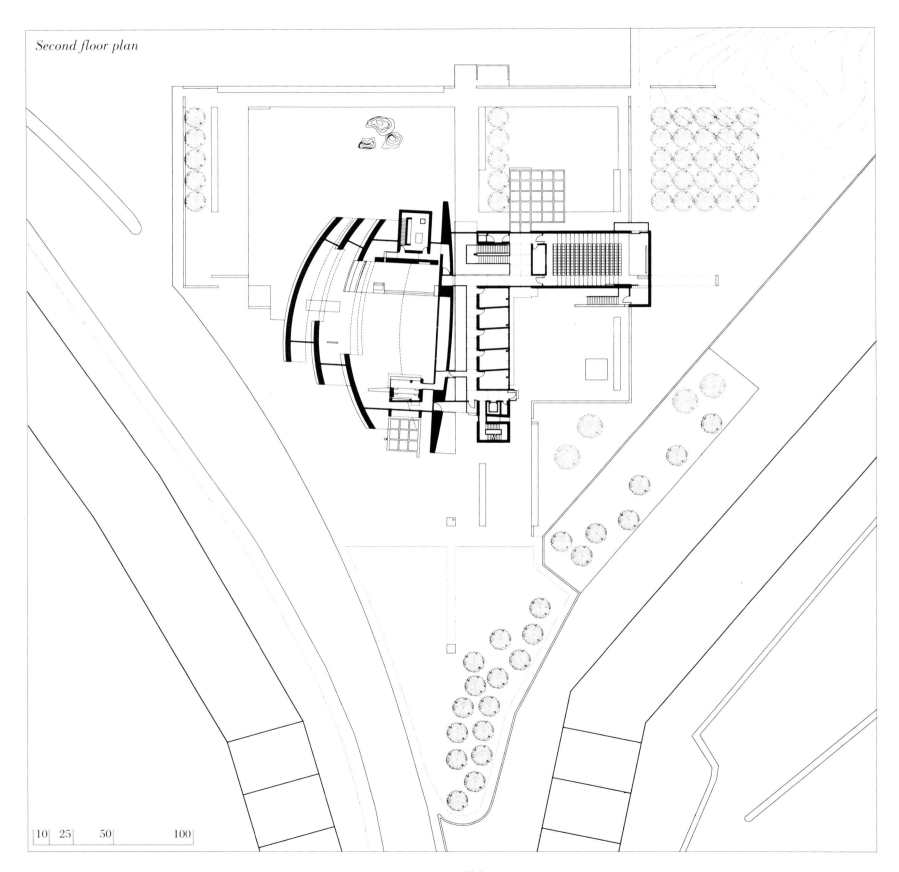

Second floor plan

|10| 25| 50| 100|

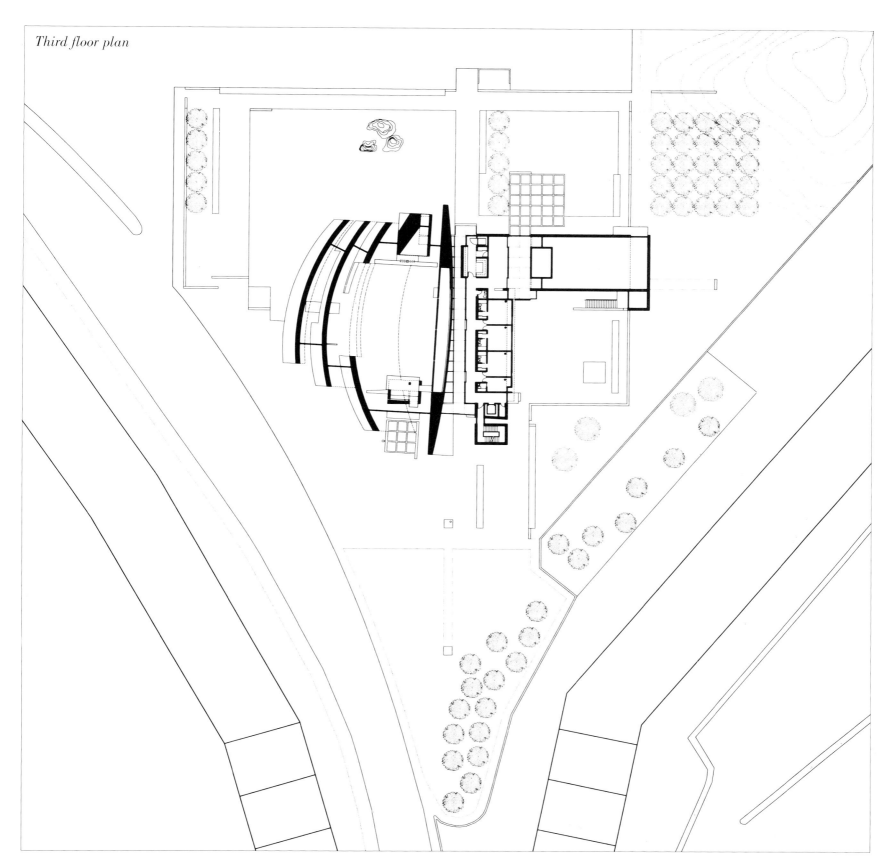

Third floor plan

415

East elevation

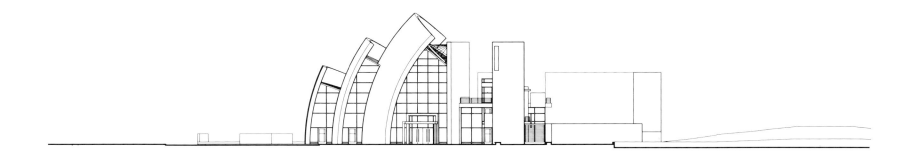

Cross section looking west

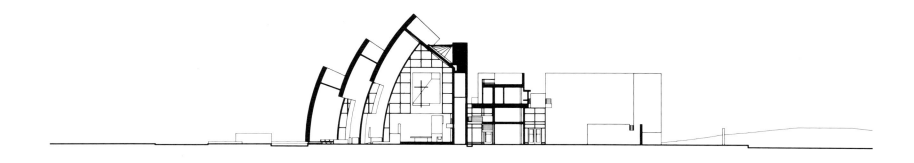

Longitudinal section through church looking north

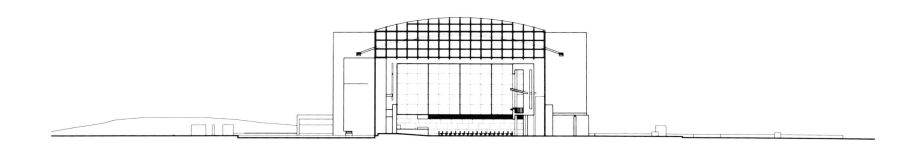

|10| 25| 50| 100|

West elevation

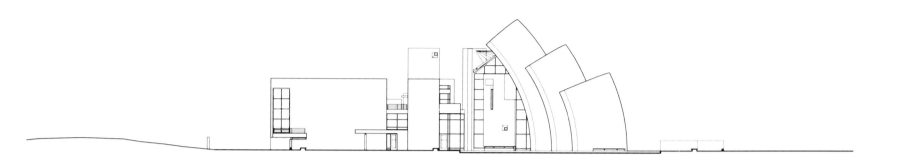

Cross section looking east

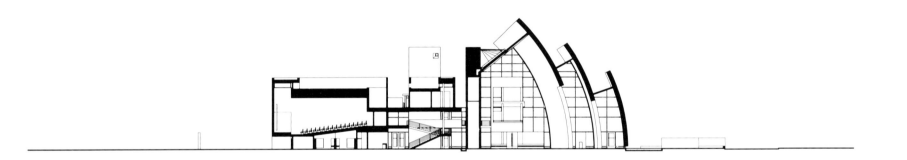

Longitudinal section through church looking south

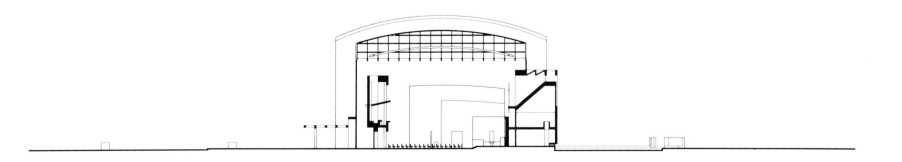

South elevation

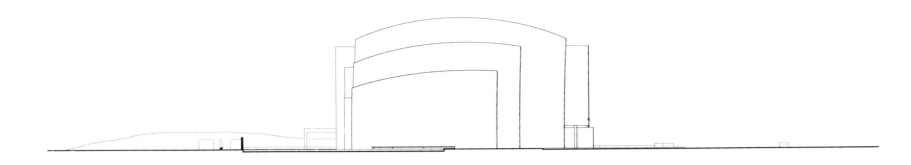

Longitudinal section through center looking south

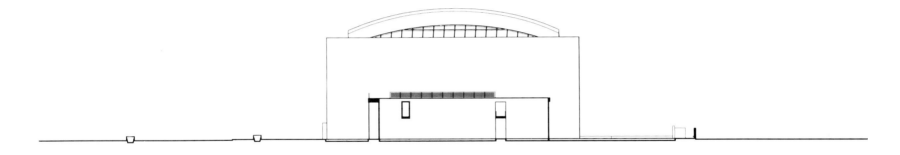

Longitudinal section through center looking north

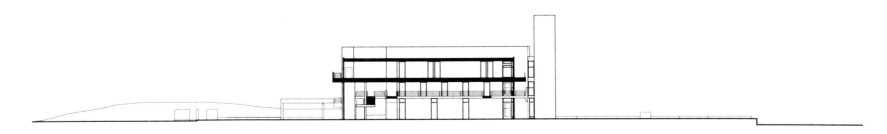

|10| 25| 50| 100|

418

North elevation

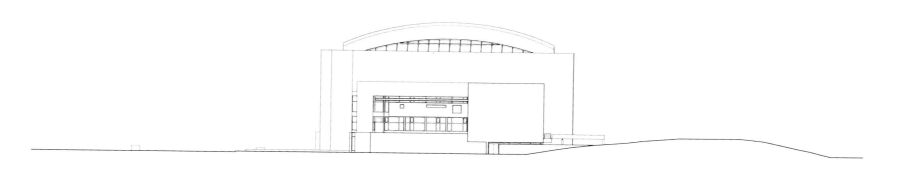

Cross section through auditorium looking south

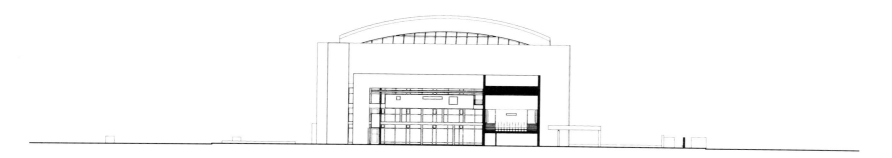

Cross section through auditorium vestibule looking south

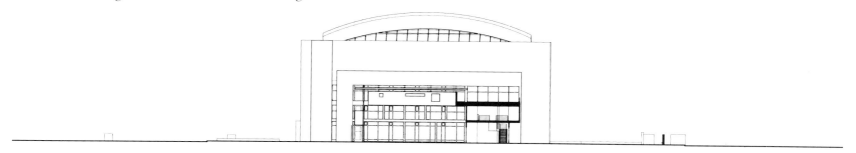

*The design of a religious struc-
ture must always evoke a sense of
the spiritual, and this challenge
is perhaps more difficult to meet
in a small church than in a large
cathedral. We felt that the most
important factor was to induce
the congregation to look upward,
toward the zenith. For this reason
we decided to enclose the volume
within three concentric shells per-
meated by light.*

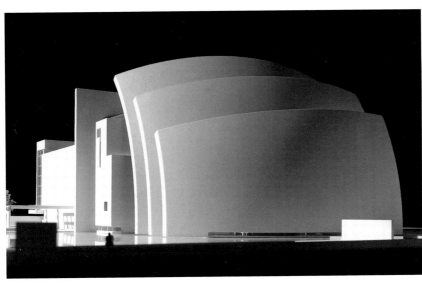

When I was asked to attend an
audience with Pope John Paul II
to show him the design of the
church, I became anxious that
inside the lugubrious confines of
the Vatican the model might not
be adequately lit. After we had
searched fruitlessly for almost
two hours within the Holy City
for some form of artificial lighting, the Pope himself arrived
with a retinue of TV cameramen
and their indispensable lighting.

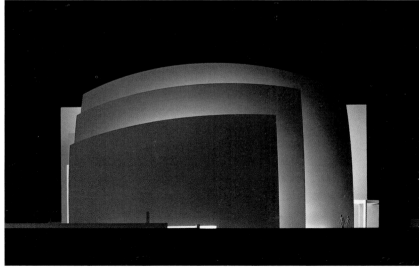

Postscript
Black on White: On Richard Meier

Richard Meier and I began our architectural careers at almost the same time, but in the early 1960s information did not flow as easily between New York and Tokyo as it does today. It was ten years later, when we both were beginning to get commissions for large-scale public projects, that we first met. That was a quarter century ago, when Meier was working on the Bronx Developmental Center, and I, the Museum of Modern Art, Gunma.

Our works have similarities and dissimilarities. Born in the same generation, we share many characteristics, but our individualities also produce many differences which show themselves in every aspect of the architectonic viewpoint, method, interpretation, and expression.

Twenty-five years ago, the Bronx and Gunma projects seemed very similar. Both used sleek aluminum panels, and, instead of simply placing the panels side by side, we both sought to produce new methods of compositional expression by innovative manipulations of the material. Even within that similarity there were differences that anticipated a future parting of the ways. After both projects were completed in 1977 I analyzed them as follows:

Although there is a similarity in our expressive methods, the difference is on the level of metaphor. In the Bronx Developmental Center, industrial metallic panels are composed in order to produce a system in which signifier and signified are in accordance. In contrast, in the Museum of Modern Art, Gunma, purely geometric elements of cubes and their surfaces—the signifiers— are rendered autonomously to produce a visual play of illusions.

In other words, I sensed the premises upon which we would diverge: engaging authentic modernism, Meier persisted in modernist architecture's morality of sustaining a straightforward connection between compositional elements and expression; I, on the other hand, was already trying to place myself on the margin of modernism and look toward the play of ideas and imagination. Being of the same generation, living in the same cultural climate, armed with similar intelligence, filling our bookshelves with a tremendous amount of similar kinds of books, using similar materials and designing similar-scale buildings, still the difference was apparent. And now, twenty-five years later, the difference in the germinal work seems to be definitive. Perhaps because the difference is so visible, we have been able to observe each other's work with a distance and sustain our friendship.

During that quarter century there were a number of professional encounters, commissions of similar projects or buildings in the same cities. In the early 1980s, we both designed large museums in American cities: Meier's High Museum of Art in Atlanta (1980–1983), and my Museum of Contemporary Art in Los Angeles (1980–1986). In Barcelona, Meier worked on the Museum of Contemporary Art (1987–1995), and I did Palau D'Esports Sant Jordi (1983–1990). In different places of the world, clients looking for similar tendencies made different choices. During those twenty-five years, our work came to look drastically different. With respect to color, the surface element, Meier has persisted in white, while I chose red, and now black. In Japan there is a custom of differentiating taste in ceramics by calling porcelain the "white kind" (shiro-mono) and china the "red kind" (aka-mono) or "black kind" (kuro-mono). While the former variation of china has a sophisticated, clean, and precise form, the latter is humble and raw. In the manner of enjoying tea, the white kind is used for serving Chinese herbal tea, while the black kind is used for Japanese powdered tea. The difference in singularities that came to express itself so unmistakably twenty-five years later was one of tastes. My early impression that Meier succeeds to authenticity and I succeed to marginality has proven itself by the subsequent development of this obvious distinction. Meanwhile, within Meier's persistent use of white, there is a clear and consistent development. When his *Smith House (1965–1967)* was finished, I pointed out in A+U *(April 1976)* that although the architectural language used in the Smith House followed the one which had been developed by Le Corbusier in the 1920s, there was a subtle transformation. I likened it to Michelangelo's transformation of Raphael's authentic interpretation of classicism into something more personal and sensuous, as described in John Summerson's Classical Language of Architecture. In Meier's work, there has been a transformational manipulation based upon his own unique senses.

Over these twenty-five years, this development has become more and more apparent. Although Meier and I shared the same initial context—Le Corbusier—we tended toward totally different directions. For instance, invoking sixteenth-century aesthetics further, it could be said that Richard Meier seeks the same freedom as Peruzzi, who flexibly transformed the perfectionist classicism of Bramante; at the same time he sustains the systematic development of Vignola, who designed the matrix of the Gesù church in 1568. On the other hand, I follow the path of conceit and metamorphosis that Giulio Romano adopted. And since 1950s Le Corbusier was no longer "white," but "red," there was no other place for me to move but directly toward "black."

Near the end of the 1990s, Richard Meier completed *The Getty Center (1984–1997)*, which is a synthesis of all "whites." And around the time of the project's completion, as a juror of a competition, he chose my design for the *Nara Convention Hall (1992–1999)*, which embodies the "blackest" of "blacks"—a culminating point of my "black" architecture. Seemingly having departed from the same standpoint, I went to "black," the polar opposite of "white," while

marveling at Meier's consistent effort to polish "white" into an ultimate form.

From staying at his house, having long trips together, and participating in the same symposia and exhibitions, I know Meier's daily life well and can say that he is totally focused on designing architecture. He endures an often severe schedule, traveling between his architectural sites scattered all over the world. This is the figure of a person who thinks only of architecture. And this life continues. And as it continues, architecture with Richard Meier's signature is being produced. Among my contemporaries, I do not know anyone who is dedicated to Architecture so fully as he.

Arata Isozaki
Tokyo
December 1998
(Translated by Sabu Kohso)

Biographical Chronology

1991
Architectural Projects Awards of
the New York Chapter of the American
Institute of Architects
Merit Award of Los Angeles Chapter
of the American Institute of Architects
Progressive Architecture Award
Lifetime Achievement Award from
Guild Hall
Honorary Doctorate of Fine Arts
from University of Naples

Plateau Tercier Master Plan
Nice, France
Setom

Rachofsky House
Dallas, Texas
1996

**Swissair North American
Headquarters**
Melville, New York
Swiss Air Transport Company, Inc.
1994

1992
Distinguished Architecture Award and
Architectural Projects Awards of the New
York Chapter of the American Institute of
Architects
Dudok Award from City Council of
Hilversum
Named Commander de l'Ordre des Art et
des Lettres by the Ministry of Culture of
France

Potsdamer Platz Master Plan
Competition Entry
Berlin, Germany
Daimler Benz AG

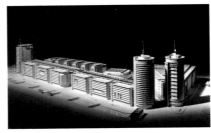

House in Wiesbaden
Wiesbaden, Germany

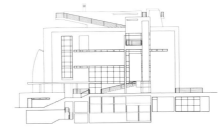

Office Furniture
Stow Davis

The site of this master plan for an underdeveloped area in the hills above Nice measures approximately 6 1/2 kilometers by 2/3 of a kilometer. The site is made up of seven hills split by numerous valleys. The potential for visual chaos in such a turbulent landscape is considerable and calls for a strong gesture to give it a sense of order, cohesiveness, and place. In determining the use appropriate to each of the hills and valleys, the visual memory of its neighbors is imposed by means of planning axes, continuation of roads, and the intermixture of building types. Around the edges, scale is consciously reduced and refined so as to provide a seamless transition with the surrounding towns and villages.

The new town center has been arranged along each side of a long green park and contains housing and cultural and commercial activities. The principal public building has the dramatic footprint of a spiraling shell. Seen from afar, the town center will bear some resemblance to the classic white hill towns that ring the Mediterranean. In following and crowning the crests of a constantly variable profile, the organic nature of the town development will establish its own unique form within this traditional character.

The level of construction refinement Meier has reached in the Rachofsky House is extraordinary. The architect expanded on his trademark vocabulary, a nearly forty year canon of principles, procedures and gestural effects that has undergone subtle, if constant, development and polishings as his firm's projects have evolved.

Set back a hundred yards from a heavily traveled road, Meier's characteristically white, metal-paneled house stands on a less characteristic black-granite podium. The podium extends some twenty-five yards in front of the building and continues behind it, phasing into two sculpture pads that lead to the pool. Beyond a pair of ancient oaks and gently sloping lawn sits a lagoonlike pond, which provides a natural counterpoint to the rectangular podium that "floats" around and under the house.

The east-facing front elevation presents a dynamic, though relatively closed wall to the street: From the side, the white plane appears suspended, almost detached from the rest of the building. Pierced by a large window near the center of the facade, this tough/elegant composition is reminiscent of Le Corbusier's Villa Stein near Paris and of the equally strong, single-window countenances of various European houses by Adolf Loos. By contrast, the highly glazed side and rear facade embrace the landscape.—Thomas S. Hines, "Richard Meier: Bridging the Public and Private Realms in a Dallas House," Architectural Digest, April 1997

Perhaps the most provocative aspect of the building, however, is that it invites us to rethink architecture's place in the realm of popular culture. Twenty years ago, Meier's purist white esthetic was frequently set in opposition to the "gray" post-modern approach advocated by Robert Venturi, Charles Moore and Robert A. M. Stern. Meier was supposed to represent the high road: high art, highbrow, Europeanized, cerebral. Post-modernists celebrated popular taste typified by the highway strip. No doubt this opposition was a useful way for some members of Meier's generation to define themselves, and the high-art image did nothing to prevent Meier from becoming the leading designer of museums.

But encountering Meier on the highway makes me think that the Whites and Grays may have had it backward. While you need a curriculum in architectural history and semiotic theory to decipher the layers of reference in many post-modern buildings (the "double coding" was once considered a strength), Swissair speaks to the senses.

The design's geometric order is not arcane. Light and spaciousness are not acquired tastes. A finely tuned glass wall rising from a green lawn gives as much pleasure to people who may never have heard of Le Corbusier as it does to those who enjoy parading their erudition. And few images are as deeply ingrained in the popular imagination as the ideal of purified desire represented by the color white.—Herbert Muschamp, "A Reason to Rubberneck on the Expressway," The New York Times, 26 February 1995

Despite all efforts to generate urban quality by urban-space relations and the interplay of indoor and outdoor spaces in this instant city, there remains a doubt with this plan (as with the other competition entries) as to the whole concept's ability to function in practice: the streets do not actually lead anywhere and after all only connect Potsdamer Platz (reduced to its transport function) with a new tunnel under the Landwehrkanal. Moreover the excessively wide street cuts the whole area in two and divides it off from the Kulturforum on the western side. The idea behind Hilmer and Sattler's urban design for the whole of the Potsdamer Platz area was "not the American city model of a conglomeration of skyscrapers, but rather the idea of a compact, complex European city." Richard Meier's work definitely shows signs of trying to embrace this idea—but the basic requirements (for the density of the development, its use and its access to traffic) imposed extremely unfavourable conditions. Meier, like others, failed to "square the circle." It remains to be seen whether the qualities of the winning design by Renzo Piano and Christoph Kohlbecker will continue to assert themselves within the development—work on this began in 1994.—Ingeborg Flagge and Oliver G. Hamm, "Daimler Benz AG," in Richard Meier in Europe, Berlin: Ernst & Sohn, 1997

Located in the residential villa area of this spa city, the site for this unbuilt project is less than a ten-minute walk from the center. The unique combination of requirements for work and residential space provided an unusual challenge for this project. The client's business sells a prestigious Swiss watch line, and he required a building that would provide a residence for his family as well as a place for his business, which employs some twelve people, seven of whom are craftsmen watchmakers.

The business portion of the program occupies the lower floors with the private residence located on the top two floors. As all of the employees come to work by car, it was necessary to utilize a compact underground garage system with stacking hydraulic elevators for maximum efficiency. Although the plan diagram of the project is based on a simple division into a service module zone serving the various program elements, it was further informed by the need to preserve a large oak tree standing close to the center of the site. The height of the building mass corresponds to the relatively high three- to four-story adjacent buildings. The westward orientation of the upper-floor living areas opens up to panoramic views of the city.

The furniture in the Richard Meier Collection was conceived as an integrated series of freestanding pieces that can be arranged in any number of configurations. The furniture is equally suitable for either private offices or an open office environment, where it could be combined to define space. Designed to be flexible and responsive to the changing needs of the workplace, the collection is provided with such features as detached pedestals and wiring channels providing for an easy transition as individual demand dictates.

Using the geometry of the square, cube, and golden section, the design of the desk established a system of proportions which were then applied, with necessary modifications, to the entire line to make a strong formal and functional interrelationship among the different pieces. While the formal vocabulary, the abstract interplay of verticals and horizontals, and the overall conception and structure are consistent, each piece is a distinct object, usable in a variety of contexts.

1993

National Honor Award from the
American Institute of Architects
Distinguished Architecture Award
of the New York Chapter
of the American Institute of Architects
Deutscher Architekturpreis Award
of Distinction

**Federal Building and
United States Courthouse**
Islip, New York
General Services Administration

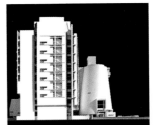

Administrative Building
Marckolsheim, France
Jungbunzlauer, S.A.

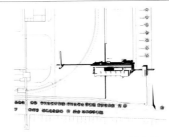

1994

Distinguished Architecture Award of the
New York Chapter of the American Insti-
tute of Architects
Elected as Honorary Fellow in the Royal
Incorporation of Scottish Architects

Museum of Television & Radio
Beverly Hills, California
Museum of Television & Radio
1996

Gagosian Gallery
Beverly Hills, California
Larry Gagosian
1995

Berliner Volksbank Headquarters
Competition Entry
Berlin, Germany

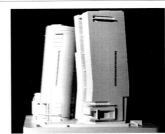

**Compaq Computer Administrative,
Manufacturing, and Distribution
Center Master Plan**
Houston, Texas
Compaq Computer Corporation

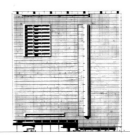

Recent architecture and art have been marked by frequent stylistic shifts. Indeed, as the century closes, with no dominant aesthetic view, the very idea of style has been called into question. Architecture, once a symbol of permanence, has wavered between superficial historical pastiche and a "deconstruction" which tends toward the ephemeral. Few mature creators have passed though this period without being tempted by one or another of the fashions of the times. Fewer still have set and maintained a clear course. In fact, an architect or an artist with a style recognizable over the years is exposed to accusations of immobility or inability to change. Yet many of the most durable works of art were born of rules as strict as the unity of time and place of the classical theater. Few would argue that Shakespeare's adherence to Elizabethan parameters prevented him from encompassing the entire range of human experience in his plays.

The rigor of Meier's design is emphasized through meticulous attention to detail, which in turn conveys an impression of quality often lacking in modern construction. It seems clear that his precisionist geometric penchant is not so much an expression of formal concern as it is a means to an end. That end is to create a space where light is an omnipresent element which itself forms the environment, where the architecture creates a feeling of well-being which may, at its best, attain a spiritual dimension.—Philip Jodidio, *Richard Meier,* Cologne: Taschen, 1995

The site for this unbuilt administrative and research building for a large biotechnical company in the Alsace region of France is part of an existing large production facility which is serviced by a railway line along its perimeter. In order to provide for easy access over the railway line, which is often blocked for long periods of time by the loading and unloading of trains, the new building was raised on pilotis to a height of 7 meters, providing for uninterruped access via a bridge to the production facility while at the same time bringing it above the flood wall of the river. Along with the placement of the office building in the northwest corner of the site, this provides the offices with dramatic views of the Rhine River and the adjacent countryside.

This is one of the few sites in the Los Angeles area that could be reasonably construed as having some degree of urbanity, and Mr. Meier has taken advantage of it. The three-story building, with a facade of glass, Mr. Meier's trademark of white metal panels and, prefiguring the Getty, a few hints of soft travertine, is a collage of geometric elements assembled in response to the needs of the street as well as to reflect the museum's interior spaces. The interiors are visible from the street, and the life of the street is visible from within the museum.

The level of attention to urbanism separates this building from much of Richard Meier's early work, which tended to be placed, like a sculptural object, in a setting and to eschew any reference to that setting. Here, however, the expanses of glass covered by horizontal sun louvers were clearly designed in response to the streetscape; so is the metal-clad cylinder that serves as an entry pavilion and central rotunda. Mr. Meier managed to avoid making the obvious gesture of putting a cylinder at the corner, and its placement near the south end of the main facade reminds us, as well as anything here, what a master of composition Richard Meier is.—Paul Goldberger, "And now, live from Beverly Hills, a new Museum," *The New York Times,* 7 April 1996

Over the last decade, the white cube that has long been a given of American galleries has been challenged by many architects trying to deneutralize spaces for viewing art. They have opened windows, added color, designed multilevel environments, and created object-specific installation, all to minimize the disparity between the subjectivity of the visitor and the objectivity of the art.

Whether it is his own building or an artwork, Richard Meier still believes in the sanctity of the object—and in the white cube as the best environment for displaying it. What Meier has asked in the design of several museums, and most recently in the Gagosian Gallery in Beverly Hills, is how far the white cube can be manipulated yet still retain its essential nature as a concentrative chamber that does not compete with the art displayed. He wants to keep the cube, but change it in order to enrich the viewing environment.

Given the scale of the nearby Getty Center, the new Gagosian Gallery in the Rodeo Drive shopping district is a trifle. But precisely because the two-story infill building is small, with a simple program, it acts as a microcosm for Meier's attitudes about how architecture should present art. . . . At the height of the artwork, the space is calm, holding viewers' attention without forcing it. Meier breaks the hermetic seal of the standard gallery without losing the qualities that made the white box such a focused, and focusing, space.—Joseph Giovannini, "Sculptural Sanctum," *Architecture,* February 1996

Located on a prominent site in Berlin near the Witzleben train station at the corner of Kaiserdamm and Messedamm, this mixed-use development serves as a highly visible urban element at the end of a major east/west connection. The two sculptural towers house the headquarters for a Berlin-based bank as well as rental offices. Apartments, retail space, and restaurants occupy adjacent low-rise perimeter buildings which complete the site. The twenty-two- and twenty-four-story towers are each organized around a central core with dramatic skylit vertical lobby spaces which run the entire height of the buildings. A podium incorporates all of the building services for the project, including parking, and serves as a unifying access plaza at the ground level.

The site consists of 744 acres located adjacent to Compaq's current headquarters campus outside of Houston. The new east campus would serve as the entry point for the entire complex and create an appropriate image for the company's leadership role in the industry. Together, the two campuses could be occupied by up to 25,000 people at any one time, with parking for the same number of cars. Development on the site was concentrated so as to minimize disturbance to the woods and lake while taking maximum advantage of the inherent beauty of the site for its occupants. Internal transportation between the two campuses was to be kept to less than fifteen minutes by foot. Several options were considered to achieve this, including the use of electric carts and shuttle buses.

The administration building, shown here, rises well above the tree-top height of the buildings on the west campus and was designed to create a strong physical image for Compaq when viewed from afar. Its transparent glass facade provides sweeping views of the site and allows for an efficient open-plan interior.

1995
Deutscher Architekturpreis Honorable
Mention
Progressive Architecture Award
Crystal Award from the World Economic
Forum
Interior Design Best of Category Award
Elected to the American Academy of
Arts & Sciences

**Federal Building and
United States Courthouse**
Phoenix, Arizona
General Services Administration

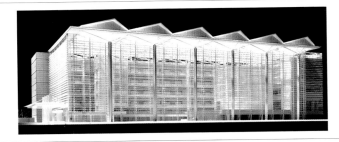

Neugebauer House
Naples, Florida
1998

Swiss Re Headquarters
Competition Entry
Kingston, New York
Swiss Re American Corporation

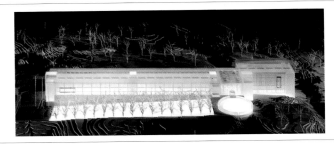

Grand Piano
Rud. Ibach Sohn

1996
Louis H. Sullivan Award from
the Chicago Athenaeum
Lifetime Achievement Award for
Architect as Artist from WestWeek '96
Golden Plate Award of the American
Academy of Achievement
Honorary Doctorate of Fine Arts from
The New School for Social Research

Church of the Year 2000
Rome, Italy
Vicariato of Rome

Museum of the Ara Pacis
Rome, Italy
Comune di Roma

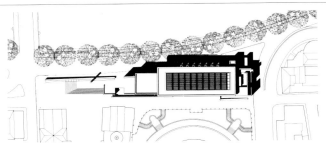

Exemplary architecture will arise from a clear constructional principle. A building is formed from what the detail is able to reveal. Good architecture is marked by the sense of order and the sense of form; at the same time, it is the spatial expression of equilibrium and totality. Leonardo defined the principles of all proportional systems and aesthetic values, for example, in his drawings of the human body and geomet-rical figures. He based his architecture on dimension and proportion.

In detail, inner laws are transformed into the beauty of the essential. Nevertheless, detailing requires efficiency in its application—in constant dialogue with the possibilities and the limits of technology. With head in hand, and nowadays also with the computer, the architect can clearly develop his intentions and his statements, with the surprising realization that detailed explorations impart diversity and importance to the building. Details are not compulsive; neither are they master-pieces that appear complete; rather, they give us the possibility of an obvious trans-formation of ideas. In Richard Meier's most recent American buildings we find many such details which, with their great wealth of ideas, extend the limits of archi-tecture to the benefit of its overall poten-tial. As ever: without details, no architec-ture!—Werner Blaser, "Making a Virtue out of the Seam," in *Richard Meier: Details,* Basel: Birkhäuser, 1996

No other architect in the twentieth century has so profoundly understood, reinter-preted, and extended the canonical lan-guage of Le Corbusier. Corb's ability to carve architecture out of solid mass has been artfully assimilated with the analyti-cal intelligence of Walter Gropius and the detailing and formal planning of Mies van der Rohe, creating new forms and meanings of unique rigor and intensity.

It is in this respect that Meier is both clas-sical and ultra-modernist. The plan always generates the form. The section generates movement and scale. You can "read" a Meier facade simply by reading the plan and section. The apparent simplicity belies a rigorous intellectual reduction of the program into its constituent elements.

There is nothing ephemeral or indetermi-nate in a Meier house. Everything, down to the smallest detail, has its exact place within an overall scheme of things—even the design and position of the cutlery and silverware. As in a Renaissance palazzo, nothing can be added or subtracted with-out upsetting the balance of the whole. The equilibrium is absolute. The enameled surfaces of his steel cladding panels, for example, are treated like precious materi-als rather than factory-produced indus-trial components. The detailing is exquis-ite, as finely detailed as polished granite or pellucid Carrara marble. Where the structure is exposed, Meier always empha-sizes its solidity and formality over the lightness and nimbleness of a structural frame.—Sir Richard Rogers, "Richard Meier's Ideal Villas," in *Richard Meier Houses,* New York: Rizzoli, 1996

The Swiss Re Headquarters building is orientated on an east-west axis to take full advantage of the southern sun and prevailing winds from the northwest. Because of the dramatic contours of the site, what is apparently a three-story building when approached from the street actually houses conference cen-ters, employee dining, and other sup-port functions under the east wing and three additional office levels under the west wing.

The building has been designed to pro-vide all employees with access to day-light and fresh air. The building makes maximum use of renewable energy sources and visually connects every workspace to the surrounding natural environment. Office space is arranged in 70-foot lease spans with operable win-dows on the north and a three-story linear atrium on the south. The atrium opens to the north above the roof and is designed to draw air through the north wall and across the office floor on temperate days in the spring and fall, and to collect and recirculate heat generated by the low southern sun in the winter. Exterior sun-screens shade the atrium glass in the summer when the sun is high in the sky, but permit light from the low winter sun. Light shelves are provided along the southern edge of the office areas to bring natural daylight as far as possible into the usable floor area.

Resting lightly within three rectilinear supports, instead of sitting on top of the usual columnar posts, this new design for a grand piano appears to hover above the ground. For this radically re-envisioned grand piano, the sinuous curve of the instrument has been internalized within a luminous black box.

A piano recast as a rectilinear object in space can be employed as a more cooper-ative player in any spatial ensemble, free to be integrated into both geometrically regulated spaces and more casual set-tings. The curve becomes apparent only when the lid is raised, and then it appears as the edge of a void in which the piano's lyra rests.

The design of the piano is a composition of sculpted volume, a composition of planes and mechanized elements. A sin-gle stainless steel curved bar driven by a motor elegantly raises and lowers the top. When the lid is closed, the curved bar descends through the piano into the space beneath. The lid over the keys is also mechanically actuated, lifting gently away from the hands and folding up. This graceful folding and unfolding of the piano's sealed black volume is a moment of transformation that announces the beginning and end of its playing.

Here, for the first time, Meier's genius is revealed, which reminds one of Bramante's when, at the dawn of the sixteenth cen-tury, he left luminous Milan to plunge into the Roman obscurity of St. Peter's. It is right that Meier prevailed, since he did not present a design, but ten virtual designs that were abandoned at half-way. They will grow, they will clash, and they will eliminate or condition one another.

And the church will rise, magnificent and astonishing, from this ideational mecha-nism, from these ten possibilities thrown down on the roulette wheel of chance, silence, and noise of the Casilino. Of the six competitors, Meier seemed the man least suited to conceiving a "finished" church. Honor to the jury that understood him, rewarding not a solution but an open problem. We are announcing in here: it will be a masterwork. Bramante reached Rome bringing with him the glimmering of Santa Maria delle Grazie. Meier reached us after the experience of the Atheneum of New Harmony, Indiana. He will not repeat Bramante's inexcusable mistakes; no mafia and no bribes. He will excavate the form of a new Christianity, that of a fabulous age in which a pope, John Paul II, after two thousand years of anti-Jewry, came to the synagogue to re-embrace his "major brothers. . . ." This competition is a hymn to those who want a truly modern architecture, one that is daring in its avant-garde impetus, hereti-cal, without nostalgia, revolutionary, of the future because impregnated with his-tory.—"Richard Meier in Bramante's Place," Bruno Zevi, *L'architettura* #484, July 1996

Through a deliberate promenade architec-turale, the visitor to Meier's buildings is confronted with a process of visualization. This process ends in an optic perception play of interior and exterior along the abstract structures of the architecture. Such perceiving of the architecture through an optic game finally leads to two different realities: that of the two dimensions of the canvas in painting and that of the three dimensions of architec-ture.

In this context, the surface becomes the decisive intermediary that makes it possi-ble to demonstrate the relation between architecture and art, and the autonomy of the architectural channels is what nour-ishes those aspects that prove the pictorial qualities of Meier's architecture, aspects which follow the example of the surface of an image in painting and the surface of the plan in the context of a given urban site, thus acquiring importance. Neverthe-less, we are not speaking of a differenti-ated pictorial architecture—as in Stir-ling's Neue Staatsgalerie in Stuttgart— that symbolically evokes the figures or metaphysical pictorial spaces of De Chirico, works composed of elements of building history and which thus endeavor to reintroduce poetry into archi-tecture. The pictorial quality of Meier's architecture is not inscribed in an object, but in the channels of pure abstraction.— Stephan Barthelmess, "Transparency and Perspective," *A & V: Richard Meier In Europe (Monografías 59),* 1996

Coordinated Street Furniture
New York, New York
Adshel Inc.

Kolonihavehus
Copenhagen, Denmark
Kolonihaven International Challenge

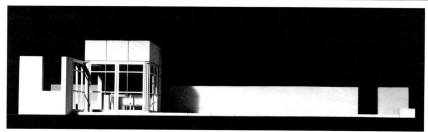

Crystal Cathedral
Hospitality and Visitors Center
Orange Grove, California
Crystal Cathedral Ministries

1997
Gold Medal of the American Institute
of Architects
Praemium Imperiale
Distinguished Architecture Award and
Architectural Projects Awards of
the New York Chapter of the American
Institute of Architects
Elected to *Interior Design* Hall of Fame

Tan Residence
Kuala Lumpur, Malaysia

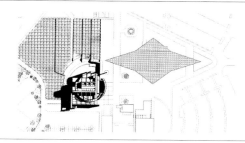

Glasgow Exhibition House
Glasgow, Scotland
Wimpey Homes Holdings, Ltd.

Tag McLaren Headquarters
Woking, Surrey, England
Tag McLaren Holdings, Ltd.

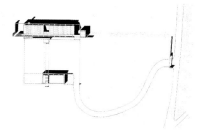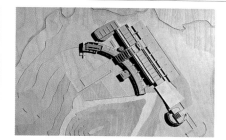

Responding to a request for proposals from New York City, we designed a line of coordinated street furniture which consists of bus shelters, newsstands, automatic public toilets, computer information kiosks, and litter/recycling bins. Rather than imitating the drama of the city's streets, we have designed a unified and adaptable line that will become an oasis of convenience and security.

Two complementary lines were developed. "Metropolis," shown here on the left, was designed to be used throughout the city. It's signature cantilevered roof and tapering profile approaches invisibility with a transparency that enhances safety. It is elegant and refined and makes a minimal impact on the busy sidewalks of New York.

In response to the city's request for a design that was even more compatible with landmark buildings and historic districts, "New Amsterdam," shown here on the right, was created. These structures are distinguished by their symmetry, balanced proportions, and graceful silhouette. They are designed to complement historic contexts, adding to their richness and appeal.

This contemporary interpretation of the nineteenth-century Danish urban summer garden pavilion, or Kolonihavehus, is one of fourteen designs submitted by international architects for an exhibition in 1996. The brief was to design a pavilion housing a 65-square-foot room without a kitchen or bath. Our design for the Kolonihavehus is an abstract composition in point, line, plane, and volume. A sim-

ple wall of native stone implies an unimposing separation between the public world and the more private realm beyond. The wall is a datum against which a private "precinct" is claimed from nature by a stone podium as an island in the surrounding landscape. The podium is slightly elevated to reinforce the separation between the order and geometry of its rigorous machinelike objects and

carefully cultivated garden against the uncontrolled nature of the surrounding landscape beyond. The Kolonihavehus is a carefully crafted jewel box of metal and glass created and placed with the classic proportions of the golden mean regulating geometry. It is designed to open out completely on three sides, transforming itself into a more canopy-like structure when in use.

The Crystal Cathedral Ministry has a history of commitment to architectural excellence. The new Hospitality and Visitors Center will be located in a tripartite arrangement with the Crystal Cathedral, which was designed by Philip Johnson in 1980, and the Tower of Hope, designed by Richard Neutra in 1966 as the administrative offices for the Garden Grove Community Church. The resultant court-

yard is a contained outdoor room shared by three buildings of different but compatible modern architectural expression.

The partially concentric, multistory Hospitality and Visitors Center will provide reception facilities for visitors to the campus, including a gift shop and lobby at the entry level, an auditorium and café at the lower level, and archives,

exhibition space, and storage at the upper levels.

The exterior finishes are selected to be compatible with the building's architectural context. Clear anodized aluminum window-wall components and metal skin are matched to the window system of the Crystal Cathedral, and the Palos Verdes Stone replicates the stone color and

coursing design by Richard Neutra for other campus facades. The architecture of the new Hospitality and Visitors Center is transparent, light, and inviting, but through the integration of partial stone closures, the facility also has timeless qualities of weight, stability, and permanence.

Located on a sloped suburban site with exceptional views, this house is organized around a vertical plane that screens views and noise from the busy suburban street and provides a monolithic backdrop for the living spaces, which are oriented north towards the view. The opaque entry elevation contrasts the north elevation, which is fully glazed and articulated with terraces and sunshades.

Entry is via a 12-meter-long bridge that parallels the street and connects the parking court to the entry vestibule. The dynamic oval form of the vestibule serves to receive and redirect the path of circulation through the opaque wall toward the views. A sequence of one- and two-story volumes house the living room, dining room, kitchen, and pool areas. On the second level, a small library overlooks

the living room and is connected by an interior bridge to the bedroom areas. The master bedroom is housed on the third level with a lush roof garden which creates a continuity from inside to outside and provides a richly landscaped foreground to the distant views. Located one level below entry is a 450-square-meter gallery that opens to a terraced formal garden.

The facade materials have been selected with respect for the wet Malaysian climate. A combination of glazed terracotta, ceramic tile, enameled aluminum, and glass form a moisture resistant skin that is easily maintained. The architecture also responds directly to the intense year-round sun by integrating exterior sunscreens into the facade to protect glass areas from direct sun exposure.

The city of Glasgow designated 1999 as the Year of Architecture and Design and asked us to design an exhibition house to be open for tour groups and then sold to a private client. The program called for a four-bedroom house with additional parking for visitors during the exhibition.

The prominent sloping site has panoramic views to Glasgow and the

mountains beyond. A sequence of manipulated views of the surrounding landscape was created from the approach and site entry to all interior living spaces, which were orientated back towards the city. The roof profile was designed to gather south light and summer breezes from the opposite direction. The low horizontal form of the house appears almost as a wall in the open landscape separat-

ing the public and private areas of the site. The facade was composed as an abstract image inspired by the simple proportions of local Scottish manor houses.

Located in the lush countryside of Surrey some 40 miles southwest of London, this new headquarters building for TAG McLaren Holdings would incorporate a 50,000-square-foot Visitor and Learning Center along with a 350,000-square-foot headquarters building. TAG McLaren is a diverse technology company that includes a Formula One racing team, a composition group, an electronics group, an aero-

dynamic division and a Formula One manufacturing group. Each group would be incorporated into separate but related sections of the building with distinct entries. Amenities such as a six-hundred-seat cafeteria, health club, and banking center will be centralized. Tours of the facilities would be common, and different levels of circulation would be used to accommodate visitors with varying secu-

rity clearances. The Visitor and Learning Center would display up to fifty racing cars and would include an auditorium for video and film projection, hands-on technology exhibits, and lecture rooms and work stations for technology seminars.

Four preliminary schemes, two of which are shown here, were developed for discussion with the client. Each included

a large water element in the forecourt of the headquarters building, with staff parking to the rear. The Visitor and Learning Center is located near the eastern public entry to the site. A large portion of the site was left in its natural state and the buildings are integrated into the landscape with rich indigenous plantings.

Indoor/Outdoor Seating
MABEG Kreuschner GmbH

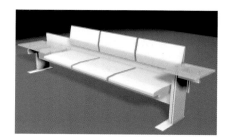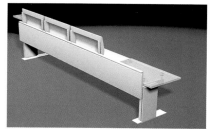

1998

National Honor Award from the
American Institute of Architects
Distinguished Architecture and Interiors
Architecture Award of the New York
Chapter of the American Institute of
Architects
Gold Medal of the Los Angeles Chapter
of the American Institute of Architects
Honorary Doctorate of Fine Arts from
Wheaton College

Deutsche Post Building
Competition Entry
Bonn, Germany

**Peek & Cloppenburg
Department Store**
Düsseldorf, Germany

Headquarters for Bayer AG
Competition Entry
Leverkusen, Germany

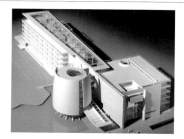

Westwood Promenade
Los Angeles, California
Christina Development Corporation

Scottish Parliament
Competition Entry
Edinburgh, Scotland
The Scottish Office

This line of indoor/outdoor seating was designed to be used in limited seating arrangements that would create unique compositions in space. Rather than the endless repetitive patterns that are often seen in large public spaces, these clusters would create a dialogue with their surroundings.

Based on a clear geometry, the flexible design allows for different configurations such as L- or U-shaped layouts. The bench is available with two, three, or four seating units that can be combined with one or two side tables of white frosted glass or metal. They can be freestanding, presented back to back, or wall mounted. Numerous finish options in select colors are available including perforated aluminum, flat metal, and leather.

This open competition for a new headquarters building for the Deutsche Post in Bonn is prominently located in Rheinhaue Freizeit Park with commanding views of the Rhein and the city of Bonn. In addition to office space, the program called for retail and conference facilities. Every effort has been made to insert the new complex into the site with minimal effect on the exisiting surroundings both natural and built. The overall height of the new building has been limited to that of the adjacent Langer Eugen building and has been placed out of its sightlines.

Two twenty-six-story office tower slabs sit on a low plinth which contains a conference center and underground parking for one thousand cars. The office towers are serviced by a central lobby and elevator cores linked by a series of double height reception areas that afford views of the city and the river. The volume of the auditorium is expressed as a turtle-shaped shell that appears to be hovering over a band of clerestory glazing, which brings light into the space but also provides views of the interior and radiates light at night when the stage is lit for performances. The retail facilites are located in a curved two-story building with a covered arcade which creates a semicovered pedestrian "street" facing a paved plaza.

Located in the main retail district of Düsseldorf, this prominent corner site is bounded on one side by a traditional European pedestrian shopping street, Schadowstrasse, and on the other by the elevated Berliner Allee. Situated on the existing site of the Peek & Clopperburg flagship store, this new project accommodates the strict requirements inherent in a large commercial space with the heavy traffic of people and creates a unique building which can become a landmark in the city.

The building form wraps and engages the site with a sweeping curve, acting as infill and reinforcing the context, but also stands independently as a distinct sculptural object. The solid base and walls are textured stone and metal panel. The glass curtain wall is expressed as a floating skin that addresses the corner.

The building is incorporated into the landscape of the Karl Duisberg Park on a site adjacent to the current Bayer headquarters building, the Bayer Hotel, and staff restaurant. The main approach is from the Kaiser Wilhelm Allee to the north, along which the existing context buildings are organized. The five-story building is comprised of three main components: the Entrance Pavilion, the Board of Management Building, and the Corporate Divisions Building. All are connected by an "interior street" and atrium which serve as the circulation spine.

The Entrance Pavilion is a truncated ellipsoid enclosing a cylindrical internal space, which, through a configuration of white opaque external skin panels, glazed and opaque surfaces, and through a relationship to the cooling water surface of a reflecting pool, will create a pleasant transition zone—a kind of garden pavilion but also a shelter from the bustle and noise of Kaiser Wilhelm Allee during peak hours of the day. It is intended to serve not only as the entrance to the new headquarters but also as a gateway to the park.

Through an angled, five-story-high wall one enters a lobby with a security desk which controls access to the Board of Management reception to the west and to the "interior street" which leads south to the Corporate Divisions tract.

Westwood Village is an enclave of pedestrian-oriented retail and commercial space located adjacent to the UCLA campus in West Los Angeles. It services both the university and the surrounding residential and business districts. In order to retain the unique character of the area, the Westwood Development Plan has set guidelines that limit density and height of new construction. In addition, they identify architecturally significant cultural resource buildings that must be preserved and restored as part of any new development in the area.

Our master plan for the Westwood Promenade incorporates four cultural resource buildings and eight other existing buildings in a strategy that creates continuity and scale through the use of repetitive architectural elements. These elements include doors and associated canopies, horizontal fascias, skylights, proportional glazing, stone slab entry thresholds, and freestanding display cases associated with each retailer's sidewalk frontage. The set of architectural elements are scaled and detailed to be compatible with cultural resource facades, but are also used to compose new facades and bridging facades. New skylights and floor openings have been designed to bring daylight into the middle of existing dark retail areas. An overlay of mid-block pedestrian crosswalks provides easy access to alleys and secondary courtyards, and weaves a new layer of pedestrian-scale activity into the existing village fabric.

The site of the new Scottish Parliament Building is prominently located in Edinburgh at the eastern end of the Royal Mile across from Holyrood Palace. As part of an invited competition for design concepts that would give an appropriate form to this significant new building in Scottish history, we developed five preliminary schemes, three of which are illustrated here. Our proposals consist of a combination of built form and exterior space. The two main built forms are the Members' Building and Foyer, which is triangular in plan, and the circular Debating Chamber. Parliament Square would face onto Holyrood Palace, and the second open space, the Queensbury House forecourt, is treated as a landscaped garden covering the MSPs' parking garage beneath.

The Parliament Building consists of a top-lit, wedge-shaped foyer attached to a seven-story office block. The accommodations for the Ministers are in the upper part of the office block in a two-story penthouse/loggia which has commanding views to Holyrood Palace and to Edinburgh Castle. The Members' Restaurant and the Press Cafeteria are housed in a sculptural element at the southern end of the office building. This glazed form faces west and overlooks the forecourt of Queensbury House, which is preserved as a historical structure.

Selected Bibliography

General

Aldersey-Williams, Hugh. "Meier's Magic for Europe." *The European*, 3–9 July 1997, p. 15.

Blaser, Werner. *Richard Meier Details*. Basel: Birkhäuser Verlag, 1996.

Cassarà, Silvio. *Richard Meier*. Bologna: Zanichelli Editore, 1995. Reprinted in German. Basel: Birkhäuser Verlag, 1996. Reprinted in Spanish. Barcelona: Editorial Gustavo Gili, 1997.

Ciorra, Pippo, ed. *Richard Meier*. Includes "Richard Meier o la rappresentazione della modernità" by Livio Sacchi. Milan: Electa, 1993.

Costanzo, Michele; Vincenzo Giorgi; and Maria Grazia Tolomeo; eds. *Richard Meier/Frank Stella: Arte e Architettura*. Exhibition catalogue. Includes "Richard Meier and Frank Stella: A Conversation about Architecture and Art." Milan: Electa, 1993.

Fernandez-Galiano, Luis, ed. *Arquitectura Viva Monografías 59: Richard Meier in Europe*. Includes "Houses and Museums: Meier in America" by Jorge Sainz; "A European America" by Tzonis Alezander and Liane Lefaivre; "Modern or Contemporary" by Joseph Giovannini; "Transparency and Perspective" by Stephan Barthelmess. May/June 1996.

Five Architects/Twenty Years Later. Includes "The Five After Twenty-Five: An Assessment" by Kenneth Frampton; Introduction by Steven W. Hurtt; "Recollections" by Ralph Bennett. University of Maryland, 1992.

Flagge, Ingeborg, and Oliver Hamm, eds. *Richard Meier in Europe*. Berlin: Ernst & Sohn, 1997.

Futagawa, Yukio, ed. Includes an interview with Richard Meier. *GA Document Extra 08*, 1997.

Galloway, David. "Europe's Love Affair With an American Architect." *International Herald Tribune*, 18–19 July 1992, p. 7.

———. "Richard Meier, Master Builder." *Inter Nations German-American Cultural Review*, 6 October 1993, pp. 40–47.

"Richard Meier: style in context." *Art in America*, January 1995, pp. 40–47.

Haito, Masahiko, and Midori Nishizawa, eds. *Richard Meier and Frank Stella: Architecture and Art*. Exhibition catalog. Includes "Meier's Toad and Stella's Garden" by David Galloway; "Ecstasy of the Artificer: On the Architecture of Richard Meier" by Seiken Fukuda; "Thoughts on Frank Stella" by Richard Meier; "Walls and Frank Stella" by Masahiko Haito. Akira Ikeda Corporation, 1996.

Hales, Linda. "Modernist With a Mission." *The Washington Post*, "Home" section, 6 February 1997, pp. 10–11, 14, 16.

Izzo, Ferruccio, and Alessandro Gubitosi. *Richard Meier Architetture/Projects 1986–1990*. Includes essays by Vittorio Magnago Lampugnani, Alberto Izzo, Camillo Gubitosi, Ferruccio Izzo. Naples Exhibition Catalogue, Palazzo Reale, 21 June–21 July, Florence, Italy: Centro Di, 1991.

Jodidio, Philip. *Richard Meier*. Cologne: Taschen, 1996.

Lange, Alexandra. "Richard Meier: Leaving Los Angeles." *Graphis 314*, March/April 1998, pp. 40–55.

Lewis, Roger. "Another Look at the 'New York Five.'" *The Washington Post*, 12 December 1992, p. E12.

Mas, Jean, ed. *Richard Meier Architect* (CD-ROM). Includes commentary by Henri Ciriani, Kenneth Frampton, Andre Rousselet, Frank Stella, Ezra Stoller. Lugano: Victory Interactive Media, 1995.

Meier, Richard. *Richard Meier Architect 2*. Includes "Works in Transition" by Kenneth Frampton; "The Second Installment" by Joseph Rykwert; Postscript by Frank Stella. New York: Rizzoli, 1991.

Nesbitt, Lois. *Richard Meier: Sculpture 1992–1994*. New York: Rizzoli, 1994.

Nickson, Elizabeth. "Master Builder." *Patek Philippe*, no. 2, 1997, pp. 3–7.

Powell, Kenneth. "The Famous Five." *Perspectives on Architecture*, February/March 1997, pp. 34–40.

Richard Meier Houses. Includes "The Dance of Composition" by Paul Goldberger; "Richard Meier's Ideal Villas" by Sir Richard Rogers. New York: Rizzoli, 1996. Reprinted in Italian. Milan: RCS Libri & Grandi Opere, 1996. Reprinted in London: Thames & Hudson, 1996.

Viladas, Pilar. "Lost in the Stacks." *The New York Times Magazine*, 5 October 1997, pp. 66–67.

Webb, Michael. "Romantic Modernist." *Korean Architects*, no. 153, May 1997, pp. 60–67.

Zevi, Bruno. "Richard Meier and the Language of Baalbek." *L'architecttura*, November 1993.

Barcelona Museum of Contemporary Art

Arnaboldi, Mario Antonio. "The Museum of Contemporary Art." *L'Arca*, April 1996, pp. 6–15.

Audusseau, Martine. "Meier a Barcelone." *D'Architectures*, December 1995.

Bohigas, Oriol. "El Museu d'Art Contemporani de Barcelona." *La Municipal de Barcelona*, March 1993, pp. 23–27.

———. "Museum of Contemporary Art of Barcelona." *Diseño Interior*, no. 53, 1996, pp. 56–67.

Buchanan, Peter. "Aloof Abstraction." *Architecture*, February 1996, pp. 70–79.

Capella, Juli, and Quim Larrea. "Barcelone et Richard Meier." *L'Architecture d'Aujour-d'hui*, December 1995, pp. 40–41.

———. "Eine unerwartete Liebergeschichte. . . ." *Architektur*, April 1996, pp. 42–53.

Cervello, Marta. "Museum of Contemporary Art." *Domus*, December 1995, pp. 7–17.

Cohn, David. "A Fine Romance." *World Architecture*, no. 41, 1995, pp. 96–99.

"Coup de blanc dans les vieux quartiers de Barcelone." *Connaissance des Arts*, February 1996, pp. 52, 56–59.

Futagawa, Yukio, ed. "Museum of Contemporary Art." *GA Document 46*, February 1996, pp. 8–43.

Galloway, David. "In Barcelona, a 'Cathedral' of Art Awaits Definition." *International Herald Tribune*, 8 December 1995, p. 11.

Hoyet, Jean-Michel, ed. *Techniques & Architecture*. Includes "An American Dream" and "Transformations in Ciutat Vella." pp. 33–41. June/July 1996.

Massot, Josep. "MACBA: Barcelona abre su museo mas contemporaneo." *La Vanguardia Magazine*, 12 November 1995, pp. 34–51.

Montaner, Josep Maria. "Mostly Solo Compositions." *Lotus 90*, September 1996, pp. 39–41.

Permanyer, Lluis. "Im Dienste der Kunst?" *Bauwelt*, May 1996, pp. 1010–17.

Richards, Ivor. "Interactive Languages." *The Architectural Review*, April 1993, pp. 22–37.

———. "White City." *The Architectural Review*, March 1997, pp. 34–41.

Richard Meier, Barcelona Museum of Contemporary Art. Includes "Urban Promenade as Architectural Promenade" by Dennis L. Dollens; "A Big White Mass Shines over a Plaza" by Federico Correa. New York: The Monacelli Press, 1997.

Riding, Alan. "A Modern 'Pearl' Inside Old Barcelona." *The New York Times*, 10 May 1995, p. C13.

Rudolph, Karen. "Museum of Contemporary Art, Barcelona" and "Light is a Transient Medium: Interview with Richard Meier." *ERCO Lichtbericht 52*, August 1996, pp. 4–11.

Von Peininger, Enrique. "Richard Meier White." *Licht & Architektur*, July–September 1996, pp. 74–77.

Zeitz, Rudiger. "Mensch, Meier." *Design Report*, April 1996, pp. 62–65.

Canal+ Headquarters

Beaudouin, Laurent. "Canal+ Building in Paris." *A+U*, no. 268, January 1993, pp. 46–71.

"Cadrage Sur La Ville." *Architecture Interieure Cree*, November 1992, pp. 115–21.

Edelman, Frederic. "Company Storefronts: The quality of the new headquarters of Canal Plus, Shell France and C3D may indicate the end of a long lethargy." *Le Monde*, 14 January 1992, p. 16.

Fillion, Odile. "La Leçon de Canal +." *Le Moniteur*, 26 June 1992, pp. 80–81.

Forster, Kurt W. "Carácter corporativo: nuevo sede de Canal+ en Paris." *Arquitectura Viva*, no. 30, May/June 1993, pp. 90–95.

———. "Stella televisia sul palcoscenico urbano." *Domus*, September 1992, no. 741, pp. 29–41.

Futagawa, Yukio, ed. "Canal+." *GA Document 34*, September 1992, pp. 8–29.

Gubitosi, Alessandro. "Architecture with a Plus." *L'Arca*, February 1993, pp. 50–59.

Loriers, Marie-Christine. "Precision Audiovisuelle: Canal+." *Techniques & Architecture*, November 1992, pp. 18–28.

Mas, Jean. "La Lumière en Mouvement." *L'Architecture d'Aujourd'hui*, June 1992, pp. 111–14.

Moore, Rowan. "A Vision in White, by an American in Paris." *The Independent*, 14 April 1993, p. 13.

Muschamp, Herbert. "On a Clear Day, You Can Watch Television." *The New York Times*, 7 February 1993, p. 32.

Progressive Architecture. Includes "The Message in the Medium" by Jean-Louis Cohen;

"Bien Venue" by Thomas Vonier. December 1992, pp. 44–53.

Régnier, Nathalie. "Canal Plus: Un Scenario Bien Orchestre." *Le Moniteur*, 8 February 1991, pp. 68–71.

Slessor, Catherine. "White Heat." *The Architectural Review*, December 1994, pp. 58–62.

"Television Company Building, Paris." *Detail*, June/July 1993, pp. 298–305.

Tempest, Rone. "America's Designs on Europe." *The Los Angeles Times*, August 25, 1992, p. 1.

Church of the Year 2000

Bussel, Abby. "Meier & Partners Wins Vatican Church Competition." *Architectural Record*, August 1996, p. 11.

Castellano, Aldo. "The Church of the Year 2000." *L'Arca*, September 1996, pp. 12–17.

———. "The Church of the Year 2000." *Ecclesia*, August/September 1996, pp. 44–67.

"The Church of the Year 2000." *A+U*, no. 319, April 1997, pp. 40–53.

"The Church of the Year 2000." Includes "Tra teologia e architettura" by Giacomo Grasso; "Richard Meier in Bramante's Place" by Bruno Zevi. *L'architettura*, no. 484, July 1996, pp. 66–80.

Ciorra, Pippo. "Richard Meier and Peter Eisenman: Talent and Ideas." *Casabella*, December/January 1997, pp. 106–7.

Doig, Allan. "Richard Meier's Church for the Year 2000 in Rome." *Church Building*, no. 44, March/April 1997, pp. 14–15.

"Etwas Modernes für Rom." *Werk, Bauen + Wohnen*, March 1997, p. 66.

Garofalo, Francesco. "The Church of the Year 2000." *Casabella*, December/January 1997, p. 88.

Hartmann, Rachel. "Richard Meier baut die Jubilaumskirche in Rom." *Kunst in Judentum*, November 1996, pp. 274–79.

Louie, Elaine. "Church for the Third Millennium." *The New York Times*, 20 June 1996, p. C1.

Mazzoleni, Emilio. "La chiesa? Va a gonfie vele." *Carnet*, August 1997, pp. 110–19.

Muschamp, Herbert. "Architecture of Light and Remembrance." *The New York Times*, 15 December 1996, section 2, pp. 1, 44.

"Progetti per la Chiesa del 2000, Roma." *Zodiac 17*, May 1997, pp. 116–27.

"Richard Meier: Wesentlich in Weiss." *Wohn! Design*, April 1996–January 1997, pp. 88–93.

Rosso, Renata. "Whiter than White." *World Architecture*, March 1997, no. 54, pp. 58–59.

Sebastini, Cinzia. "White Sails in the Roman Suburbs." *Ecclesia*, January/February 1998, pp. 24–31.

"Una chiesa per il Duemia: La Moltiplicazione degli spazi." *Chiesa Oggi: Archittetura e comunicazione*, vol. 22, 1996, pp. 16–19.

Zevi, Bruno. "Kostel pro rok 2000." *Architekt*, January/February 1997, pp. 13–21.

Espace Pitôt

Brausch, Marianne. "Montpellier. L'Enprente de Richard Meier." *Le Moniteur*, 26 May 1989, pp. 110–13.

"Espace Pitôt." *Bauwelt*, 6 October 1995, pp. 2126–31.

"Richard Meier." *Montpellier Architectures 1977–1992*. Montpellier, France: Ville de Montpellier, 1993, pp. 32–37.

"Montpellier: Folie de la Ville." *D'Architectures*, March 1994, pp. 33–38.

Euregio Office Building

Allenspach, Christoph. "Ganz in Weiss." *Facts*, 26 March 1998, pp. 146–51.

Barreneche, Raul. "Meier's White Turns Green." *Architecture*, February 1996, p. 136.

Hollenstein, Roman. "Pittoreske Spätmoderne." *Neue Zürcher Zeitung*, 10 July 1998.

"Kein 'Fast-Building'-dafür ein Qualitätsbau." *Basler Zeitung*, 4 April 1997, p. 29.

Windhöfel, Lutz. "Der Lichtendurchflutet Boulevard." *Basel Landschaftliche Zeitung*, 2 April 1998.

Gagosian Gallery

Futagawa, Yukio, ed. "The Gagosian Gallery." *GA Document 46*, February 1996, pp. 78–81.

"The Gagosian Gallery." *A+U*, no. 328, January 1998, pp. 70–77.

Giovannini, Joseph. "Sculptural Sanctum." *Architecture*, February 1996, pp. 88–91.

Iovine, Julie V. "State of the art gallery." *The New York Times Magazine*, 10 December 1995, pp. 94–95.

"Richard Meier à Beverly Hills." *Abitare*, July/August 1996, p. 135.

Whiteson, Leon. "Gallery Talk." *Elle Decor*, December 1995, pp. 50–53.

The Getty Center

"Acropole d'Art: The J. Paul Getty Center, Los Angeles." *Techniques & Architecture*, no. 408, June 1993, pp. 54–59.

"Acropolis moderna." *Clarin*, 22 December 1997, pp. 6–8.

"Amerikas Bastion der Kunst." *Berliner Morgenpost*, 13 September 1997.

Amery, Colin. "Getty's Acropolis: any colour but white." *Financial Times*, 4 November 1991.

Andersen, Kurt. "A City on a Hill." *The New Yorker*, 29 September 1997, pp. 66–72.

———. "A Grand New Getty." *Time*, 21 October 1991, p. 100.

Architecture. Includes "Art vs. Architecture" by Allan Schartzman; "Faulty Towers" by Aaron Betsky; "Ready for Art?" by Dave Hickey. December 1997.

Architectural Review. Includes "Meier's Magic Mountain" by Ivor Richards; "Playing to the Gallery" by Michael Brawne. February 1998, pp. 30–51.

Arnaboldi, Mario Antonio. "Il Getty Center a Los Angeles." *L'Arca*, March 1992, pp. 4–11.

Bachmann, Wolfgang. "The Getty Center in Los Angeles." *Baumeister*, February 1998, pp. 16–27.

Bonetti, David. "Triumph of the Will." *The San Francisco Examiner*, 7 December 1997, pp. 18–22, 24, 36–39.

Book, Jeff. "Edifice Complex." *Departures*, November/December 1997, pp. 216–223, 273–276.

Boschmann, Hella. "Wie Getty Millionen Berge versetzten." *Die Welt*, 8 April 1997, p. 3.

Bradaschia, Maurizio. "Meier per 'Getty.' " *L'Architettura*, no. 8, 1993, pp. 54–58.

Brawne, Michael. *The Getty Center, Architecture in Detail*. London: Phaidon Press, 1998.

Campbell, Robert. "A Critical Tour of the Getty." *Architectural Record*, November 1997, pp. 106–7, 197.

Caruso, Michelle. "New crest for culture in Getty Center." *Daily News*, 17 December 1997, pp. 16–17.

Colacello, Bob. "Meier's Moment." *Vanity Fair*, April 1997, pp. 332–39, 376–79.

Cooper, Frederick. "El Centro Getty." *Arkinka*, February 1998, pp. 14–50.

Cornwell, Tim. "Getty takes high art to Hollywood." *The Independent*, 9 December 1997.

Costa, Florencia. "Richard Meier a Los Angeles: The Getty Center." *Abitare*, March 1998, pp. 146–53, 182.

D'Arcy, David. "Billion Dollar Getty Opens." *The Art Newspaper*, December 1997, pp. 1, 29–33.

———. "Lights, Camera, Getty." *Los Angeles*, November 1997, pp. 84–91, 169–70.

Decker, Andrew. "Gettyworld." *ARTnews*, May 1996, pp. 110–16.

DeMichelis, Marco. "The Getty Center, Los Angeles." *Domus*, December 1997, pp. 38–49.

Filler, Martin. "The Citadel of Light." *House Beautiful*, December 1997, pp. 100–103, 140.

———. "The Getty Gets Ready." *Architecture*, February 1996, pp. 80–87.

———. "Meier's Marvel." *Harper's Bazaar*, October 1995, pp. 208–211.

Forgey, Benjamin. "The Getty Center Sets Its Site." *The Washington Post*, 27 October 1991, pp. G1, G5.

———. "Getty's Big Address." *The Washington Post*, 14 December 1997, pp. G1, 4.

Frampton, Kenneth. "Una acrópolis cultural." *Arquitectura Viva*, May/June 1992, pp. 18–23.

Futagawa, Yukio, ed. "Getty Center." *GA Document 55*, July 1998, pp. 8–49.

Gandee, Charles. "Modern Man." *Vogue*, December 1997, pp. 284–89, 346.

The Getty Center Design Process. Includes an introduction by Harold Williams; "The Architect Selection and Design" by Bill Lacy; "The Architectural Program" by Stephen D. Rountree; "The Design Process" by Richard Meier. Los Angeles: The J. Paul Getty Trust, 1991.

"Getty Unveils Mega-Museum." *Art in America*, no. 12, December 1991, p. 136.

Gillette, Jane Brown. "Western Civ." *Landscape Architecture Magazine*, December 1997, pp. 52–61.

Glueck, Grace. "From Quirky Little Gallery to Behemoth." *The New York Times*, 13 October 1991, sec. 2, pp. 31, 34.

Goldberger, Paul. "Can the Getty Buy Design Happiness?" *The New York Times*, 13 October 1991, sec. 2, pp. 1, 31.

———. "The People's Getty." *The New Yorker*, 23 February/2 March 1998, pp. 178–81.

Goodale, Gloria. "New Getty Center Shouts Strong Message from Mountaintop." *The Christian Science Monitor*, 28 June 1996, p. 10.

Graaf, Vera. "Ihr Lebenwerk, Richard Meier?" *Architektur & Wohnen*, August/September 1997, pp. 102–5.

Gruber, Michael. "A Look at Making in the Meier-Getty Model Shop." *Architecture California*, 1994, pp. 32–41.

Hales, Linda. "The Getty: Views on Architecture, Views of Los Angeles." *The Washington Post*, "Home" section, 6 February 1997, p. 15.

Hamm, Oliver G. "Die Alte und die Neue Welt." *Bauwelt*, 13 February 1998, pp. 302–13.

Herrera, Philip. "Lights, Camera, Action!" *Town & Country*, December 1997, pp. 178–87, 210–14.

Hohmeyer, Jurgen. "Tempelstadt fur die Kunst." *Der Spiegel*, no. 50, 1997, pp. 235–39.

Hollenstein, Roman. "Eine Alhambra fur Los Angeles." *Neue Zurcher Zeitung*, 15 November 1991, p. 65.

Hughes, Robert. "Bravo! Bravo!" *Time*, 3 November 1997, pp. 98–105.

———. "The Beauty of Big." *Time*, Special Issue, Spring 1997, p. 54.

Januszczak, Waldemar. "Getty's white elephant." *The Sunday Times*, 28 December 1997, pp. 10–11.

Jodidio, Philip. "Le Monastére de Brentwood." *Connaissance des Arts*, November 1994, pp. 124–51.

Ketcham, Diana. "No garland for Getty garden." *The San Francisco Examiner*, 17 December 1997, pp. B1, 6.

Kimmelman, Michael. "The New Getty, Dream and Symbol." *The New York Times*, 16 December 1997, pp. E1, 3.

Knight, Christopher. "Modernist Delivers the Unimaginable." *The Los Angeles Times*, 2 December 1997, p. A1, 21.

Laube, Helene. "Meiers Musentempel am Pazifischen Ozean." *Cash*, no. 28, 11 July 1997, pp. 38–39.

Los Angeles Times Magazine. Includes "Shining City on a Hill" by Nicolai Ourousoff; "His Defining Moment" by Steve Proffitt. Special Issue, 7 December 1997.

Macdonald, Marianne. "If God is in the detail . . . " *Observer Life*, 7 December 1997, pp. 12–17.

Mack, Gerhard. "Eine Festung als kulturelles Symbol." *St. Gallo Tagblatt*, 17 December 1997.

———. "Zu wenig sexy fur private Sponsoren." *Cash*, no. 51/52, 19 December 1997, pp. 60–61.

MacRitchie, Lynn. "The Getty citadel of culture opens its doors." *The Financial Times*, 29/30 November 1997, p. VII.

Making Architecture. Includes an introduction by Harold Williams; "The Clash of Symbols" by Ada Louise Huxtable; "A Concert of Wills" by Stephen D. Rountree; "A Vision for Permanence" by Richard Meier. Los Angeles: The J. Paul Getty Trust, 1997.

McGuigan, Cathleen, with Emily Yoffe. "A Lavish Place in the Sun." *Newsweek*, 21 October 1991, p. 64. Reprinted in *Newsweek* international edition, 11 November 1991.

———. "A Place in the Sun." *Newsweek*, 13 October 1997, pp. 72–74.

Meier, Richard. *Building the Getty*. New York: Alfred A. Knopf Inc., 1997.

Meisler, Stanley. "The House that Art Built." *Smithsonian Magazine*, December 1997, pp. 82–92.

Minervino, Fiorella. "Getty in Olipmo per l'arte." *Corriere della Sera*, 10 December 1997, p. 22.

Minetti, Maria Giulia. "L'Acropoli della California." *Specchio*, 31 January 1998, pp. 54–66.

Montaner, Josep M. *Museos Para el Nuevo Siglo*. Barcelona: Gustavo Gili, 1995, pp. 132–35

Moore, Rowan. "Getty's shining city on a hill." *The Daily Telegraph*, 6 June 1997, p. 25.

Morgenstern, Joe. "Getty Opens Mammoth Hilltop Center to Public." *The Wall Street Journal*, 16 December 1997, p. A16.

Muschamp, Herbert. "A Mountaintop Temple Where Art's Future Worships Its Past." *The New York Times*, 1 December 1997, pp. A1, 18.

Neffe, Jürgen. "Eine Affäre mit dem Licht." *Der Spiegel*, no. 17, 1997, pp. 206–10.

Newman, Morris. "Raising the Getty." *Progressive Architecture*, January 1995, pp. 63–75.

Ourousoff, Nicolai. "West Coast Showdown." *Harper's Bazaar*, November 1996, pp. 256–58, 268.

———. "Realizing a Utopian Goal in Center that Doesn't Cohere." *The Los Angeles Times*, 1 December 1997, pp. A1, 23.

Pastier, John. "Getty Center Design Unveiled in Los Angeles." *Architecture*, November 1991, pp. 21–22.

Pearson, Clifford. "Unveiling a Modern Classic." *Architectural Record*, October 1991, pp. 80–87.

Perl, Jed. "Acropolis Now." *The New Republic*, 26 January 1998, pp. 25–31.

"Perspectives: Richard Meier's Getty Center." *Progressive Architecture*, February 1992, pp. 103–7.

Plagens, Peter. "Another Tale of Two Cities." *Newsweek*, 3 November 1997, pp. 82–84.

Plattus, Alan J. "Il museo e la città: la geografia della cultura." *Casabella*, January/February 1992, pp. 71–77.

Raulff, Ulrich. "The Acropolis of Hollywood." *Frankfurter Allgemeine Zeitung*, 28 October 1995.

———. "The California Monks of Mount Pathos." *Frankfurter Allgemeine Zeitung*, 16 December 1997.

Reese, Thomas F. "The Architectural Politics of the Getty Center for the Arts." *Lotus 85*, 1995, pp. 6–43.

Reese, Thomas, and Carol McMichael Reese. "Richard Meier's New Getty Center in Los Angeles." *A+U*, January 1998, pp. 6–69.

Reeves, Phil. "Dream Without a Theme." *The Independent*, 30 October 1991, p. 17.

"Richard Meier—The Getty Center." Includes "A Citadel for Los Angeles and an Alhambra for the Arts" by Kurt Foster; "Richard Meier's Getty Center" by Henri Ciriani. *A+U*, Special Issue, November 1992.

"Richard Meier—Getty Center Los Angeles." *Casabella*, February 1997, pp. 76–77.

Richards, Ivor. "Californian Acropolis." *World Architecture*, September 1992, no. 19, pp. 54–57.

Rocco, Andrea. "Usa e Getty." *Carnet*, November 1997, pp. 147–55.

Rosenbaum, Lee. "View from the Getty: What Its Billions Bought." *Art In America*, May 1998, pp. 92–97, 138.

Rykwert, Joseph. "Acropolis with hover-tram." *London Times Literary Supplement*, 9 January 1998, pp. 15–16.

San Diego Union Tribune. Includes "Modern master makes museum a site to behold" by Ann Jarmusch; "Promised landmark" by Robert Pincus. 14 December 1997.

Stein, Karen D. "The Getty Center, Los Angeles, California." *Architectural Record*, November 1997, pp. 72–105.

Streisand, Betsy. "A new Getty for the people." *U.S. News & World Report*, 22 December 1997, pp. 58–59.

Tasset, Jean-Marie. "Naissance du plus grand musee prive du monde." *Le Figaro*, 12 December 1997, p. 4.

Taylor, Jennifer. "Art, Architecture and Los Angeles." *Design Book Review*, Winter 1994, pp. 67–73.

Trebay, Guy. "L.A.'s Museum Complex." *Village Voice*, 15 April 1997, p. 30.

"The unrepentent modernist." *The Economist*, 7 February 1998, pp. 87–88.

Vagheggi, Paolo. "Un'Acropoli per Hollywood." *La Repubblica*, 11 December 1997, p. 41.

Vidler, Anthony. "Architecture as Spectacle." *The Los Angeles Times*, 3 May 1998, pp. M1, M6.

Wallach, Amei. "Getty Museum Expands." *New York Newsday*, 11 October 1991.

Watson, Peter. "Bastion of high culture." *The Daily Telegraph Magazine*, 15 February 1997, pp. 40–45.

———. "The cultural high ground." *The Sunday Times*, 14 December 1997.

Webb, Michael. "Getty's World." *Blueprint*, no. 82, November 1991, pp. 28–30.

———. "King of the Hill." *Buzz*, February/March 1991, pp. 64–68.

The Hague City Hall and Central Library

"City Hall and Library." *Architecture in the Netherlands*, Rotterdam: NAi Uitgevers Publishers, 1996, pp. 42–49.

Davies, Colin. "Dutch Modern." *Architecture*, February 1996, pp. 98–107.

Diaz, Tony. "El sentido de la práctico: Richard Meier en La Haga." *Arquitectura Viva*, no. 388, March 1989, pp. 17–19.

Futagawa, Yukio, ed. "City Hall and Central Library." *GA Document 46*, February 1996, pp. 56–77.

"Hague City Hall." *SD*, no. 31, 1998, pp. 32–35.

Hamm, Oliver G. "Der wahre weiße Riese." *Bauwelt*, 11 August 1995, pp. 1635–41.

Library Builders. London: Academy Editions, 1997, pp. 126–33.

Richards, Ivor. "Heart of the Hague." *The Architectural Review*, January 1996, pp. 40–49.

Stadhuis Bibliotheek : The City Hall / Library Complex by Richard Meier in The Hague. Includes an interview with Richard Meier; "The quest for the City Hall" by Fred Feddes; "The City Hall as a Pivot of Urban Renewal" by Victor Freijser; "A Public Library in a Prominent Place" by Olof Koekebakker; "The Atrium, Livable Climate and Technology" by Ed Melet. Rotterdam: NAi Uitgevers, 1995.

Van de Bilderdijkstraat Naar Het Spui: De Geboorte Van Een Nieuwe Centrale Openbare Bibliotheek. The Hague: Dienst Openbare Bibliotheek, 1992.

Vantisphout, Wouter. "Richard Meier in Holland." *ANY Magazine*, no. 16, 1996, pp. 40–44.

Vermeulen, Paul. "Verzengend." *Archis*, September 1995, pp. 16–27.

Wislocki, Peter. "Rhythm and Counterpoint." *World Architecture*, no. 41, 1995, pp. 100–105.

Hans Arp Museum

"Arp-Museum 1999 eröffnet." *Bonner Generalanzeiger*, 2 April 1997.

"Arp-Museum Rolandseck." *Bauwelt*, 1 March 1996, p. 426.

"Ganz in Weiß." *Sudwest Presse*, 12 February 1996.

Maurer, Caro. "Beautiful View: Richard Meier and the Arp Museum." *Bonner Generalanzeiger*, 12/13 October 1996.

"The New Arp Museum Comes Into Being." *Art Magazine*, August 1997, p. 112.

Parade, Heidi. "Rose Götte: Es soll beim Arp-Museum bleiben." *Bonner Generalanzeiger*, 22 May 1997, p. 5.

"Projekt: Hans Arp-Museum in Rolandseck." *Kunstzeitung*, 6 February 1997, p. 16.

Hypolux Bank Building

Barthelmess, Stephan. "Zwei Amerikaner in Europa: Richard Meier und Frank Stella mit Projekten in Luxemburg, Rom und Ulm." *CCHeidenheimer Neue Presse (Neue Wurttembergische Zeitung)*, no. 168, 24 July 1993.

Danner, Dietmar. "Zinseszins: Richard Meiers Hypolux-Bank." *AIT*, December 1993, pp. 22–29.

Delluc, Manuel. "Siege de Banque au Luxembourg." *L'Architecture d'Aujourd'hui*, February 1994, pp. 64–67.

Futagawa, Yukio, ed. "Hypolux Bank Building, Luxembourg." *GA Document 40*, July 1994, pp. 34–47.

Galloway, David. "Der Dialog Als Program Die Hypobank in Luxemburg." *Hypobank International S.A.*, 1993.

Gazzaniga, Luca. "Richard Meier: Edificio per una banca, Lussemburgo." *Domus 755*, December 1993, pp. 25–35.

Hollenstein, Roman. "Zeitgenössische Architektur in der Bankenfestung: Bauten zwischen Banalität and Kunst in Luxemburg." *Neue Zurchner Zeitung*, no. 191, 20 August 1993.

Illies, Florian. "Hier ist dein Geld." *Frankfurter Allgemeine Zeitung*, 28 January 1994.

"Weise Bank fürs schwarze Geld: die Neue Hypobank von Richard Meier." *Baumeister*, 10 October 1993, p. 8.

Islip Courthouse and Federal Building

Dunlap, David W. "Putting a New Face on Justice." *The New York Times*, 19 July 1998, section 11, pp. 1, 18.

Gragg, Randy. "Monuments to a Crime-Fearing Age." *The New York Times*, 28 May 1995, pp. 36–39.

Landecker, Heidi. "Court Houses." *Architecture*, January 1996, pp. 64–85.

Rappaport, Nina. "New Courthouses Around New York." *Oculus*, April 1996, pp. 6–7.

Wise, Michael. "Architecture on Trial." *Metropolis*, May 1995, pp. 99–151.

Museum of Television & Radio
Dietsch, Deborah K. "Broadcast News." *Architecture*, November 1996, pp. 100–107.
Futagawa, Yukio, ed. "Museum of Television & Radio." *GA Document 49*, November 1996, pp. 50–61.
Goldberger, Paul. "And now, live from Beverly Hills, a new museum." *The New York Times*, 7 April 1996, section 2, p. 32.
"Museum of Television & Radio." *Paesaggio urbano*, July–October 1997, pp. 112–19.
Whiteson, Leon. "Richard Meier in Beverly Hills." *Bauwelt*, 25 October 1997, pp. 2302–05.
———. "TV Museum Both Formal and Inviting." *The Los Angeles Times*, 2 June 1996, pp. K1, K5.

Neugebauer House
Dal Co, Francesco, ed. "Un aliante di fronte al mare." *Casabella*, no. 646, June 1997, pp. 22–27.
Futagawa, Yukio, ed. "Neugebauer House." *GA Houses 52 Project 1997*, April 1997, pp. 104–7.
"Villa in Florida." *Ville Giardini*, September 1997.

Phoenix Courthouse and Federal Building
Barreneche, Raul. "Meier's White Turns Green." *Architecture*, February 1996, p. 137.
Progetto. Includes "Federal Building & United States Courthouse" by Maurizio Unali; "Architetture invulnerabili" by Livio Saachi. No. 1, July 1997.
"Progressive Architecture Awards." *Architecture*, May 1996, pp. 118–21.

Rachofsky House
Dietsch, Deborah K. "Howard's House." *Architecture*, July 1997, pp. 72–79.
Futagawa, Yukio, ed. "Rachofsky House II." *GA Houses 37 Project 1993*, March 1993, pp. 90–93.
———. "Rachofsky House." *GA Houses 51*, March 1997, pp. 70–85.
Giovanelli, Francesca. "White Cube." *Moebel Interior Design*, March 1998, pp. 36–41.
Hines, Thomas. "Bridging the public and private realms in a Dallas House." *Architectural Digest*, April 1997, pp. 118–25, 214.
von Westersheim, Kay. "Bauen fur die Kunst." *Architektur Aktuell*, January/February 1998, pp. 54–65.

Research Center for Daimler-Benz
"Daimler-Benz Forschungszentrum." *Bauwelt*, 19 November 1993, pp. 2358–59.
Flagge, Ingeborg. *Richard Meier: Daimler-Benz*. Stuttgart: Gerd Hatje, 1994.
Futagawa, Yukio, ed. "Daimler Benz Research Center." *GA Document 40*, July 1994, pp. 8–23.

Royal Dutch Paper Mills Headquarters
"Due edifici europei di Richard Meier." *Casabella*, April 1993, pp. 12–19.
Futagawa, Yukio, ed. "Royal Dutch Paper Mills Headquarters." *GA Document 34*, September 1992, pp. 30–43.
Gubitosi, Alessandro. "The Dialectics of Image." *L'Arca*, March 1994, pp. 4–11.
Kloos, Maarten. "Presence, Not Illusion: Richard Meier in Hilversum." *Archis*, July 1992, p. 3.
Metz, Tracy. "Richard Meier Builds a 'Big House' for KNP." *NRC Handelsblad*, 2 June 1992, p. 15.
Pearson, Clifford. "Working Couple." *Architectural Record*, March 1993, pp. 52–61.
"Royal Dutch Paper Mills Headquarters." *A+U*, no. 275, August 1993, pp. 34–53.
Staal, Gert. *KNP Corporate Office Hilversum*. Netherlands: KNP, 1992.
Toy, Maggie, ed. "Aspects of Minimal Architecture." *Architectural Design*, vol. 64, July/August 1994, pp. 54–57.

Swissair North American Headquarters
Colwell, Carolyn. "School of Design." *New York Newsday*, 30 October 1993, pp. 30–31.
Dunlap, David. "For Swissair, Modernism on the Long Island Expressway." *The New York Times*, 22 April 1992, p. D25.
Futagawa, Yukio, ed. "Swissair North American Headquarters." *GA Document 46*, February 1996, pp. 44–55.

Kroloff, Reed. "Swiss Precision." *Architecture*, February 1996, pp. 92–97.
Muschamp, Herbert. "A Reason to Rubberneck on the Expressway." *The New York Times*, 26 February 1995, p. 42. Reprinted in Italian. *Casabella*, October 1995, pp. 63–65.

Ulm Exhibition and Assembly Building
Bächer, Max. "The Stadthaus at Ulm and the Cathedral Square." *Domus*, February 1995, pp. 7–22.
Barthelmess, Stephan. "Richard Meiers Stadhaus." *Schwäbische Zeitung*, 27 May 1992.
Canella, Guido, ed. "Exhibition and Assembly Building, Ulm, Germany." *Zodiac 9*, March/April 1993, pp. 180–96.
"The Civic Center in Ulm." *Lichtbericht 47*, November 1994, pp. 10–13.
Futagawa, Yukio, ed. "Exhibition-Assembly Building." *GA Document 18*, April 1987, pp. 7–12.
———. "Exhibition and Assembly Building." *GA Document 40*, July 1994, pp. 24–33.
Galloway, David. "Richard Meier, Master Builder." *Inter Nations German-American Cultural Review*, 6 October 1993, pp. 40–47.
Jodidio, Philip. "La Quadrature du Cercle." *Connaissance des Arts*, December 1994, pp. 96–105.
Metz, Tracy. "A Circle in the Square." *Architectural Record*, October 1995, pp. 90–99.
"Richard Meier: Stadthaus in Ulm." *Bauen en Beton*, 1995, pp. 34–43.
Richard Meier: Stadthaus Ulm. Includes "Richard Meier and the Urban Context" by David Galloway; "The Urbanization of Architecture" by Stephan Barthelmess. Niederstotzingen: International Creative Management, 1993.
Richards, Ivor. "Square Deal." *The Architectural Review*, June 1995, pp. 38–45.
Rumpf, Peter. "Square of Circles." *Bauwelt*, 14 January 1994, pp. 96–101.
Sack, Manfred. "Luxury? Why Not." *Die Zeit*, 19 November 1993, p. 63.
———. *Richard Meier Stadhaus Ulm*. Stuttgart: Axel Manges, 1994.
Ullman, Gerhard. "Vergnugliches Schauen." *Werk, Bauen + Wohnen*, 6 June 1994, pp. 14–15.

Weishaupt Forum
Barthelmess, Stephan. "In Germania un museo privato di Meier." *Il Giornale Dell'Arte*, July/August 1992, no. 102, p. 20.
Blaser, Werner. *Weishaupt Forum/Richard Meier*. Includes introduction by Richard Meier; essay by Claudia Rudeck. Schwendi, Germany: Max Weishaupt GmbH, 1993.
"Due edifici europei di Richard Meier." *Casabella*, April 1993, pp. 12–19.
Futagawa, Yukio, ed. "Weishaupt Forum." *GA Document 34*, September 1992, pp. 44–57.
Glusberg, Jorge. "Tecnica, estetica y creacion." *Arquitectura*, 18 January 1995, pp. 2–3.
Hamm, Oliver. "Meier IV." *Deutsche Bauzeitung*, 6 June 1992, pp. 8–9.
Richards, Ivor. "Visionary Weishaupt." *The Architectural Review*, March 1994, pp. 53–57.
"Weishaupt Forum." *A+U*, no. 275, August 1993, pp. 54–72.
"Wenn Schwarz und Weiss Zusammenfinden." *Häuser*, May 1992, pp. 8–9.

Photographers

Collaborators

The people listed here are among those who worked in the office and assisted on the buildings and projects in this book.

New York Office
Maria Alataris
Jeff Barber
Peter Bochek
Wolfgang Brandl
Karin Bruckner
Peter Burns
Amedee Butt
Michael Calvino
Ron Castellano
Renee Cheng
Miles Cigolle
Nancy Clark
Adam Cohen
Peter Coombe
Donald Cox
Adam Cwerner
Benjamin Darras
Stephen Dayton
Mark Dizon
Amy Donohue
Timothy Collins Douglas
Michael Duncan
Robert Edwards
John Eisler
Peter Felix
Gary Fischer
Renate Fischer
Diederik Fokkema
Francina Foskey
Robert F. Gatje
Kevin Gordon
Lisa J. Green
W. Jeffrey Greene
Stephen Harris
Christopher Haynes
Daniel Heuberger
Anne Hinsman
Abigail Hopkins
Raphael Justewicz
Gunter Kaesbach
Bernhard Karpf
Andrew Kim
Jeffrey King
Julian King
Marcus Klein
Christina Kohm
Jah-Hee Koo

Tobias Kraus
Beat Kuttel
Robert Lewis
John Locke
Reynolds Logan
Knut Luscher
Bernhard Lutz
Richard Manna
David Martin
Paul Masi
Michael Misczynski
Jun-ya Nakatsugawa
Marc Nelen
Alex Nussbaumer
Ana O'Brien
Matthias Oppliger
Alfonso Perez-Mendez
Matteo Pericoli
Thomas Phifer
Hans Put
John Quale
Mihai Radu
Gilbert N. Rampy, Jr.
J. Gregory Reaves
John Reed
James Richards
Rijk Rietveld
Marc Rosenbaum
Thomas Savory
James Sawyer
Stefan Scheiber
Alan Schwabenland
Joseph Shields
David Shilling
Jennifer Stevenson
Carlos Tan
Michael Thanner
Joerg Thorissen
Michael Vinh
David Walker
Birgit Werner
Dukho Yeon
Birgit Zwankhuizen

Los Angeles Office
Robert J. Ashley
Gregory Baker
John H. Baker
Donald E. Barker
Michele Baron
Roger Barrett
John Bender
Daniel Benjamin
Therese Bennett

Donald Berges
Peter Berman
Manuel Bouza
Karen Bragg
Shari Brukman
Florencia Costa
Angelo Costas
James Crawford
David Davis
Carlos Dell'Acqua
Victor DeSantis
Lori East
Maurice Edwards
Tom Farrell
Eric Fisher
Francis Freire
E. Jon Frishman
Tami Gam
Rozan Gacasan
Dean Geib
Pavel Getov
Estabrook Glosser
Derek Gonzales
Paul Goodenough
Rick Gooding
Stefan Gould
Tom Graul
Michael Gruber
Jason Haim
Gavin Harris
Jeff Heller
Dennis Hickok
Tom Hoos
Michael Hootman
Glen Irani
Richard Kent Irving
Glen Ishida
James Jackson
Bijoy Jain
Gudlaug Jonsdottir
Kamyar Kamran
Anne Katata
Kathy Kikuno
Christine Kilian
Caroline Kreiser
Bernard Kummer
Robert Larson
Jean Lem
Stephen Levine
Mario Madayag
James Matson
Hiroshi Matsubara
James Mawson
Neil McLean

Mark McVay
Paul Mitchell
Milena Murdoch
John Murphey
Ronald J. Musser
Lonnie Nakasone
Alexis Navarro
Kevin O'Brien
Olivia Ocampo
Carlo Paganuzzi
Michael Palladino
Martin Pease
John Petro
Eric Randolph
Renaldo Raya
Averill Vic Schnider
Joanne Scott
Anne Seol
Timothy Shea
Lilia Skutnik
Mark Sparrowhawk
Bruce Stewart
Richard Stoner
Krishna Suharnoko
David Swartz
Aram Tatikian
Phillip Templeton
John Thomann
Norman Title
George Todorovich
Jeffrey Turner
Laszlo Vito
Thomas Vitous
Philip Warde
J.F. Warren
Bruce Weinstein
Malvin Whang
John Woell
Harry Wolf
Alex Wuo
Terrence Yuan Young
James Yu
David Yuguchi
Tom Zook